Twentieth-Century Honky-Tonk

BABYLON BOOKS

Twentieth-Century Honky-Tonk

THE AMAZING UNAUTHORIZED STORY
OF THE CAIN'S BALLROOM'S FIRST 75 YEARS
★★ 1924-1999 ★★

JOHN WOOLEY &
BRETT BINGHAM

BABYLON
BOOKS

ISBN-13: 978-1-948263-57-3

Babylon Books Publishing

Cover and Interior Design by Müllerhaus Legacy.

Photo Acquisition by Brett Bingham and John Wooley unless
otherwise noted.

ACKNOWLEDGMENTS

Back in the mid-1990s, Tulsans Russ Florence and Steve Higgins began laying the groundwork for a book on their hometown Cain's Ballroom, amassing many pages of interviews, notes, and research material. For various reasons, that book never came to fruition, but when Russ and Steve heard about our project, they unselfishly allowed us complete access to everything they'd collected on the Cain's.

Much of what they gave us turned out to be invaluable to the creation of this book. They were both first-rate interviewers, and some of the people they talked with—notably promoter R. C. Bradley—were not around when we began our own interviewing. For that and many other reasons, *Twentieth-Century Honky-Tonk* is a far better work for the efforts, and kindness, of Russ and Steve. We take this space to sincerely thank them, and to hope in print that the book we've built over the past several years is worthy of the top-flight work they did a quarter of a century ago.

We're grateful to many other people for their memories, insight, assistance, and willingness to share whatever they had with us. Glaringly absent from the following list are most of our interview subjects. That's because the reader will encounter their names and words in the text, not because we aren't deeply thankful to them all. Believe us—we are. In fact, we're doubly thankful to people like Glenn White, Larry Shaeffer, Ray Bingham, and the late Chris Tyler, who supplied us with material for the book in addition to sitting down and talking to us for the record. Shaeffer's wholehearted support of what we were doing, in fact, was incalculably important, since he was the owner of the ballroom from the mid-'70s to the end of the century.

Others, both living and no longer with us, who have contributed in significant ways to *Twentieth-Century Honky-Tonk* include, in alphabetical order, Robert Bishop, Billy Byrd, Randy Cale, Jason Collington, Ed Davis, Susan Ellerbach, John Hamill, Brad Harris, Debbie Jackson, Bobby Koefer, Randy Krehbiel, Dr. Guy Logsdon, Barbara Martin, Wayne McCombs, Kassie McCoy, Deborah Millaway, Jesse Morris, Mickey Payne, Brad Piccolo, Michael H. Price, Mike Ransom of tulsatvmemories.com, Don and Phyllis Rhodes (who did some wonderful volunteer research for the book), Clint Russell, Harvey Shell, Duane "Bear" Smith, Rachelle Vaughan, David Ward, Rosetta Wills, and Jamie Wooley.

Big thanks also to our designers, Laura Hyde and Kristin Stroup, as well as Kayloni Alexander, Doug Miller, Jared Casci, and Alexandra Seifried at Müllerhaus Legacy in Tulsa. Having worked on Müllerhaus projects for years, co-author Wooley knew both the staff and their work were uniformly excellent, and we feel that it was a real coup to get artists of this caliber to produce and design *Twentieth-Century Honky-Tonk*.

Ditto for Bill and Lara Bernhardt at Babylon Books. As is the case with Müllerhaus, they have been a blessing to us on both a personal and professional level.

And while their tenure as the ballroom's owners are outside the scope of this book, we must thank Jim, Alice, Chad, and Hunter Rodgers, as well as Danny Finnerty, who piloted the venue into the 21st century. At this writing, the Rodgers family has owned the Cain's for the better part of two decades, maintaining and augmenting the hall's international reputation with both musicians and music fans of all stripes. The story of the Rodgers era is still being written, and it's a good one. Someday, it will surely end up between covers.

A note to our interviewees: If we talked to you but none of your quotes ended up in this book, it's not because you didn't give us any good material. It's because we simply had far more than we could use and still keep the book a manageable size—which is a major reason we used the end of the 1900s as a stopping point. Even if you can't find any of your words in here, please know that each of you helped lay the foundation upon which *Twentieth-Century Honky-Tonk* was constructed, and we will always be grateful.

— *John Wooley and Brett Bingham*

PROLOGUE

Yes, I've seen them all
From the House of Blues to Carnegie Hall
And I've heard Tommy Duncan sing
But when it's party time and I'm ready to honk
I go to the timeless honky-tonk
There just ain't no place like the Cain's

– FROM "NO PLACE LIKE THE CAIN'S," WRITTEN BY DON WHITE

It's the House That Bob Built. The Carnegie Hall of Western Swing. Tulsa's Timeless Honky-Tonk.

A long time ago, it was the Louvre. A little later, it became the Cain's Academy of Dance. At the very beginning, it didn't even *have* a name.

And the night Tulsa-based singer-songwriter Don White first performed "No Place Like the Cain's" for his hometown crowd, the venerable Cain's Ballroom was going through the first stages of a metamorphosis, of adapting, of becoming something else.

Since the mid-1930s, when it became ground zero for the spread of an exciting new form of danceable music that would eventually be known as western swing, the Cain's had been considered a country joint. Texas expat Bob Wills and the Texas Playboys had a lot to do with that perception; from the mid-'30s into the early '40s, they had parlayed their Cain's dances and clear-channel radio broadcasts into stardom, especially in the American Southwest. And, while many listeners could tell that this stuff was different from the "hillbilly" music of the time— the kind of music played by acts on radio's *Grand Ole Opry* and elsewhere—it was still conveyed predominantly with stringed instruments played by musicians dressed in cowboy outfits. So the Texas Playboys were perceived in a general way as a hillbilly band, and their dancehall headquarters as a place where country folks went to have fun and let off a little steam.

This perception continued long after World War II broke up the band. Bob headed off to serve his brief stint in the military, and brother Johnnie Lee Wills took over the job of leading the band that broadcast from the Cain's. Western swing loosened its grip on listeners and patrons in the late '50s, following the rise of rock 'n' roll and other factors, but a succession of Cain's managers and owners continued to book country-style acts there, with varying degrees of success.

By the time White debuted "No Place Like the Cain's," however, big changes were in the air. A group of young promoters, including R.C. Bradley and Jeff Nix, had begun leasing the place from the owner (who referred to her lessees as "hippies"—a not completely unfounded characterization), running some different, more youthful acts onto the Cain's stage. Country music still had a place in the spotlight, but it was a different kind of country, one represented by the emerging Texas-based singer-songwriters and others who had at least a modicum of rock in their souls.

Don White, for example. Although White would ultimately write songs for contemporary country recording acts like the Oak Ridge Boys, Rosanne Cash, and Suzy Bogguss, and land his own solo deal with ABC Paramount, at the time he wrote "No Place Like the Cain's" he was a Tulsa performer struggling to take his career to the next level.

"That was in the mid-'70s, when I made my first trip to Nashville," White recalled in an interview for this book. "I only lived there about a year and a half. I couldn't get anything going. So R.C. and Nix would hire me to do a solo gig, give me 250 or 300 bucks to open a show, and I'd come back to Tulsa and do that. Then I'd go back to Nashville and pay my rent.

"I was over at my mom's house one day when I was back for a show, and I thought, 'Man, those guys have been so nice to me. I need to write a song about the Cain's.' So I sat in the little house out behind my mom's one afternoon, and I wrote that song down on a piece of paper. And that night at Cain's, in the middle of my show, I sat down on a chair, got the paper out, and told the crowd, 'Hey, y'all. I sat down and wrote this little song today. It's about Cain's.' I said, 'I didn't have time to memorize it, so if I read the words, you'll understand, won't you?'

"And they all went, 'Nooooo!' Which I thought was real funny."

Live music you can choose
Rock and roll or the country blues
Right here, you'll hear the best of western swing

The dancin's good, the music's great

Why right here is where Bob Wills used to play

There just ain't no place like the Cain's

For the first 75 years of its life, the Cain's Ballroom showed a remarkable ability to adapt to changes, a resiliency that kept it bouncing back like its alleged and legendary spring-loaded dance floor. From high-toned dancing academy to the epicenter of western-swing music, Nashville-star stopover to outlaw-country haven to a place where some of the most outré acts imaginable played on the same stage as up-and-coming rock superstars, the Cain's has been a constant presence not only in the night life of Tulsa, but in America's popular culture as well.

As it wended its way through the twentieth century, this classic old honky-tonk may have faltered a time or two. But every time, it rose again, to make more history and give the world more music.

There was—and is—indeed, no place like the Cain's.

CAIN'S

BALLROOM
DANCING

Inseparably interwoven with the history of Tulsa and its development is the name of W. Tate Brady, now a wealthy merchant and mine owner who has a wide and favorable acquaintance here. His marked enterprise and diligence have not only been factors in his personal success, but have also contributed to general progress.

— FROM *A HISTORY OF THE STATE OF OKLAHOMA* BY LUTHER B. HILL (THE LEWIS PUBLISHING COMPANY, 1909)

Wyatt Tate Brady, evidence suggests, was at least superficially a young man right out of the pages of a Horatio Alger novel. Wildly popular during Brady's childhood, the Alger books, sporting titles like *Luck and Pluck* and *Strive and Succeed,* all centered around a similar theme: a boy rises from challenging circumstances and, by applying himself and striving tirelessly and diligently, manages to become a wealthy capitalist—or, at least, a solid middle-class businessman. The Alger narratives all dealt with that era's American Dream, and the books were eagerly perused by millions of youngsters. It's likely that young Tate Brady was one of them, inspired by those up-from-the-gutter stories of shiny-faced youngsters persevering and triumphing in the hardscrabble business world of the late 19th century.

According to an entry in *The History of the State of Oklahoma*—published when Brady was in his late thirties—he'd started as "a small boy in a humble clerkship...embarking in business on his own account when but seventeen years of age." By that time, he would've been living in Nevada, Missouri, having left his native Forest City, Missouri, with his family at the age of 12. He hit Tulsa in 1890, when he was twenty.

Both he and the city had some growing to do. *The History of the State of Oklahoma* called Tulsa "an embryo city" with a population of "not more than fifty" at the time Brady blew into town. "[Few] would have believed that it would prove a city for a successful business career," added author Hill, "but Mr. Brady foresaw the possibilities here and time has proved the wisdom of his judgment."

Brady's decision to stay in Tulsa and his subsequent success as a businessman, politician, and city founder became reflected in the names around the area north of town where he settled: Brady Street, the Brady Theater, the Brady Arts District, and the Brady Heights neighborhood, where he built a mansion styled after that of Confederate general Robert E. Lee.

However, to quote the wise title of one of Bob Wills and His Texas Playboys' greatest hits, time changes everything, and Brady's apparent affinity for the values of the antebellum South—he was also the Oklahoma commander of the Sons of Confederate

Veterans—ended up getting him, or at least his name, into trouble more than a century after he first arrived in town. As *Tulsa World* writer Randy Krehbiel put it in a July 1, 2019 story, "An indefatigable town booster and signer of the original city charter, Brady fell out of favor about a decade ago when his vigilantism and involvement in a scheme to move black Tulsans out of the Greenwood District following the 1921 Tulsa Race Massacre became more widely known." He reportedly did a stint in the Ku Klux Klan (and, also reportedly, renounced the racist organization later in life).

So, in the summer of 2013, after much input, both for and against, from community members and civic leaders, the Tulsa City Council made the head-scratching decision to amend Brady Street to M.B. Brady Street, reflecting the name of the Civil War photographer Mathew B. Brady—whose relationship to Tulsa was, to be charitable, remarkably tenuous. (At the time, some suggested that naming the street after comedian Wayne Brady, the late actor Scott Brady, or one of the characters on the TV sitcom *The Brady Bunch* would've been just as appropriate.) Five years later, the council changed the street's name to Reconciliation Way, which made much more sense, as the John Hope Franklin Reconciliation Center (named after the famed Oklahoma-born historian) sits very near the former Brady Street.

****

According to writer Rik Espinoza's story on the city's founding fathers, which ran in the May 18, 1977 *Tulsa World*, Brady was working as a traveling salesman when he first arrived in town. His wares were shoes, and although his potential customer base was only around half a hundred souls—or about a hundred soles—he was hardly dissuaded by those small numbers. Deciding he liked the looks of the place, Brady set up shop in the northern part of the town, buying a small frame building, 16 feet wide and 32 feet long, a block away from the Frisco Railway tracks on North Main Street. And there he set up a shoe shop that evolved into a mercantile store, offering a variety of goods.

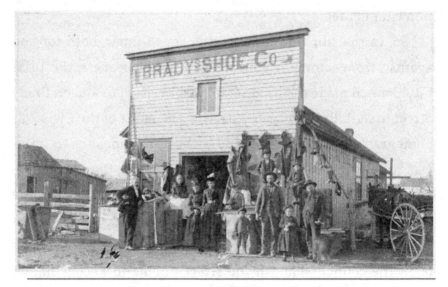

The Brady Shoe Company operated from 1893 to 1898. Pictured are Andrew Brady, Mary Liz Brady, John L. Brady, and Guy McCraken.

"Day by day the business grew in volume and also advanced in the confidence and respect of the buying public," wrote Hill in *The History of the State of Oklahoma*. He also noted that—at the time of the book's publication in 1909—the store had vastly expanded in both size and inventory. It was now the Brady Mercantile Company, with annual earnings of $100,000.

Brady's other successful ventures included the two-story Brady Hotel—the first Tulsa hotel with bathtubs—at the corner of North Main and North Second (which later became Brady Street), and, beginning in 1893, a wide-ranging northeastern Oklahoma coal-mining operation. And he continued to add to his real-estate holdings.

"He hoped Tulsa was going to grow north," wrote Espinoza in his *Tulsa World* piece, "and bought extensive properties on that side of the railroad tracks."

As he went along, Tate Brady also became one of the leaders of the developing city. In 1897, he journeyed with a handful of others to the district court in Muskogee in a bid to get the Indian Territory town of Tulsa officially incorporated. According to Espinoza's article, Brady's name was one of 20 signatures on the petition, which had the desired effect.

Later on, Brady held local offices, including town alderman (essentially, the equivalent of a city council member) and school board president. And, in the great American tradition, he kept expanding his business empire—which is the reason he appears in this book.

In 1924, when he was 54 years old, Brady decided to construct another building on North Main, the street where Brady Mercantile and the Brady Hotel already stood. Constructed of native sandstone and brick, the new building was intended to be a garage (and probably a dealership) for Hupmobiles, then-popular Detroit-built cars in the same general price range as Chevrolets or Fords. It's unclear whether any new Hupmoblies actually made it to 423 N. Main Street, however, and if they did, it was for a very short time. Perhaps Brady's deal with the automaker fell through, or he pulled the plug for financial or other reasons. Sources indicate the building was used as a schoolhouse for a little while after that, and then, in a transformation that would last far, far longer than either Hupmobile garage or school, Brady's newly built property became what it seems, in retrospect, to have been destined for all along: a dancehall.

****

Apparently, it was Tate Brady himself who christened the hall the Louvre, although the reason he would name a Tulsa dance emporium after the famous museum in Paris, France, remains a mystery. The exact chronology of all of its incarnations from 1924 to the end of that decade can't be pinned down, either. We do know that sometimes it was a relatively genteel establishment, at other times something less so. We also know that touring bands sometimes performed there, including an orchestra led by Muskogee native Clarence Love. "[W]hat you call the Cain's now wasn't the Cain's then," Love said in an interview with John Wooley that was published in the April 1985 *Tulsa Magazine*. "It was the Louvre. I played there before Bob Wills changed it to the Cain's.... A lot of people think of Cain's, they think the Wills boys started it. But I was playing there in my teens."

Love and his band were African-American, but even in those rigidly segregated days in Tulsa (the infamous Greenwood race massacre had taken place in 1921, its epicenter just a few blocks east of the Louvre), their appearance at the venue doesn't necessarily mean it catered to black clientele at some point; Love's orchestra was a "sweet" band, along the lines of the Guy Lombardo orchestra, that played for predominantly white audiences throughout its career. It was, in essence, a "society" orchestra, which suggests that the patrons of the Louvre, at least during part of its existence, came from Tulsa's middle and upper classes.

At other times during the '20s, however, the Louvre seems to have drawn a less savory crowd. This would've been during its dime-a-dance days, a period in the life of the club that was explained by O.W. Mayo, longtime business manager for Bob and Johnnie Lee Wills and an owner of the Cain's, in a July 1986 interview conducted at the dancehall. "This building was built in 1924, and it was first used for a garage," Mayo said. "Then, they put a dance floor in here, and they ran a jitney dance. Do you know what a jitney dance is? The men paid ten cents to dance with the girls, and the girls got all the dancing free."

The era of the dime-a-dance, taxi dance, or jitney dance (a "jitney" was slang for a nickel then, so it actually cost two jitneys per dance at most places) ran from the 1920s through the Great Depression, providing attractive and light-on-their-feet young women a chance to make a little income by dancing with men willing to pay for the privilege. Usually, the man would buy tickets at 10 cents a throw, pick a woman to dance with, and give her a ticket per dance. At the end of the night, she'd present her accumulated tickets to management and draw as much as a nickel for each one.

While these events shouldn't be confused with the dance lessons that would come along after Madison Cain took the place over in 1930, it's likely that the female dancers sometimes provided basic instruction in various steps. Most times, though, the paid dancers at the Louvre simply provided companionship for lonely men at a dime per song—even as they kept an eye out for trouble. In a December 12, 1970 *Tulsa World* article, Tom Wood wrote that "males paid 10 cents a dance to jostle females around the floor between gang fights." Five years later, in a December 10, 1975 story, *Tulsa Tribune* reporter Doug Darroch elaborated on Wood's pithy observation:

> *Periodically during Oklahoma prohibition, no liquor was allowed in the ballroom. A pass system was inaugurated and those going in and out received ink stamps on their hands. When the doorkeeper decided a fellow had had enough stamps and outside drinks, trouble sometimes ensued. There were some better fights in the vestibule over readmission arguments than in any professional ring.*
>
> *It was not a place for the faint of heart.*

Darroch called those wild days "the beginning of the Cain's tradition," and in many ways, he's right. Certainly, the dancing and fighting and loosely enforced illegal drinking all swirled together during the golden days of Bob Wills' reign at the hall. While he and his musicians were busy honing and perfecting a new kind of danceable, jazzy music that would come to be known as western swing, many of his audiences were sneaking out into the alley behind the bandstand to enlist the services of a bootlegger. But before all of that began, a new period of restraint settled over the ballroom.

That came about in 1930, when the aforementioned Madison Cain, a successful dance instructor, happened along, offering to lease the place. And once he'd made the deal, he banned alcohol, insisted on proper dress, and strove in other ways to give the place some class.

After all, the hall at 423 North Main Street was now trumpeting his name for all the world, or at least Tulsa, to see. It was right there on the sign over the sidewalk: "Cain's Dancing Academy," renamed by and for its new operator, Madison W. "Daddy" Cain.

Tate Brady, however, was not around to witness the transformation. In August of 1925, deeply upset by the death of his firstborn son, John Davis Brady, in an automobile accident and—by some accounts—vexed by financial reverses, he had taken his own life.

CAIN'S ACADEMY OF DANCING

A WORD TO THE WISE

About this school of Dancing. It behooves us to state
that we are proud to be able to hold this wonderful slogan,
"The Worlds Largest School of Ballroom Dancing." At this
~~time~~ we specialize in ballroom dancing only.

I am presenting to the people of Tulsa, and vicinity *ever*
one of the most able staff of teachers that I have ^been able
to procure in my 32 years of professional career.

In ~~I am~~ presenting <u>William T. Davis</u>, a graduate pupil of
G. Hepburn Wilson and the American National College of Danc-
ing, and also a pupil of the great Maurice Halton, the
"Waltz King" of the world, All schools are of New York City. *w*
I feel confident you will ~~all~~ be well pleased with his
instructions.

Now for the lady instructor, Nita Bassett. I feel like
I have lots of help in presenting her. This is the lady teach-
er that became so famous in my school here in 1926, when the
"Charleston" was such a rage. Miss Bassett a
"Ballroom" and featured the "Charleston." At
is specializ

We have
times.

$1.50 pe
Those wh

Ol' Daddy Cain, he never had anything but a modern type of music, because he was teaching ballroom dancing, waltzes and foxtrots and what have you, and he built his dance audience from his dance classes and vice versa. What played regular was...a little small combo. That's the type of music that he played.

— O.W. MAYO, IN A JULY 1986 INTERVIEW WITH JOHN WOOLEY

Tulsa-based historian Harvey Shell swears that he once saw a *Ripley's Believe It or Not* newspaper cartoon from a long time ago that spotlighted a couple of dance instructors who worked out of the same building. One was a fellow named Abel. The other was a man named Cain.

No, they weren't brothers, and one of them didn't murder the other and then try to hide his deed from the Almighty, as was the case with their biblical namesakes. We're not sure what happened to Abel—the dance instructor—when he and Cain went their separate ways, but we do know something about Madison Wade Cain, aka "Daddy" and occasionally "Professor," whose work as a teacher of popular dance steps brought him to Tulsa and the ballroom that still bears his name.

An Illinois native born September 12, 1874, Cain spent his youth and early adulthood in that state. A United States Federal Census entry from 1900, uncovered by researcher Phyllis Rhodes, finds the 25-year-old bachelor living in Jasper, Ill., and working as a "restaurant person." At some point after this he traveled to New York, where he became a student at the famed Castle House on Long Island, founded by star dancers Vernon and Irene Castle. The exact dates of his tutelage there, however, are not clear. An obituary from a Tulsa newspaper, published on June 23, 1940—one day after Cain's death—claimed that "Mr. Cain went to New York from a small Illinois town where he was born, and after several years in New York he came directly to the oil capital." In fact, he spent years in Oklahoma City and Drumright before settling in Tulsa—the "oil capital" referred to in the story—in the late '20s.

In 1907, for instance, the year of Oklahoma's statehood, Cain was headquartered in Oklahoma City, teaching dancing with a man named L.E. Buttrick. (In a July 8, 2008 interview for this book, western-swing historian and collector Glenn White told Brett Bingham that Buttrick later bought the City Auditorium and changed the name to the Ritz Ballroom. After he sold it, it became the Trianon, a kind of Oklahoma City analogue to the Cain's. It no longer exists.) A newspaper ad from January 8th of that year for Cain and Buttrick's dance academy offers "Two-Step and Waltz taught on a guarantee," with a $3 charge for ladies and

$5 for gentlemen. The hall was located at 25½ West Main Street in Oklahoma City.

Cain and Buttrick later split, with Cain moving his base of operations to 212 ½ West First Street, where he established Cain's Academy of Dancing (with "America's Finest Ball Room and Reception Parlors," according to a print advertisement of the time). By 1912, he'd expanded into Tulsa, where he offered dancing and dance lessons at a couple of different halls, the Euclid and the Orcutt, as well as at other venues, some of which he apparently ran. An ad from the July 4, 1912 *Tulsa Daily Democrat*, for instance, featured a head shot of Cain with a notice that dancing would begin at 7 p.m. at a place called Cain's Pavillion, and the 1940 Tulsa newspaper piece cited earlier contained this information: "His first studio was in the Genet building in the 100 block [of] South Boston Avenue. He later moved to other locations and several years ago ill health forced him to sell the dance hall at 423 N. Main St., which still bears his name. Previously, Cain's academy was located at 927 E. Second St."

In 1915, however, he was running an Oklahoma City eatery called the Manhattan Café—reverting to his former profession— although it's likely he was still in the dance-instruction business as well.

When the 1920 census was taken, Cain was living in Drumright, 30 miles west of Tulsa, where he also operated a Cain's Academy of Dancing. According to researcher Don Rhodes, this Cain's was located on West Fulkerson Street, and, when Cain and his wife moved to Tulsa later in the decade, the building was taken over by the American Legion. (Later, Bob Wills and His Texas Playboys would play dances in that same Legion Hall, which means that Wills, technically, performed in *two* Cain's Ballrooms.)

Drumright Newspaper Article, September 13, 1927

By the time he and his wife, Alice, had acquired their new home in Tulsa, Cain was a big name in regional ballroom-dancing circles, especially in the northeastern Oklahoma area. As the newspaper obituary put it, "He was the first dancing master of any importance to come to Tulsa."

As mentioned earlier, Cain had studied dancing with Vernon and Irene Castle in their studio on Long Island—working with, among many others, a fellow instructor named Arthur Murray. While Murray is better known today, thanks to the franchised dance studios that still bear his name, the Castles were the ones who raised America's consciousness about ballroom dancing in the very early part of the 20th century. In their time, the British-born Vernon and his New York-native wife were major American celebrities. Tremendously popular stars of vaudeville and early motion pictures, their smooth and graceful dance moves went a long way toward creating a national market for instructors like Daddy Cain, dance-educated people who could teach regular folks how to step out on the floor in the Castle style.

Just when he hooked up with Vernon and Irene Castle is a bit of a mystery. The many advertisements viewed by the authors for Cain's dance instruction don't mention his affiliation with the superstar Castles until the 1919 *Gusher*, Drumright's high school yearbook, where a small ad identifies M.W. Cain as a "Teacher of Ball Room and Fancy Dancing" and "GRADUATE OF CASTLE SCHOOL OF DANCING" in New York City. Does that mean that he studied at Castle House *after* he'd been teaching for a while, or, as the newspaper obituary indicated, that he headed east after working in the restaurant business, took lessons with the Castles, and then returned to Oklahoma to teach for the first time? Evidence points to the former, with Cain likely heading to New York somewhere around 1915 or 1916. World War I had begun revving up then, but Cain was in his early forties and therefore not likely to have his instruction interrupted by military service. (Vernon Castle, on the other hand, joined Britain's Royal Flying Corps in 1916, flew well over 100 combat missions, and died in a 1918 plane crash in Fort Worth, Texas, where he'd been instructing young pilots for the war effort.)

In his December 1970 *Tulsa World* article on the history of the Cain's, Tom Wood described Daddy Cain as "a short, bald, bull-like man who was light on his feet for a heavy man." When he waltzed into the old Louvre dancehall, he changed the name but kept at least one of the fixtures—Max Kessler, who'd been the regular pianist at the place.

"At that time, Mr. Cain was a well-known dancing instructor, and during those years I was never sick and never late to work," the old ivory-tickler told writer Doug White for a story in the May 29, 1979 *Tulsa Tribune*.

Along with Kessler, Madison Cain later got significant help from a right-hand man named Howard Turner. That's according to Don Mayes, Turner's stepson, who told Brett Bingham in a 2011 interview that Turner had grown up on a farm in Washington County, Pennsylvania, and gone to work for Southwestern Bell as a teenager. Later, he came to Oklahoma City, where other members of his family lived, and finished high school. "I think he decided then that he wanted to be in dancing," Mayes said. "That's when he got a crack with Madison Cain."

Mayes doesn't know how the two got together. But chances are, if a young man was interested in dance instruction and living in Oklahoma, Cain would've been at the top of his list of people to meet. Turner may also have been teaching in the area and attracted Cain's attention for that reason.

Whenever that meeting did happen, the dancing master must've been impressed. Turner began working for Daddy Cain as an instructor, and when Cain took over the building in 1930, renaming it the Cain's Academy of Dance, he brought Turner in to help manage the place. Mayes says that his stepfather also painted signs for the ballroom and performed various other tasks under Cain's employ, including supervision of the dime-a-dance nights that continued from the Louvre days.

When Cain and Turner assumed control of the dancehall, the Great Depression was underway and Oklahomans' earnings, in the heart of the Dust Bowl, were driven down by both the bad economy and the forces of nature. Because of that, it's logical to arrive at the conclusion that the taxi dances and the actual dance lessons at the ballroom during this time were one and the same—that people who could no longer afford lessons costing several dollars could at least come up with a dime per dance to learn the new steps.

That's the accepted wisdom. But it's probably wrong.

Brett Bingham's collection includes an undated, typed, and hand-corrected letter promoting the Cain's and two of its instructors, William T. Davis and Nita Bassett. Apparently copy for a promotional sheet—written by either Howard Turner or Cain himself—it touts the Cain's as "The World's Largest School of Ballroom Dancing," adding, "We have depression rates this season to meet with the times," a line that suggests it was written in the first few years of Madison Cain's ownership. The quoted rates are $1.50 per lesson or a "term" of eight lessons for $10. Previous students could get four lessons for $5. Not outrageous sums by any means, but much higher than the dime-a-lesson price that's been passed down through the generations as fact.

Then, there are the recollections of Bob Phillips. In a 2012 interview with John Wooley, he talked about his youthful days in Tulsa, during the Depression, when dancing was a major pastime for him and his friends. (The "program dance" he refers to means that there was a printed program made up for the evening, perhaps listing the total number of dances available for the evening and/or the names of the taxi dancers. It's not clear if *all* the jitney dances at the Cain's during that time had programs.)

Said Phillips:

In 1936, my older brother and I both signed up for six lessons at the Cain's. It was a six-lesson program for a dollar a lesson. I took five lessons and ran out of money. My older brother took

*all six. There were probably 20 in a group, with an instructor
for each group.*

*The dime-a-dance thing was different. It was a program
dance, and you could dance a dance with any of the girls
in the program for a dime. I went to lots of those. It was a
good way to exercise what you'd learned in the lessons. But
some people would come who didn't know how to dance
and weren't taking lessons.*

Whatever the cost, Daddy Cain and Howard Turner certainly
weren't hurting for takers. Turner told the *Tulsa World*'s Tom
Wood that, at the height of the dance school's popularity, "We had
555 people enrolled and an average of 275 students attended.... A
hundred-dollar night meant a lot of dancing." Turner figured that
was "the world's largest ballroom class"—a sentiment echoed in
the typewritten sheet quoted above.

As mentioned in the previous chapter, Cain insisted on a certain amount of decorum at his place, including proper dress and
no alcohol on the premises. Of course, patrons could still score
illegal hooch on the outside, but it wasn't as easy, nor as cost-ef-
fective, to partake and return. "Daddy Cain wouldn't allow liquor
inside," Turner explained to Wood, "and a person who went outside to drink had to pay to get back in."

The academy's high-water mark for enrollees came in 1933. In
January of the next year, 59-year-old Madison Cain would suffer
a stroke, rendering him unable to continue dancing. He died six
years later, leaving his widow, Alice, an estate of $857,466, accord-
ing to Wood's story—a fortune in those times.

After Cain's stroke, he left the management of the place as well as the instruction up to Turner, who would continue heading up dance lessons for many more years. He would also become the *de facto* manager of the place, and it was in that capacity that he became involved in the story of the ballroom's first and most famous house band, as well as in the popularization of a new musical form known as western swing.

****

"There were a lot of good people who worked at Cain's," wrote Texas Playboys piano player "Brother" Al Stricklin in his book *My Years with Bob Wills* (the Naylor Company, 1976, written with Jon McConal). "One was Howard Turner, the dance instructor.... Howard was kinda nervous and fidgety, but he was very friendly and likeable."

Stricklin was the man who'd put a strange new trio called the Wills Fiddle Band on the Fort Worth, Texas, airwaves a few years earlier, back in 1930—the same year Madison Cain had purchased the Louvre and renamed it. The month after Cain was stricken, that band's namesake moved a new, albeit ragtag, group of musicians to Tulsa, desperate for a chance to make it big—or, at least, to earn a living. (Stricklin would not join them until the next year.) After heading north from Waco, Texas for presumably greener pastures, they'd been run off a big Oklahoma City station by their leader's vengeful ex-employer and, in desperation, headed to Tulsa. Luckily for them, they'd find a radio home there and, several months later, a regular place to play and broadcast their dances—thanks in part to Howard Turner.

The band, of course, was Bob Wills and His Texas Playboys. And the place was the Cain's Dancing Academy.

****

Before going into the story of Wills and the Cain's, where the music that would become known as western swing grew up and lit out across the country and the world, it's our sad duty to explode one of the longest-lived and most persistent myths about the ballroom itself.

When Daddy Cain leased the building in 1930, he pulled out the old oak floor and installed one made of maple, which ended up lasting nearly eight decades. And under that maple floor, as everyone familiar with the place knows, he installed truck springs at intervals, to give the dancers a little extra bounce. The story of the springs is very specific, right down to the brand. They were made for Dodge trucks, heavy duty and built to last.

The legend of Cain's spring-loaded dance floor is absolutely ubiquitous. Historians and journalists and authors have spread the word about it for decades, and so have musicians. In a March 22, 1995 interview for a proposed book about the Cain's, music historian Guy Logsdon told interviewers Russ Florence and Steve Higgins that a pair of notable Tulsa musicians had tried to emulate what Daddy Cain did.

"When [drummer] Shirl Cummins and [steel-guitarist] Speedy West built the Caravan Ballroom [in 1963], they couldn't get the springs, so they went out and bought old tires," Logsdon recalled. "The dance floor at the Caravan is based on a 12-inch grid. They took the rubber tire treads and put them underneath every twelve inches throughout that dance floor—I was there and watched them do it.

"It adds a little bit. Not like springs. But they built the Caravan so the dance floor would give a little. It is not wood on top of concrete. So the second-best dance floor in Oklahoma is the Caravan Ballroom's."

We know, then, that at least one tire-tread-undergirded dancehall exists in the world. And, possibly, one enhanced by truck springs is somewhere out there as well.

It is, however, not the Cain's.

The decades-old myth was quietly exploded in late December of 2007, when Dean West and his 70-person crew from Tulsa's West Construction tore out the old floor, after an architectural study showed restoration to be unfeasible. Underneath it, they found a few broken pieces of glass and other inconsequential odds and ends—but not a sign of any springs, truck-sized or otherwise.

"I thought it might be a good joke to throw some springs in there," said a laughing West in an August 10, 2009 interview conducted for this book, "but I wasn't gutsy enough to do it."

If he had, those would have been the only springs ever to be found under the Cain's floor. Something accepted as fact by practically everyone who'd ever heard of the ballroom was, in reality, just a tall tale, intentionally or unintentionally started a very long time ago and perpetuated to this day.

Which is not to say, however, that the old floor didn't have a bit of spring to it.

"It did, but that was actually because the framing members were undersized," explained West. "It was framed with 2x6s, and the girder beams that the joists rested on were 10 to 12 feet apart—but the joists spanned two girders. So if you jumped on one side, it would teeter and raise someone standing beside you up, making it feel like it was spring-loaded."

****

During 1933, the ballroom's big year for fox trots, two-steps, waltzes, and tangos, the members of a hardscrabble Texas outfit headed by a charismatic, headstrong fiddler named Bob Wills were struggling to get themselves established with a radio station, a task made harder by the considerable clout of the fiddler's former boss, one W. Lee "Pappy" O'Daniel. (The two father figures—"Daddy" Cain and "Pappy" O'Daniel—figure heavily in the early days of Bob Wills and His Texas Playboys, albeit in different ways.) O'Daniel, later a major political figure in the state, had been for years the president and general manager of Burrus Mill and Elevator Company in Fort Worth, and it was in that capacity that he had hired Wills and other musicians to perform on radio as the Light Crust Doughboys, promoting the company's Light Crust Flour. (In those days, when baking was an everyday task in many of the country's homes, the flour market was far more competitive than today's consumers of baked goods might realize.)

Music historians point to the Light Crust Doughboys—and their predecessors, the Aladdin Laddies and the Wills Fiddle Band—as the earliest examples of what are now known as western-swing groups, and it's no coincidence that Wills was in all three of them. But both Wills and O'Daniel possessed significant

egos as well as different ways of looking at things, and almost from the moment of Wills' hiring in January 1931 (following a short stint in which the group played a morning show touting the company's products for free—or on spec, to put it in today's terms), the two seemed to be locking horns about one thing or another. Although it may be considered a somewhat fanciful recreation of the first meeting between Wills and O'Daniel, the account in the 1938 book *Hubbin' It: The Life of Bob Wills* by *Tulsa Tribune* writer Ruth Sheldon (which was privately printed and offered for sale for a dollar on Wills' radio shows from the Cain's) is instructive. The following exchange of dialogue comes after Wills—who in this telling came up with the Light Crust Doughboys name himself but hadn't seen much success with his freebie radio stint for Burrus Mills—decides he needs to plead his case with O'Daniel himself:

Bob pushed his way into O'Daniel's inner office and waited patiently for recognition. O'Daniel, an impressive figure, continued to busy himself with papers on his desk. In a few minutes he said coldly, "What did you want to talk to me about?"

"The main thing is, I want a job," Bob blurted. "I'll drive a truck, sweep the floor or anything. But I want a job."

"So you want to work?" O'Daniel said amusingly. "It's out of the ordinary for a musician to want to work, isn't it?"

"I've always worked and I sure know what hard work is," Bob retorted indignantly.

"Well that puts a different light on it if you're sure you want to work."

O'Daniel was silent a minute or two, and then offered to take on the program again paying each of the boys $7.50 a week. In addition to that, Bob would have to drive a flour truck every day. [Guitarist] Herman [Arnspiger] would join the bull gang loading and doing heavy work, and [vocalist] Milton [Brown] would call on bakers pushing sales.

After a few weeks, O'Daniel relieved the Light Crust Doughboys of their day jobs, but he still insisted that they work an eight-hour day, practicing when they weren't on the air. He also began writing continuity for their broadcasts and appearing as the show's announcer. He started composing poems he could read on the program. And he asked the band to come up with music for some of his verses, resulting in blatantly sentimental numbers like "Beautiful Texas" and "I Want Somebody to Cry over Me."

He also made the Doughboys stop playing dances. They'd been performing regularly at a Fort Worth spot called Crystal Springs, gigs that were a major source of income for the band members. But O'Daniel insisted they give up Crystal Springs and instead spend more time touring towns in Texas, playing stage shows and functioning as goodwill ambassadors for Light Crust Flour.

He accompanied that edict with a raise in pay. But Wills and Brown both chafed at the new restriction. "O'Daniel didn't believe in dancing or drinking," Guy Logsdon explained to reporter Sue Smith for a May 16, 1982 *Sunday Oklahoman* article. "Bob and Milton Brown preferred playing for dances and they enjoyed a good drink."

They also must've enjoyed the adulation they began receiving from their listeners. In a taped interview done around the early '60s, Wills told his interviewer—whom the authors believe to be Lee Ross, a former Wills vocalist—that the "thrill highlight" of his career to that date had not been with his own band, but with the Light Crust Doughboys and their "rambunctious" crowds:

We...had a limousine, played in the back, just three of us, and...they'd be so rambunctious we'd have to keep driving. We had speakers on top, and we couldn't stop. They would have turned it over with us [in it]....

We've been a lot of places they just couldn't handle them [the crowds]. We'd have to drive on out, throwing dollars, five-dollar bills, windows cracked at the top about that much.

[People] pushing in there [saying], "I want a Doughboy,"
and stuff like that. We had to move on. We couldn't stay. We
played to over 100,000 people in Wichita Falls—sitting off a
quarter of a mile, up on housetops. We had big speakers.
I've never seen nothing like that. Ever.

In September 1932, Brown—like Bob, a strong personality and natural leader—decided to split from the Doughboys and form his own band. Ostensibly, the reason was that he felt he was losing too much money by not playing dances. Another reason, however, probably had to do with the professional rivalry (as opposed to the personal friendship) between Brown and Wills concerning the leadership of the group. Taking along his brother Durwood, who sometimes played with the Doughboys, and putting together several other top-notch musicians—including the Oklahoma-born steel-guitar innovator Bob Dunn—Brown formed Milton Brown and His Musical Brownies. The group did well, and Brown, a seminal western-swing figure, might have rivaled Wills for popularity if his life hadn't ended in a post-show single-car wreck only a few years later, in 1936.

Meanwhile, the Light Crust Doughboys—featuring vocalist Tommy Duncan, who'd been hand-picked by Wills as Brown's successor—were steadily gaining in popularity, with the canny O'Daniel creating a growing radio network for the broadcasts. Using telephone lines to send the shows to different affiliates, he got the Doughboys program onto several other stations in Texas, and as far northward as Oklahoma City's KOMA.

But Wills wasn't particularly happy with many of O'Daniel's decisions, and a series of annoyances and conflicts led to his own departure. One thing that needled Wills was the fact that Brown had returned to their old dancehall, where he was prospering. "He was making more money in one night at Crystal Springs than Wills made at Burrus Mill all week, and Wills knew it," wrote Charles Townsend in the definitive Wills history, *San Antonio Rose: The Life and Music of Bob Wills* (University of Illinois Press, 1978). "He deeply resented the fact that O'Daniel's arbitrary decision was costing him dollars he desperately needed."

The band had grown larger, and Bob regularly petitioned O'Daniel about raises for him and his men, but he was usually turned down. Wills also wanted his brother Johnnie Lee in the band, but instead O'Daniel kept him driving a truck for the company rather than releasing him to play music. There were other conflicts between O'Daniel and members of the Wills family, including Bob's father, Uncle John Wills, who was living on a farm owned by O'Daniel at the latter's insistence.

And then there was an incident in late August, 1933, detailed in Sheldon's *Hubbin' It*, that was apparently the tipping point. Fort Worth had just legalized beer, and, Sheldon wrote, "Bob and the boys took their instruments and wandered from beer tavern to beer tavern helping the rest of Fort Worth drink up all the beer and playing wherever they went."

The next morning, Bob was AWOL from the program. Because O'Daniel didn't like alcohol and Bob Wills did, they'd had other problems along this line. This time, though, Bob's fondness for the high life led to his firing.

Although evidence indicates that the imperious O'Daniel might have given a properly chastened Wills another chance, the bandleader instead seized the opportunity to light out on his own. Vocalist Duncan and bassist Kermit Whalen threw in with Bob —leaving only two members of the band with O'Daniel—and with Johnnie Lee liberated from his mill job and playing tenor banjo (an important rhythm instrument in those drumless days), the group headed about 90 miles south to Waco. The Light Crust Doughboys were known there, so it didn't take much for the new group to get a show (on station WACO at 12:30 p.m., opposite the Doughboys program). A Waco fireman named Bill Little, who was a huge fan, found them some quick bookings in the area. But he made one misstep. When the ads for the first dance came out in the Waco papers, it touted the group, which had temporarily reverted to the earlier "Bob Wills Fiddle Band" moniker, as "(formerly Light Crust Doughboys)."

That little parenthetical identification brought a $10,000 lawsuit from O'Daniel on behalf of the mill, which soon landed the parties in Waco district court. Wills, with a couple of rookie attorneys, ended up beating the charge brought by his former employer, who appeared, according to Ruth Sheldon, with "a battery of lawyers from Fort Worth and Dallas." Not a man easily dissuaded, O'Daniel appealed to a higher court; the case kicked around until 1935, when the district court's decision was upheld.

Meanwhile, a Texas businessman, who'd just left a nine-year job with the Cities Service oil company, dropped by a Waco dance his brother-in-law was promoting. At the time, the ex-oil company employee was weighing offers from General Tire, American Oil, and Phillips Petroleum, but his initial encounter with the group playing the dance would nudge his life in another direction entirely.

His brother-in-law was the fireman, Bill Little. The band the man saw was Bob Wills' group.

And the man himself? He was Oliver Wheeler Mayo, who would become a major figure in the lives of Bob and Johnnie Lee Wills, as well as in the history of the Cain's Ballroom.

$50,000.oo **REWARD**

KIDNAPPED!

LOST, STRAYED OR STOLEN

A young man about the size of a widow woman, rosy cheeks, blue eyes and sunset golden hair, a dislocated eyebrow on his upper lip, a little patch of spinach on his chin, barefooted with a pair of hightop boots on, wearing a corn-beef overcoat with sauer kraut lining; has an empty sack on his back containing 50 skylines and 100 assorted railroad tunnels. Last seen was following a crowd of 999 people on their way to St. Patrick's Dance at Cain's Dancing Academy.

MORAL: In order to reduce these crowds to a more normal size we have added an extra dance night each week to better accommodate all the people. We are now dancing, Tuesday, Thursday and Saturday nights.

CAIN'S ACADEMY

927 East Second   TULSA   Phone 2-1950

Bob Wills and His Texas Playboys circa 1934, shortly after arriving in Tulsa

Bob Wills and His Texas Playboys circa 1935 from the stage of
Cain's Academy of Dancing

CHAPTER 03

We went to Waco and spent about six months down there. But I was raised in the cotton country and I knew when the cotton went out we'd better try to get someplace, move on, so we went to Oklahoma City first and stayed there a week and just got started good and O'Daniel had us throwed off of that station. Then we jumped on over into Tulsa. KVOO.

— Bob Wills, in an undated recording (circa the early '60s) with an interviewer the authors believe is Texas Playboys bassist-vocalist Lee Ross

The first time O.W. Mayo encountered Bob Wills and his group, it was at the American Woodmen Lodge in downtown Waco, where Mayo's fireman brother-in-law had booked the group.

"I saw them and they were sweating and so forth, and they didn't have any transportation," he recalled in his 1986 interview with Wooley. "They had an old Buick that was just a wreck that they had borrowed from somebody in Fort Worth to get down there in."

Mayo, on the other hand, owned a nearly new '32 Plymouth—"in good shape, a four-door, and it would haul six," he remembered. Fire-department rules about moonlighting forbade Mayo's brother-in-law to do much more than book the dances. Mayo, being between jobs, had no such restrictions, and he figured he might lend them a hand, and some transportation assistance, until he had to leave and report to whatever full-time job he ended up taking.

"So I said, 'Bob, I'm marking time here for a while, and I know the territory pretty well, and if I can help you I'll be glad to,'" related Mayo.

"He said, 'I sure would appreciate it.'"

With that exchange, a business and personal relationship began between Bob—and Johnnie Lee—Wills and O.W. Mayo that would last for decades. Together, they'd make their way out of Texas to Oklahoma, hooking up with a powerful radio station and ultimately establishing themselves at the Cain's Ballroom, transforming that dance studio/dancehall into the Carnegie Hall of western swing.

Once assured that Wills would appreciate his help, Mayo started booking the band and managing its finances. And when the wire came from Phillips Petroleum for Mayo to report November 1st to Amarillo for a new position that would, as he recalled, put him in charge "of all the company-operated stations in eastern New Mexico and west Texas, from the panhandle clear to the Rio Grande," Wills—according to Townsend's *San Antonio Rose*—talked him out of going and officially offered him a job.

"That," Townsend wrote, "was one of the wisest moves Wills ever made."

So was re-establishing himself and the band in Oklahoma, although it's not clear who came up with the idea. *Hubbin' It*, which Sheldon penned with the participation and approval of Wills, unsurprisingly names him as the instigator of the trip.

"When the Doughboy program had been broadcast from KOMA Oklahoma City quantities of fan mail had been received from that area," she wrote. "The majority of it was addressed to Bob personally. He figured that there would be enough interest in his personality there to keep them from starving to death."

"That's why I went to Oklahoma," Wills affirmed in the recorded interview excerpted at the beginning of this chapter. "I checked the mail all the time pretty close that was coming in to O'Daniel and the Doughboys, and most of our mail, the big majority, was all from Oklahoma. So it looked like it was the only way to go."

Wills also realized that the group had done well in Waco in great part because there had been a good cotton crop that year. A former field worker himself, he knew that much of the disposable income in the region would have been spent once winter arrived, and things didn't have a chance of getting appreciably better until the next fall. In Sheldon's telling, he even had to convince his new business manager about the necessity of the move.

"Mayo argued with Bob against going to Oklahoma, pointing out that they were doing well in Waco making as much as $170 a night," wrote Sheldon, "and it would be foolish to go where they could not be sure of the possibilities of succeeding."

For his part, Mayo told Wooley that he "saw the potential" in Wills and his band, and that he felt that they needed to get beyond Waco, where local broadcaster WACO "was just a small station. If you got over 50 or 60 miles away, you didn't hear it."

Certainly, lurking in the back of both of their minds was the idea of putting some miles between them and Pappy O'Daniel, who was still hell-bent on pursuing the damage suit against the band. (According to one oft-expressed school of thought, he'd underestimated Wills' popularity and was, essentially, trying to sue him back into the Doughboys.)

Mayo, Bob, and the band quickly found out, however, that O'Daniel's harassment didn't stop at the Red River. In January of 1934, Wills and Mayo visited Oklahoma City's KOMA, only to be told that they couldn't have a show on the station because the Light Crust Doughboys—which had continued with different personnel after Bob's departure—were still on the air there, and the program generated good income for KOMA. O'Daniel, of course, rode herd over the Doughboy broadcasts and would not stand for a Wills show on the same station.

So they tried a rival broadcaster, WKY, which agreed to give the band a shot.

During their stint in Waco, Bob had begun calling his group the Playboys. "It was a natural adaptation," explained Sheldon in *Hubbin' It*, "since they had been called 'Doughboys' for so long and thought of themselves always as the 'boys.'" (Interestingly enough, the Johnnie Lee Wills band that made the Cain's its base after Bob left was called All the Boys or, simply, the Boys or his Boys.) But once they crossed into Oklahoma, he added the name of the state where the band was born, and the group became Bob Wills and His Texas Playboys.

That's the name they played under when they began their WKY shows, probably in very early February. And it's the name they kept when they left the Oklahoma City airwaves, after only five broadcasts.

The reason? Once again, it was good old Pappy, as Mayo explained:

We were on the air just about a week, and one morning, Daryl McAllister, the program director, called me and said, "I want to see you and Bob in the studio." So we went down and he told me what had happened. O'Daniel had called the manager of that station [WKY], the big shot, and told him he'd been figuring on moving his show from KOMA over to WKY, but as long as they had Bob Wills on, he wasn't going to consider it anymore. He gave him such a talk that he

thought all he had to do was kick Bob off the station and
he'd have the Light Crust Doughboys show. I said, "Let us
talk to him." But Daryl wouldn't. You couldn't talk to the
manager of the station.

McAllister, however, told them of a new outlet, KTUL, that had recently signed onto the airwaves in Tulsa, and offered to call there on behalf of the band. They took him up on it, and when McAllister got a positive response, Wills, Mayo, and Everett Stover—the former WACO station manager who had joined the band as announcer and trumpeter—headed up the road to Tulsa.

It was a cold and foggy Oklahoma morning, and the mood inside the car was just as gloomy. While the band's plum days in Waco might have ended when the cotton money was all spent, the group still had a following there, as well as a radio show with a sponsor, the Jones Fine Bread Company. Bob and the band had pinned their hopes on WKY—Stover had even quit his job at WACO to throw in with Wills—and now they were headed to a smaller station in a smaller city, still hounded by O'Daniel.

Mayo may have been grasping at straws when he came up with the idea of holding off on visiting KTUL. It may have been a notion born out of desperation; certainly, he realized what a battle it would be to attract a sizable audience from broadcasts over a brand-new station that didn't have a lot of wattage. Whatever the motivation, the decision to begin elsewhere set Bob Wills' feet onto the path that led to the Cain's Ballroom, and from there to the kind of stardom most acts can only dream about.

* * * *

"On our way over [to Tulsa], I said, 'Bob, KVOO radio is over there, and they're a 25,000-watt station. This station we're going to is only a 500-watt station,'" Mayo recalled to Wooley. "'Let's go see KVOO first, and we might get a chance to get on that station.'"

The three agreed on that course of action, and upon hitting town, found a barbershop on First Street and got shaves, so that they could look as presentable as possible when they arrived unbidden at the KVOO offices, which were then in the downtown Wright Building, behind the Tulsa post office. As luck would have it, general manager William B. Way wasn't in. The receptionist, Mayo remembered, told them, "If it's important, I know where he is, and I can get hold of him."

"We said we thought it was pretty important, and told her who we were," he added, "so she called him. And Bill Way, who was [famed oilman and KVOO owner] Bill Skelly's right-hand man, came in, and we gave him a song and dance."

Apparently, Way was not an easy sell. In a letter written to Wills, Mayo, and the group in February 1939, acknowledging the band's five successful years on the station, he recalled that first meeting:

> *Selling me on the idea that our station needed an*
> *orchestra, that our public was interested in a group*
> *of Texas kids with no particular claim to glory, was*
> *not easy. When I finally relented, due entirely to your*
> *superlative ability to sell yourselves, there still was*

considerable doubt in my mind. Now I am convinced
that you knew exactly what you were talking about
when you said you'd prove a success.

Once he'd had his resistance worn down, Way told the trio to get the rest of the band members, all of whom were staying in an Oklahoma City boardinghouse, to the station as soon as possible. KVOO normally signed off at midnight, but Way agreed to leave the station on the air for another hour so he could try the group out that night.With only a couple of hours to go before showtime, the rest of the guys roared in from Oklahoma City, setting up for the broadcast in the basement of the Wright Building. And at midnight, going in to February 9, 1934, Bob Wills and His Texas Playboys made the first of what would be thousands of broadcasts for the 25,000-watt flamethrower, whose call letters stood, appropriately, for "Voice of Oklahoma."

"[We] said we'd give a picture of the band to the one who sent a letter or card from the furthest distance," noted Mayo. "That winning card or letter came from Oakland, California. We were clear-channel, and they didn't have all these little stations going, so we didn't have much interference."

(The "clear-channel" designation, in those strictly AM radio days, meant that there were hardly any stations with a similar frequency within their broadcast pattern, so KVOO could be heard relatively clearly for hundreds of miles—which is how the Playboys' broadcasts got to the West Coast, and sometimes beyond, especially after KVOO doubled its power to 50,000 watts a few years later.)

Way was impressed enough by their midnight tryout to give Bob Wills and His Texas Playboys a regular show, although in its early days it bounced around from morning to afternoon to evening and was what was termed a sustaining program or a "sustainer." That meant it was unsponsored, so the band got no money for doing it. However, it was well worth the effort because it introduced the band to the listening public. That exposure translated into offers to play dances and other events, with the band, in turn, using the radio shows to let people know about their live appearances.

"We'd just tell 'em we were available for dance engagements and schools and so forth," explained Mayo about their radio strategy, "and pretty soon the letters began to come in, and the calls came in, and in a week's time we were playing every night."

Predictably, W. Lee O'Daniel tried again to sabotage the band, phoning up Way and laying out the same sort of line he'd used to get Wills dumped from WKY. Way, however, didn't bite, and assured Mayo, Wills, and the boys that they had a home on KVOO.

(Way's shrugging-off of O'Daniel must've meant a great deal to the boys, after all the bedevilment he'd caused them since Wills had left the Doughboys. Their feelings toward Way, and his boss Skelly, go a long way toward explaining why Mayo included big pictures of those two non-performers right along with the famed recording-star photos he later put up on the Cain's walls.)

According to Townsend, during the first year or so of the Wills broadcasts over KVOO, O'Daniel kept turning up like the proverbial bad penny, even though it was clear that William B. Way was beyond coercion or intimidation. Then, in 1935, Bob's former boss was let go by Burrus Mill and Elevator Company. Although

Those delightful entertainers whose enchanting melodies and sparkling gaiety have charmed you over the air-waves . . .

Meet Them Face to Face
—STARTING TODAY! . . .

Your Radio Favorites
ON THE STAGE

TEXAS PLAYBOYS

—Out from "behind the mike"

IN PERSON

combined with a cast of delirious funsters in a swift-moving, tune-laden laff production!

—Four—
BIG PERFORMANCES TODAY
at—2:17, 4:34, 6:50, 9:24

Screen
A mighty, thrill-jammed drama of terrific action—and conquering love!

JACK HOLT
WHIRLPOOL

Also PAUL HURST in "There Aint No Justice"

26c
12:30 to 7:00

A "Screen Souvenir" McNamee News

Liberty

Oklahoma City Newspaper Ad
May 27, 1934

he quickly put together a new group, W. Lee O'Daniel's Hillbilly Boys, and got his own Hillbilly Flour on the market, Pappy O'Daniel was far less formidable without the clout of the big well-established Fort Worth mill behind him. So he apparently decided he'd try a new tack with Wills.

"He had the guts to try to make a merger with his Hillbilly Boys and Bob Wills and His Texas Playboys after he didn't have Burrus Mill's money to fight us," Mayo told Townsend, who added that, unbeknownst to Mayo, O'Daniel had made a pitch to take over as Bob's manager.

Of course, that didn't work either. But there may have been one other attempt by O'Daniel to cut into Wills' deal. If O'Daniel was indeed responsible, it was at the least an audacious, not to say *desperate*, move.

The authors heard this little-known piece of musical history from Wills expert Glenn White, whose vast collection includes a 1934 ad from an Oklahoma City newspaper, advertising the Texas Playboys and illustrated with, among other things, representations of young women in chorus-girl attire.

When I went up to see Mr. Mayo one time, I showed it [the ad] to him. Two things would ruffle his feathers: something with scantily clad women, and W. Lee O'Daniel.

I showed him that clipping, and I said, "That wasn't y'all, was it?"

"No," he said, "it wasn't. Where did you find this?"

"Well, it was in the paper about May of '34, a few months after you were already in Tulsa. This bunch was at a theater [in Oklahoma City]. It looks like they're advertising a group of singers and novelties and comedy and all that stuff."

He said, "That wasn't us. That was in the paper?"

I said, "Yes sir, but nobody knows that but me."

I got to analyzing this thing, and what I think happened was that W. Lee O'Daniel put a bunch on the road with some scantily-clad girls dancing around, trying to hurt Bob, and something changed his mind and he backed off. It's just too coincidental that they were out at the same time, and he was out to get them anyway.

If that show was in fact masterminded by O'Daniel, it was just one in the long line of his failed attempts to re-insert himself into

Bob Wills' career. After a few more years, his passion for chasing Wills apparently faded, and O'Daniel entered Texas politics. He was elected governor of the state in 1938, following a campaign that featured extensive public appearances with his Hillbilly Boys in support. Then, in 1941, he became the only politician ever to defeat Lyndon Johnson in an election when he squeaked by the future U.S. president in a race for the United States Senate.

According to *San Antonio Rose* author Charles Townsend's entry on O'Daniel in *The Handbook of Texas Online* (www.tshaonline.org), once Pappy became governor, he took his Hillbilly Boys with him to the state capitol and got them jobs with the government. They also got together to play a weekly show from the governor's mansion.

"Most of the musicians never saw the inside of the mansion," Townsend wrote. "They played the show on the front porch and were never invited inside."

* * * *

Wills and the Playboys, meanwhile, needed a place in Tulsa to have as a base, somewhere in town where they could play regularly. After a few months of broadcasts over KVOO, they'd generated plenty of potentially regular patrons for local dances. Now all they needed was a venue where they could go, say, once a week, between their out-of-town gigs.

It wasn't the Cain's Ballroom, though. At least, not at first. Instead, it was a second-story dancehall built over a garage at Second Street and Madison Avenue. The place was called the Pla-Mor, and it would later be utilized by steel-guitarist Leon McAuliffe, after he'd left Bob and formed his own band, as well as a number of early Tulsa rock 'n' rollers. About half the size of the Cain's, according to Mayo, it was the Thursday night place to see Wills and the Playboys live for the better part of a year.

Then, along came some nurses, with an offer for a gig in another, bigger hall.

"It was New Year's night, nineteen-hundred-and-thirty-five," Mayo told John Wooley for a March 5, 1993 *Tulsa World* story. "It was a benefit for the nurses of Morningside Hospital, which is now Hillcrest. We were playing down at the Pla-Mor on Second Street, and they came to us to ask us to play their dance. They sold the tickets and everything, and we told them that under the circumstances, we wanted to chip in too, so we played it for $100."

Cain had suffered his debilitating stroke a year earlier, so he wasn't on the premises. But Howard Turner was, and he either saw for himself or heard about the crowd that Wills and the Playboys drew—which, Mayo noted, "opened his eyes about the possibilities." After that successful engagement, Mayo made a deal with Cain's management—probably Turner and Alice Cain, Madison's wife—to move the band's base from the Pla-Mor to Daddy Cain's place for the regular dances.

"We started playing a Thursday night dance there, on a percentage," recalled Mayo in the 1993 interview. "We got 65 percent and they took 35."

(Here, we should note that Turner's stepson Don Mayes related a persistent family story that has Turner seeing Bob and the Playboys perform in Texas and, impressed, going to Daddy Cain's hospital bed and recommending that they bring the band to the ballroom. While the part about Texas doesn't quite synch up,

Turner may well have taken in the band at the Pla-Mor; Mayes has an undated newspaper ad, possibly predating Turner's affiliation with Cain, that reads: "Learn to dance. Pla-Mor Ballroom Dancing Academy. Howard Turner, instructor.")

Whatever the circumstances that led to it, the move was a good one for a number of reasons. Of course, the musicians were happy about not having to lug their instruments up a flight of stairs. But more important, the Cain's was twice as big as their former venue, and therefore able to accommodate far larger crowds.

"We was putting 1800, 2000, sometimes 2200 people in the place," Wills told his interviewer in the previously mentioned recording. "Mayo liked to have fainted. He was used to us playing that little Pla-Mor, you know, with a fourth of them [the crowd] being able to get in."

The once-a-week job became a twice-weekly event, and the noontime radio broadcasts, which had begun at the KVOO studios, were moved to the Cain's, where hundreds of enthusiastic fans, admitted free, greeted each show.

Meanwhile, ballroom-dancing lessons continued at the Cain's, with Alice Cain insisting that the crowd maintain decorum according to the rules put in place by her husband—and not only during the instruction sessions, but at the evening dances as well. It was only natural that the worlds of ballroom dancing and Wills' more earthy approach would collide, and they did.

Here's how Wills himself remembered it in the recorded interview, recalling that the cost to get in was 40 cents a person, with Alice Cain in charge of the room:

Alice Cain

She's standing on the sidelines one night, and I keep seeing her pluck couples off the floor and the law take 'em out. So finally I called one of the laws over—that was old Briggs, who worked with me years later, for years— and I said, "What in the world's happening to these people here? They're dancing and you're taking them out."

He said, "They don't have a tie on and they've got their sleeves rolled up, and she wants them with a tie and coat on."

Here we are up there with our sleeves rolled up and no ties on, and the sweat pouring down us—it wasn't air-conditioned. So I just got down and went and talked to her.

She said, "Well, they can go home and put on a tie and a coat and get back in."

"I'm sorry, Miz Cain, but that won't work," I said—we started this off, this so-called Ford idea—"We're Fords, not Cadillacs. We're charging a Ford price, and you cannot afford to run these boys out of here because they haven't got a tie and coat. If they're dancing with me, they're gonna dance like they are or there won't be no dance here next Saturday night. Now that's the way it is. Just stop it tonight. No more going out the door."

We had quite a wrangle there, but didn't no more go out the door.

After that, as Wills remembered it, he told Mayo, "You get out there Monday and make some kind of deal with her, or I'm not touching the place anymore."

I said, "I mean it. You're not going to treat them people that
way." She's here with just a piano player, playing to 15, 20
people [on the dance nights the Playboys weren't there] and
lucky if they had that many, then all of a sudden she's run-
ning them out that door.
So he went out there and, luckily, he bought it from her.
And of course we went on running the dance the way
I figured it should have been run. My goodness. Those
kids, some of them, didn't even have a coat or a tie. It was
Depression days then. Throwin' 'em out was ridiculous to me.

So, according to Mayo's 1986 interview, he and Bob got a bank loan and took over the place. "In 1937," he said, "we bought Daddy Cain's lease out. We leased it from the [Tate] Brady estate through an insurance company that had a loan against it and was doing all the collecting. When we leased it, we put this [drop] ceiling in, and we put in an air-conditioner—it was washed air, water-circulation."

By that time, although the dance lessons still continued under the tutelage of Howard Turner—who performed other tasks for the new management as well—the Cain's Ballroom was far better known for the music played by its famed inhabitants, Bob Wills and His Texas Playboys, than for the ballroom-dance training that had begun in the '20s.

Its fame wasn't just local, or even regional. Thanks to a pairing of the hall with a radio station that reached into most of America, people all over the country knew the name of the Cain's Ballroom. Bob and his Playboys, KVOO, and the Cain's formed a powerful three-strand rope that lassoed in millions of listeners, and it's time now to take a closer look at that partnership, and how it got going.

Cain's in the 1930s

Sometime during 1934, KVOO moved its studios from the Wright Building onto the 32nd floor of a six-year-old skyscraper called the Philtower. Financed by famed area oilman Waite Phillips, the structure rose impressively into the sky a few blocks from the station's previous digs in downtown Tulsa.

Nineteen-thirty-four was also the year that Bob Wills and His Texas Playboys went from doing a sustaining program to a sponsored one. "In September 1934, just one year after Wills left the Light Crust Doughboys, KVOO signed a contract with the makers of Crazy Water Crystals for a program at 12:30 p.m.," wrote

Charles Townsend in *San Antonio Rose*. "The sponsor's contract required that Bob Wills and His Texas Playboys play the show. Still no pay. But Wills was convinced he could build a good dance circuit with this prime time."

Although the sponsorship didn't benefit the band in a direct financial way, it had the effect of stabilizing the program, because the revenue went to KVOO. Station management put the show into a regular noon-hour slot, which meant it aired at a time when everyone from office personnel to field workers took their lunches, often gathering around their primary source of entertainment, the radio, while they ate. KVOO also sweetened the pot by giving Wills and the boys an extra 15 minutes of airtime each day; Crazy Water had only contracted for a quarter-hour show, but the broadcast ran from 12:30 until 1 p.m. every day but Sunday.

****

At this point, a reader, far removed from those pre-antibiotic days of the 1930s, could be forgiven for wondering just exactly what Crazy Water Crystals *were*.

They were what might now be called a natural, or "folk," remedy. Ostensibly made from ingredients found in nature—in this case, spring water from Texas that had been boiled down in a factory until only crystalline minerals remained—Crazy Water Crystals were recommended as treatment for a variety of ailments, from kidney disease and diabetes to upset stomach and constipation.

The crystals came along during a national mania for mineral water, which was then being touted as a potential curative for just about anything. America's infatuation with the stuff had begun around the turn of the century and was still going in the mid-'30s, when Crazy Water Crystals—so named because a mentally ill woman had apparently been rendered sane by repeated drinks from the springs that yielded the crystalline medication—sponsored the Playboys show.

Did Crazy Water Crystals actually work? Well, apparently some people thought they did, and that number included C.W. Parker of

Seminole, Oklahoma, who saw fit to compose a paean to the band and its sponsor very soon after the program went on the air. The correspondence is dated September 17, 1934, and it came to the authors from the collection of Playboys saxophonist Robert "Zeb" McNally.

Here, reproduced in its entirety, is Mr. Parker's versification:

Here's to Crazy Water
Bob Wills and all his Gang,
With all ther songs and "tootin"
Their Lingo and their Slang.
Of all the entertainers
Here and there and everywhere,
There is no better program
Ever sent out on the air.
And, Boy, those Crazy Crystals
When you're feelin' down and out,
Will really work you over
Make you sing and dance and shout.
You'll forget the family Doctor
There'll be no ache nor pain,
You'll hark back to your Childhood
And be a Kid again.
So call the corner Druggist
Let's get started, now, today,
Cause those Crazy Crystals
Will make you want to play.
So here's to Bob and Everett,
June, Tom and all the Gang,
One long cheer for Crazy Water
She's gone over with a "Bang."

("June" was guitarist June Whalin, who would, along with his bassist-steel guitarist brother Kermit, soon leave the band. "Tom" was vocalist Tommy Duncan, who wouldn't.)

Crazy Water Crystals sponsored the Texas Playboys program until late in 1935, a period of some 14 months. During that time, Wills not only moved into the Cain's and began doing the noontime broadcasts from there; he also began adding band members, picking up such important musicians as drummer William "Smokey" Dacus (making the Texas Playboys the first "hillbilly" band—a term Bob hated, according to his daughter Carolyn—to include drums), pianist "Brother" Al Stricklin, and a young steel-guitarist named Leon McAuliffe, who'd just left the Light Crust Doughboys in Fort Worth.

While that period saw Bob Wills and his band gain its first foothold on the national stage, it also marked the beginning of the end for Crazy Water Crystals. According to the Museum of Quackery website (www.museumofquackery.com), the head of the American Medical Association's Bureau of Investigation at the time found that the crystals produced in the Crazy Water Crystals plant in Mineral Wells, Texas, were actually Glauber's salt, a sodium sulfate compound used as a horse laxative and diuretic by veterinarians. Given those properties, the name of the AMA's investigator, Dr. Arthur J. Cramp, can be seen as an amusing coincidence.

Of course, it may simply have been that sodium sulfate was the primary mineral in the springs, and the crystals were being produced as advertised. But the 1935 report by Dr. Cramp surely put a crimp in Crazy Water's operations. The company, based in Mineral Wells, Texas, had been sponsoring a lot of broadcasts by what were then known as hillbilly acts, but evidence indicates the outfit cut back after the mid-'30s. Wills was probably not the only artist cut loose by Crazy Water, as the whole national mineral-water mania was receding at the time.

In 1940, the Federal Trade Commission ordered the Crazy Water Company to "cease and desist from misrepresentation concerning their products," listing a host of diseases and afflictions that Crazy Water could not claim to treat. An FTC press release from December 20 noted, "The Commission finds that the products possess no therapeutic value in excess of those of a cathartic or laxative, plus a tendency to temporarily neutralize excess gastric acidity."

That was enough, though, for some of its devotees. Crazy Water Crystals continued to be sold, and swallowed, into the 1950s.

****

It's easy to overlook the fact that the Crazy Water Crystals lunchtime program did *not* mark the first time Wills and his Playboys broadcast from the Cain's Ballroom. After making the deal with Howard Turner to stage their regular dances there instead of the Pla-Mor, the band soon added a dance on Saturday night as well as on Thursday. And, through an arrangement with KVOO, they began to air an hour of each dance—from 11:05 p.m. until midnight on Thursdays, and from midnight to one a.m. on Saturdays.

Perhaps Wills and Mayo considered that time frame lucky; after all, it had been an hour-long midnight broadcast that had won them a spot on the station and given their efforts a much-needed boost. Now they were getting to be well established not just in the Tulsa area, but in the 37 other states that KVOO's big signal reportedly reached.

"Why, I remember one time, when we had that midnight broadcast here back before the war," the great guitarist and arranger Eldon Shamblin (who joined Wills in 1937) told writer Wayne Mason for a January 18, 1970 *Tulsa World* story. "There was a bunch of people up in Wisconsin who chartered a rail coach and came to Tulsa. Just to dance. Can you imagine it?"

Years later, in 1995, Shamblin told interviewer Steve Higgins that during one stretch in the late '30s, over the Christmas holidays and into the new year, the Playboys did "two weeks in a row, Thursday, Friday, and Saturday...and we averaged three thousand people [per night] for those six nights."

It's hard to imagine how crowds of that size could fit into the ballroom, even given the number of people who were outside dealing with bootleggers, drinking, smoking, romancing, or simply grabbing a breath of air at any given time. As drummer Smokey Dacus noted in an episode of the OETA television series *Tulsa Magazine*, taped at the Cain's in 1992, "You put 1200 [in here], you've got a crowd."

That program also featured Shamblin, who reminisced about the Thursday and Saturday dances to host Jack Frank. "This thing would be packed," he said. "Solid people. If they was dancing, you couldn't even see them dancing, it was so crowded. They didn't even have room to dance."

For someone living in these days of media saturation, it's difficult to imagine a time when only sound and not moving pictures comprised the broadcast entertainment in America's living rooms. Radio broadcasts, including those from the Cain's, required listeners to create the visual elements in their own minds, perhaps with the help of newspaper or magazine photographs. And when they finally got to compare the reality with their imaginations, as Wills fan Gene Walker did, the results could be almost overwhelming.

"I was not very old when I heard those [Cain's] broadcasts," he told interviewer Russ Florence in March of 1995, during the celebration of the 90th anniversary of Wills' birth at the ballroom. "I could just see people, crowds and crowds of people. I could just imagine so many things. When I came the first time, it was like looking at the whole world, just walking in there. I thought, 'Oh, I'm *here*.'"

****

During that formative year of 1935, Wills and the boys were busy brewing up a brand-new musical stew, throwing ingredients together that had never before been combined, cooking them from the Cain's stage, and serving the resultant concoctions hot via KVOO to midnight listeners over most of the country—who eagerly gobbled them up and craved more. Then, since the transmission line to KVOO was already installed at the ballroom, it didn't take long for Wills to realize that he could also do his 12:30 broadcasts for Crazy Water Crystals from the same bandstand.

The Cain's was also the place he rehearsed and refined the mixture of country-dance beat and jazz improvisation—mixing in elements of blues, pop, old-time fiddle tunes, and south-of-the-border music—that would eventually be known as western swing. (A term, incidentally, first applied not to Wills' music,

Bob Wills and His Texas Playboys circa 1936 from the stage of Cain's Academy of Dancing

but to that of his Southern California-based counterpart, Spade Cooley, in the 1940s.)

In their *Tulsa Magazine* TV episode, both Dacus and Shamblin told interviewer Frank that the Cain's was the place where Wills built his band and wrote, arranged, and rehearsed "all the big hits he had," according to Shamblin.

"He'd sit out here in one of them chairs...they had rows of seats out here for the studio audience while we played the [noontime] broadcast," he added. "We'd rehearse, and he'd sit and listen, and if he liked it, he'd grin. If he didn't, he'd shake his head."

Of course, when the time came to hit the airwaves, Wills was up on the stage with the rest of the boys, playing six afternoons a week for crowds that averaged around 300 souls every day, swelling to many more for special shows. But the number of audience members, many of whom brought their lunches to the Cain's and ate while they watched and listened, wasn't as important as the broadcasts themselves, which got the word out about Bob's upcoming appearances and touted the products of his sponsor—which, by November of 1935, was a product called Play Boy Flour. Wills was understandably interested in extolling the virtues of this new product; he'd worked out an agreement with the company to get a percentage of the profits from every sale.

This was far different from his Crazy Water deal. Sales of that product could've exploded or died during its sponsorship of the Playboys' noon-hour show, and neither would've had much of an effect on Wills' pocketbook. The Crazy Water Company paid the station, not Wills, for the airtime, and Wills got no money from the advertiser (or KVOO)—his sole payment was exposure to potential audiences for his dances and other public appearances. As the Crazy Water contract wound down, however, Wills and Mayo came up with the idea to buy that 12:30–1 p.m. slot themselves—at a cost of approximately $12,000 a year—and then turn around and offer it to a sponsor. As Townsend pointed out in *San Antonio Rose*, this was something of a revolutionary idea. "If Wills was not the first," he wrote, "he was among the first artists to purchase his own radio time and then sell his own show. He was as unorthodox in this respect as he was in music; but he was young, and orthodoxy meant nothing to him."

The sponsor Wills and Mayo landed was a Wichita, Kansas-based outfit called the Red Star Milling Company, a subsidiary of the giant General Mills organization. And it just may be that Pappy O'Daniel, in what appears to have been his last attempt to get his hooks back into Bob Wills, had something to do with giving them the idea.

Hubbin' It, the 1938 book sanctioned by Wills, is rather circumspect about this connection. However, it's tempting to connect some dots after reading this passage by author Ruth Sheldon: "Extremely conscious of Bob's popularity and drawing power, he [O'Daniel] came to him with a proposition. He wanted to go into partnership with Bob and sponsor flour. The idea was not a new one to Bob. He had been thinking of the same thing, but had not gone into details."

It's unclear if this was the same proposed merger Mayo told Charles Townsend about (see Chapter Three), in which O'Daniel wanted to merge his Hillbilly Boys with the Playboys, or a second attempt. It is, however, quite possible that this overture from

O'Daniel helped spur Mayo and Wills toward landing a flour-company sponsorship. (Remember, O'Daniel had hooked up with another mill after leaving Burrus, and soon he not only had his new group, the Hillbilly Boys, but a new product for those boys to promote: Hillbilly Flour.)

The deal Mayo and Wills hammered out with the Red Star Milling Company would introduce a new product to the crowded flour market. Called Play Boy Flour, it would be advertised solely by the Texas Playboys' radio shows from the Cain's. And, in return for buying the airtime for the company, Wills would get a percentage of the take from every barrel sold. "He would be the only advertising medium for it," wrote Sheldon in *Hubbin' It.*

IF YOU ENJOY OUR PROGRAM — GIVE THE BOYS A HAND. FEEL FREE TO APPLAUD AFTER EACH NUMBER.

BOB WILLS SUGGESTS
For All Home Baking
- PLAYBOY -
THE ALL PURPOSE FAMILY FLOUR
AND
WHEN YOU BUY BREAD
ASK FOR
PLAYBOY BREAD
The Energy Food
YOUR GROCER HAS IT

"Instead of the usual procedure of a company buying radio time and hiring talent to sell its product, Bob was offering talent and time in exchange for a product. For the first time a radio program could prove with exact figures how many people it influenced, as it would be brand new to the market."

Once the deal was hammered out, Bob and His Texas Playboys crafted a new song, done to the tune of "Alabama Jubilee," that they would play on the air. That's according to western-swing great Curly Lewis, whose association with the

Wills organization went back to 1936, when the 11-year-old Lewis won a fiddling competition and got to appear on a Wills broadcast. Well over 70 years later, in a 2009 interview for this book, he could still sing the lyrics.

> *That was their theme: "Play Boy Flour is now on the air, we sing its praises wherever we are. It's proven and tested for all baking plans, so buy a sack "—and then Bob would say, "Buy a sack"—"it's good or your money back."*
>
> *They used that for a long time when they were advertising Play Boy Flour, and I don't know of anybody who would know that other than me, because I don't know if it was ever recorded.*

By early 1936, sales of Play Boy Flour had "shot to the top of the graph," Sheldon wrote. Play Boy Bread was soon added to the line, and Mayo, Wills, and the Texas Playboys skillfully marketed the products not only on each noontime show, but also by occasionally leaving the Cain's to make those broadcasts from grocery stores and bakeries that carried their products. Other marketing tools, highly prized by collectors today, were cards featuring a picture of a band member along with his favorite recipe—all of which, naturally, had Play Boy Flour as an ingredient. Even business manager Mayo had his picture on a card. It instructed home bakers on how to make his ostensible favorite dessert, egg custard pie.

****

Cain's Academy Broadcast, April 1938

While children were admitted to the Cain's dances—with the younger ones being laid down to sleep on the benches that surrounded the dance floor and, sometimes, on blankets right up on the side of the stage—the Thursday and Saturday night shindigs were aimed toward grownups.

The noontime shows, however, not only attracted working men and women from Tulsa, who could make it over to the Cain's on their lunch hours, but also parents and kids doing their shopping in the city. The latter applies to a youngster named Earl Edward Basse and his mother, two characters in one of the most poignant stories to come out of all the years of the noonday broadcasts.

In the early '30s, polio was one of the most frightening diseases imaginable, and the infant Earl Edward had contracted it, leaving him paralyzed from the waist down. The Basse family lived in nearby Sperry, and Earl Edward's dad bolted a wooden chair onto a red wagon so his mother could pull him around with her when she came to Tulsa on her weekly shopping trips.

The noon broadcasts hadn't been going long when Mrs. Basse wheeled four-year-old Earl Edward into the Cain's to watch Wills and the boys do their KVOO show.

"They had people sitting around all over, in front of the stage, and she pulled him right up there in his wagon," remembered Earl Edward's brother Jack in an interview with John Wooley, for a story that ran in the February 26, 2006 *Tulsa World*. "She didn't do that with anything special in mind, as far as I know. But he was a real personable kid, and at the break, Bob came down and started visiting with him. Then, every time after that when he'd show up [at the broadcasts], Bob would visit with him a little more."

Earl Edward and other members of his family became frequent visitors to the KVOO noon-hour shows, and over the next couple of years, a special bond was forged between the preschooler and the fast-rising bandleader—the kind of bond, many have said, that typified Wills, a man who'd arisen from tough circumstances and had a deep empathy with those who faced their own challenges. Smokey Dacus gave host Jack Frank a good example of Wills' largesse in the *Tulsa Magazine* TV episode taped at the Cain's in 1992:

If I've seen this once, I've seen it at least somewhere between 25 and 50 times, right here on this floor. We'd come off a noon program, and we'd start across to get a cup of coffee or something after. And here would come some guy in overalls. He'd stop Bob back there. The story was always the same. His mother was sick. And she was always in California. And could Bob let him have five dollars to help him buy a bus ticket....

Bob would reach in his pocket and give him a hundred dollars, and the guy would thank him. Profusely. And then leave—right quick, while he was ahead.

Soon as he got out of earshot up here by the door, we'd just stand there and wait. Bob would say, "Well, he's probably lying, but I don't want to take that chance."

Other stories abound of Wills giving out money to buy clothes and other necessities, without being asked, when he spotted someone who looked needy in his audience. According to Eldon Shamblin's comments on the same television program, if Wills spotted a woman at the show wearing rags, he'd often go to Cain's secretary Ada Perry after the broadcast and say, "Take her down to one of the stores in town and buy her a complete outfit—coat, dress, shoes," and then pay for it all.

His gift to the Basse family was different, but no less commendable. In the spring of 1937, only four days after Wills' 32nd birthday, young Earl Edward passed away at the age of six. Said Jack Basse:

I don't know how he found out about Earl Edward, but he called my dad and asked if he could play at the funeral. I remember that he had Tommy Duncan and [bassist-vocalist] Joe Frank Ferguson and two or three others at the

*Christian Church in Sperry [for the funeral]. They had
one of those big limousine deals; they were on their way
somewhere to play a dance. I was 10 years old then, and I
remember one song they played was "Mother, Put My Little
Shoes Away."*

*I remember him coming to the family car and talking to
my mother and dad, big old tears coming down his face. It
was quite a tragedy for our family, but we all appreciated
what he did. And after that, it just seemed like Bob Wills
was a real person.*

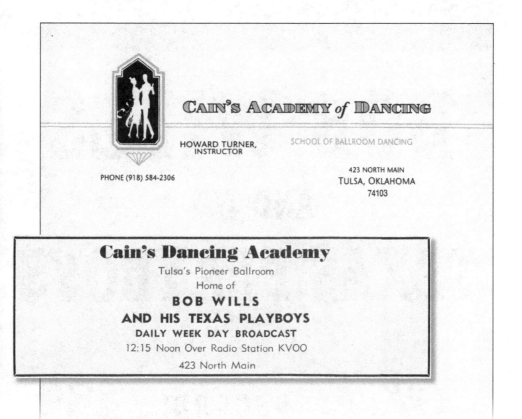

CAIN'S ACADEMY *of* DANCING

HOWARD TURNER,
INSTRUCTOR

SCHOOL OF BALLROOM DANCING

PHONE (918) 584-2306

423 NORTH MAIN
TULSA, OKLAHOMA
74103

Cain's Dancing Academy
Tulsa's Pioneer Ballroom
Home of
**BOB WILLS
AND HIS TEXAS PLAYBOYS**
DAILY WEEK DAY BROADCAST
12:15 Noon Over Radio Station KVOO
423 North Main

AMERICA'S GREATEST STRING BAND

BOB WILLS
AND HIS
TEXAS PLAYBOYS

OKeh RECORDS 35¢

See other side for complete list of his Okeh Records

05

We just lived to dance, to go out to the Cain's on Thursday and Saturday nights. It was so exciting to us. We always had a good time. We had one side of the Cain's that we danced on, a side that was our side. There was a little, oh, I don't know, jealousy there between the groups, I guess. We'd all kind of try and outdo each other.

— LORENE WILLS, BOB'S SISTER, QUOTED IN AN ARTICLE BY JOHN WOOLEY FROM THE MARCH 7, 1997 ISSUE OF THE *TULSA WORLD'S SPOT* MAGAZINE

Following the repeal of Prohibition on December 5th, 1933, the technically illegal speakeasies that had flourished throughout the country became legitimate taverns and bars. For many, especially those frequented by African-Americans and working-class whites, the primary entertainment they offered, beyond the giggle water, was recorded music on jukeboxes.

Bob Wills and His Texas Playboys would become jukebox heroes, but not for a couple of years after Prohibition's end. Although Wills had made a couple of tentative stabs at recording before coming to Tulsa and the Cain's, his recording career didn't really get going in earnest until September of 1935, when he and the Playboys traveled to Dallas to cut some sides for the American Record Company, whose labels included the budget-priced (at 35 cents, or three for a dollar, as opposed to the upper-end 75-centers) Vocalion and OKeh imprints. Although Bob had some initial confrontations with the British-born producer "Uncle" Art Satherley, who didn't quite understand what he was getting with the band, the sessions began a very successful run for Wills on those labels and, ultimately, Columbia, which took over OKeh and Vocalion at the end of the decade.

The low price and high entertainment value of the Texas Playboys' records made them not only attractive to phonograph owners in Depression-era homes, where every expenditure had to be considered carefully, but also to the bars and taverns that catered to working people, the group that comprised Wills' biggest audience. For a nickel a throw, patrons could sip their drinks (in Oklahoma, until 1959, the only legal alcoholic beverage was beer) and tap a foot to the latest Wills tunes. Surely, as was the case with many of his radio listeners, a little bit of dreaming went on as the song played out. Those who'd never been to the Cain's sat and listened and thought about what it might be like to actually be in the place with all the dancers and music and Bob Wills up there on the bandstand, in person, along with those musicians whose names he'd call on the records and the radio shows—Leon, Tommy, Eldon, Brother Al. Surely they envied their comrades who'd actually been there, who'd experienced the whole wonderful thing and could tell their friends all about it.

It's been some 80 years since Bob Wills last led the famous Cain's Ballroom house band (not counting his short-lived return in the late '50s), and the people who were grownups then are gone now. Those who danced to the Texas Playboys in the 1930s and early '40s have joined the cloud of ghosts that benignly haunt the old hall, creating its distinct aura of ancient romance and fun and music.

Reality, lapped by decades and passed down orally through the generations, becomes legend, and, in the case of the Cain's during Bob and the Playboys' reign, the crowds have undoubtedly become bigger, the fights more epic, the music grander, as each year has passed into the next.

With that in mind, let's try to picture it the way it really was.

****

It's safe to start by saying that a night at the Cain's during this era was a whirling kaleidoscope of color and sound, of thumping bass and riffing strings and brass and reeds, Tommy Duncan's mellow tones riding atop a tight and solid beat. All of it together rolled like ocean waves over the shoulder-to-shoulder crowd spread across the dance floor, the music washing through the buzz of a hundred comments and conversations, rustling dresses and scuffling boots. There were no tables on the dance floor then (although chairs were set out for the lunch-hour broadcasts), as there would be later, so the only places to sit were the benches around the walls—and, as we've noted, they were often occupied by sleeping kids.

As Eldon Shamblin remembered in our last chapter, the people could be so closely packed that real dancing was impossible—just a kind of swaying to Wills' irresistible beat. So the floor would be taken up by wall-to-wall dancers, or, given Shamblin's observations, standers and listeners. The smell of popcorn and beer (along with the distinct whiff of illegal whiskey) mingled with other pungent odors, from perfume to sweat to cigarette smoke. The evaporative-cooling system installed by Mayo in 1937, which was the best you could do for air-conditioning at the time, kept things marginally cooler in the summer but added its own water vapor to the oppressive Oklahoma humidity inside the place.

The heat was tough on the band, too, especially since the players took no breaks or intermissions. The ostensible reason for that was related by Sheldon in *Hubbin' It*: "Bob figures that the people have paid their money for music and that they should get it every minute they are there." Maybe so, but at least as important was the fact that Wills and Mayo figured if the boys kept playing through an entire four-hour dance, there would be fewer opportunities for people to get into fights. So if a Texas Playboy had to go to the bathroom or grab a soft drink during a dance, he simply left the stage as unobtrusively as he could, for as long as he needed. Then he quietly returned and resumed playing.

(Fighting, it should be noted, was a part of the Cain's ambience at the time. "Ambulance drivers recall an era of split lips and concussion patients," wrote Tom Wood in his 1970 *Tulsa World* article. "Management worked to head off gang fights.

Two bouncers—usually off-duty policemen or professional wrestlers or boxers—were on hand and the city gendarmes could be called in case of emergency.")

Although photographs from 1941 indicate that firing up cigarettes, cigars, or pipes was prohibited during the Cain's noon broadcasts—at least during that time period—that same ban was likely never in effect at the dances. Certainly, some of the boys in the band smoked while they were working: One famous Cain's story tells of Al Stricklin's piano being set on fire during a dance by cigarette butts flipped at him by drummer Smokey Dacus. Still, a steady stream of patrons moved in and out the door on any given dance night, some ostensibly heading outdoors for a smoke. And as long as they were outside, many wandered to their cars or trucks for a shot of something other than the beer and soft drinks sold inside. In addition, more than a few disagreements from indoors got settled *al fresco* as well.

There was another area that many dancers flocked to on any given night—the front or side of the Cain's stage, where they tried to attract the attention of Bob or one of his band members. Overwhelmingly, all a person wanted to do was request a certain song. At rare times, usually when alcohol was involved, someone had the notion of getting belligerent with the band. They were usually dealt with by the aforementioned bouncers—including an ex-champion wrestler named John Briggs, who tried, without much long-term success, to get the Texas Playboys on an exercise regimen during his long tenure at the ballroom. To hear former Playboys tell it, however—notably "Brother" Al Stricklin in his book *My Years with Bob Wills*—on the rare occasions they had to defend themselves against attackers, they did just fine, exercise or no exercise.

And then there were those visiting the bandstand whose attacks were subtler. In certain quarters, Wills' music was looked down on as cornball and countrified, appealing only to the lower classes—an unfair characterization on the whole, of course, but one regularly made in those days.

Unsurprisingly, attempts to put his music or musicians down irritated Bob Wills, and those who strove to make him feel small usually came out on the short end of the exchange. In the Cain's-set *Tulsa Magazine* television show mentioned earlier, drummer Smokey Dacus recalled one of those incidents, telling about a dance one night, with the crowd "16 feet around the bandstand," when an overdressed, disdainful woman stepped up to the lip of the stage and motioned for Wills. "Bob went over and leaned down," Dacus related, "and she said, 'Your music makes my teeth hurt.'

"Bob didn't change his expression or nothing. He just stuck out his hand and he said, 'If you'll let me have 'em, I'll just put 'em up here, and you can have 'em back when the dance is over.'"

"The old man didn't put up with a whole lot," added Shamblin in the same program, using his pet name for Wills. "If they started poppin' off, they done tangled with the wrong man. Boy, he would nail 'em. If they started making fun of the musicians, for example, boy, he couldn't take that."

****

While the Cain's quickly achieved its reputation as the band's headquarters, Bob Wills and business manager O.W. Mayo fielded offers from other venues as well. With Thursday and Saturday nights set aside for their hometown dances, the group members would climb regularly into the bus that took them to other territories—always getting them back in time for the daily noon broadcasts from the hall.

According to the innovative steel-guitarist Bobby Koefer, who did his stint with the Texas Playboys in the early 1950s, those Cain's-based radio transmissions stirred the band's fans to action, even if they couldn't make it to the dances themselves. Koefer got the story from Wills' right-hand man, his good friend and bandmate Eldon Shamblin.

Said Koefer:

Bob Wills on Cain's bandstand circa 1939. Note the KVOO microphone suspended from the ceiling

> *They would announce their dance dates on that noon broadcast—"We're going to be in Fort Smith tonight, and we're looking forward to seeing you folks"—and they might say they were starting at eight o'clock or nine o'clock or whatever. So those people between Tulsa and Fort Smith would figure out about when the bus might be passing by their farms or ranches, and they'd watch for 'em.*

Back then, there were not a lot of freeways or turnpikes, so there was pretty much one way [for the Playboys] to get to these places. So these people would guess at when they might be coming by, and maybe they'd go out early so they wouldn't miss 'em. And if it was cold weather, they'd just dress for it— because it was fun. It was fun to see that bus coming down the road, the Texas Playboys' bus. They might be in their yards, or standing by their mailboxes out on the road, watching just so they could wave. And they'd have the Playboys waving back, and the driver maybe giving a little toot on the horn.

Smokey [Dacus] might say, "You remember last time we went down that road? There was a whole crowd by that mailbox. Maybe they'll be there again."

So it worked both ways. The Playboys liked to see those people, and the people went crazy seeing that bus. And they'd gotten their information from listening to the noon broadcast coming out of the Cain's on KVOO.

* * * *

Back home at the ballroom, the band's Thursday night reper-toire differed a little from Saturday's, with the weekday event giving more attention to people comfortable with older dance steps. It also started and ended an hour earlier than the Saturday event, going from 8 p.m. to midnight. "On Thursday, a lot of the time, we'd have some square dancing and schottisches and stuff like that," recalled Shamblin in his 1995 interview with Steve Higgins. "On Saturday night, just a regular dance."

A "regular dance" would usually include Texas Playboys versions of hits of the day as well as tunes they'd made famous themselves. And while they were still considered a "hillbilly" aggregation by much of the country, it was clear that Wills considered his music to be well beyond that label—or for that matter, *any* glib characterization.

"We're hep," he told Newspaper Enterprise Association reporter Erskine Johnson for a piece syndicated in early May of 1944. "We're the most versatile band in America.

"Sure," he continued, "we give 'em western music like 'Mama Don't Allow No Lowdown Fiddlin' Around Here,' and 'Liza Jane,' but we give 'em rhumbas, too. And when there are jitterbugs in the joint, we get 'em so happy they can't stay on the floor. We lay it on like they want it.

"You gotta give 'em showmanship," he concluded. "You gotta work the crowd from the bandstand."

Although Wills had relocated to the West Coast by the time of that interview, leaving brother Johnnie Lee to continue the dances and broadcasts from the Cain's, his words could certainly describe the Texas Playboys' twice-weekly events at the ballroom. So do these, from Ruth Sheldon's *Hubbin' It*, which nicely outline the crowd-pleasing approach of Wills and his late-'30s Cain's-based outfit:

> *When Bob stands on the band stand and looks out over the crowd, his mind is not wandering. He is closely observing the people. In a few minutes he can grade them like he used to grade bales of cotton. He looks at them and instantly*

figures out the kind of person they are and the type of music
they would like to hear.... He and the band have a reper-
toire of over 3,600 tunes, whereas the average band cannot
play more than 50 upon a moment's notice. Thus, he has an
infinite variety of material to suit any crowd....

Few bands in the country appeal to so many different
types of people. The old folks come for square dance, jig
time, schottische rhythms. The youngsters come for his
popular, hot renditions. A smaller, more sophisticated
crowd is drawn by the way he can show his mastery of
smoother melodies.

No situations rise that he cannot handle....

In order to partake of this amazing variety of musical entertainment, all dance patrons had to do was come up with the cost
of a ticket. (As we've noted earlier, the noonday radio shows were
free to the public.) Over the years, the authors of this book have
heard from old-timers, especially ranchers and farmers in the
Tulsa area, about the huge part Wills and the boys played in their
lives. Stories abound of the workers coming in from the fields at
noon, in those days before rural electricity, and hooking a radio
up to their precious battery in order to listen to Wills while they
ate their lunches. (In the city itself, it was said, you could walk
down the street when the windows were open and never miss a
beat of the broadcast.) Many of these same folks also saved up for
weeks in order to have enough to buy a couple of tickets to a dance
at the Cain's, dropping pennies in a fruit jar or other receptacle
until they accumulated what they needed.

Wills and Mayo, always sensitive to the economic realities faced by their crowds, went to great lengths not to gouge anyone at the box office. According to Tom Wood's 1970 *Tulsa World* story, the cost of a ticket was only 35 cents in 1935; by 1938, admission was $1 to get in on Thursday and $1.25 on Saturday. It may have been the height of the Great Depression, with Oklahomans and those in neighboring states grappling with the Dust Bowl as well as the national economic crisis, but the floor of the Cain's was usually packed whenever the Playboys took the stage.

"I used to be here every Thursday and Saturday night," said Jay Gibson, one of the longtime patrons interviewed by Russ Florence during the celebration of the 90th anniversary of Wills' birth at the Cain's in March of 1995. "'I can remember those real fine benches they had along the side. The women would sit over there, you know, and you went and asked them. Everybody just danced with everybody else. Just like a big family. Everybody came here, they was happy."

Admitting that he didn't know "one step from another," Gibson added that "anybody could dance to Bob Wills' music. Everybody could. If you could pat your foot, you could dance to it.

"They had the finest musicians in the world," he said, adding that he remembered Luke Wills as the bassist for the band. Of course, Luke—the third of the four Wills brothers, older than Billy Jack but younger than Johnnie Lee—recalled being on the bandstand with his oldest brother too, even though he began with a different instrument.

"I was 17 in 1937, when I did my first show with Bob's band," he told John Wooley for the March 7, 1997 *Spot* story. "I played tenor

LEFT TO RIGHT: *Billy Jack Wills, Luke Wills, Johnnie Lee Wills, Bob Wills, and their dad "Uncle" John Wills*

banjo. As a matter of fact, I signed my first Social Security card in the office of Cain's Academy. Not long after I started with Bob, Johnnie Lee started his first band, and I became his bass player."

Luke, also known as Luther J., would play with Bob and Johnnie Lee, as well as with his own band, the Rhythm Busters, for years, touring the country and plying his trade in all sorts of dancehalls and other venues. At one point, according to Don Mayes, Cain's dance instructor Howard Turner doubled as the Rhythm Busters' manager.

"We played the big ones and we played the little ones," Luke said. "But I'd have to say, with all consideration, that the Cain's was the best."

That sentiment was echoed by the youngest Wills brother, Billy Jack, who spent his own time in the bands of brothers Bob and Johnnie Lee before establishing his own group, Billy Jack Wills and His Western Swing Band, in Sacramento, California.

"I have nothing but the finest memories of the Cain's," he told John Wooley for a cover story in the July 17, 1982 issue of *OK Magazine*, a *Tulsa World* Sunday supplement. "I grew up there. This was during World War II, and I'd just turned 18. I'd go down to the Cain's to watch Bob or Johnnie Lee and just itch to get up on that bandstand myself."

* * * *

It wasn't long before Billy Jack was able to scratch his musical itch. But when he finally began playing the Cain's, it was with a Texas Playboys band that was in flux. The December 7, 1941 Japanese attack on Pearl Harbor had changed the lives of all Americans, and the members of Bob Wills' famous aggregation were no exception. (Nor were their fans. One chilling piece of Wills memorabilia is a list of requests and dedications for the announcer to read on the band's December 6 midnight broadcast, which actually ran through the first hour of Sunday, December 7. As the Japanese bombers secretly roared toward Hawaii on their deadly mission, three dedications went out from the Cain's to servicemen in Pearl Harbor—George Spencer aboard the *USS Helm*, William E. Hole on the *USS Medusa*, and Victor David. In addition, the mother of Pvt. Warren Freeman, stationed in Honolulu, requested the band play "Worried Mind" for her son.)

During those topsy-turvy months after the bombing and President Roosevelt's subsequent declaration of war, a significant

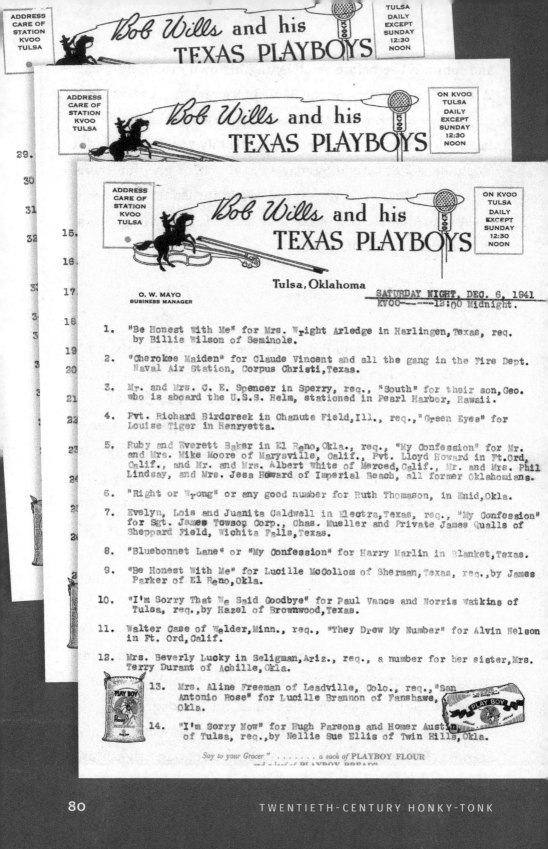

ADDRESS CARE OF STATION KVOO TULSA

Bob Wills and his TEXAS PLAYBOYS

ON KVOO TULSA DAILY EXCEPT SUNDAY 12:30 NOON

Tulsa, Oklahoma

O. W. MAYO
BUSINESS MANAGER

SATURDAY NIGHT, DEC. 6, 1941
KVOO------12:00 Midnight.

1. "Be Honest With Me" for Mrs. Wright Arledge in Harlingen, Texas, req. by Billie Wilson of Seminole.

2. "Cherokee Maiden" for Claude Vincent and all the gang in the Fire Dept. Naval Air Station, Corpus Christi, Texas.

3. Mr. and Mrs. C. E. Spencer in Sperry, req., "South" for their son, Geo. who is aboard the U.S.S. Helm, stationed in Pearl Harbor, Hawaii.

4. Pvt. Richard Birdcreek in Chanute Field, Ill., req., "Green Eyes" for Louise Tiger in Henryetta.

5. Ruby and Everett Baker in El Reno, Okla., req., "My Confession" for Mr. and Mrs. Mike Moore of Marysville, Calif., Pvt. Lloyd Howard in Ft. Ord, Calif., and Mr. and Mrs. Albert White of Merced, Calif., Mr. and Mrs. Phil Lindsay, and Mrs. Jess Howard of Imperial Beach, all former Oklahomians.

6. "Right or Wrong" or any good number for Ruth Thomason, in Enid, Okla.

7. Evelyn, Lois and Juanita Caldwell in Electra, Texas, req., "My Confession" for Sgt. James Towson Corp., Chas. Mueller and Private James Qualls of Sheppard Field, Wichita Falls, Texas.

8. "Bluebonnet Lane" or "My Confession" for Harry Marlin in Blanket, Texas.

9. "Be Honest With Me" for Lucille McCollom of Sherman, Texas, req., by James Parker of El Reno, Okla.

10. "I'm Sorry That We Said Goodbye" for Paul Vance and Norris Watkins of Tulsa, req., by Hazel of Brownwood, Texas.

11. Walter Case of Welder, Minn., req., "They Drew My Number" for Alvin Nelson in Ft. Ord, Calif.

12. Mrs. Beverly Lucky in Seligman, Ariz., req., a number for her sister, Mrs. Terry Durant of Achille, Okla.

13. Mrs. Aline Freeman of Leadville, Colo., req., "San Antonio Rose" for Lucille Brannon of Fanshawe, Okla.

14. "I'm Sorry Now" for Hugh Parsons and Homer Austin of Tulsa, req., by Nellie Sue Ellis of Twin Hills, Okla.

Say to your Grocer " . . . . a sack of PLAYBOY FLOUR

number of Wills' musicians would find themselves swapping the stage of the Cain's Ballroom for more austere and far less glamorous government quarters, their hot night-owl music replaced by early morning reveille.

One of the linchpins of the outfit was the first to declare his intentions. According to Townsend's *San Antonio Rose*, vocalist Tommy Duncan came into the Cain's for the 12:30 broadcast on December 8 and announced to his bandmates, "I don't know about the rest of you guys, but I'm going to join 'this man's army' and fight those son-of-a-bitches." Although Townsend writes that "Duncan enlisted and was soon gone," he apparently hung around for a few months before shipping out. A handwritten daily journal of the songs played on the KVOO broadcasts, kept by a fan, indicates that Tommy Duncan was still singing with the group in May 1942, although he was gone by July, as were Leon McAuliffe and Bob Wills himself. That summer, Johnnie Lee Wills had taken over leadership of the group at the Cain's, with Leon Huff his primary vocalist.

Several months before that war-induced shakeup, however, the Texas Playboys broadcasts had begun taking on a patriotic flavor. Radio presentations from the 1941–42 period include interpretations of such contemporary pop tunes as "Boogie Woogie Bugle Boy," "White Cliffs of Dover," and "Johnny Doughboy Found A Rose in Ireland." The band even dusted off a World War I-era chestnut, "Uncle Sammy's Calling You," for both their dances and noon broadcasts.

The call was real, and the toll it took on the band was real as well. As Townsend noted, "What might be called the original Tulsa (prewar) Texas Playboys band began to break up before Christmas, 1941, and by Christmas the next year it was history."

It's hard to say what might have happened with Wills and the Texas Playboys if World War II had not come along; chances are good they would have been even bigger than they were. Before the war, the group had grown to include a brass and reed section, heard to great advantage both live and on record, most notably in the huge 1940 hit "San Antonio Rose." Interestingly enough, even with that monster disc—the one Wills famously said took the band "from hamburgers to steaks"—producer Art Satherley insisted that the group lose the horns for several songs during each recording session. He felt that Wills' older audiences were put off by the more sophisticated big-band sound, and he was not without some justification for that belief. According to Glenn White, Wills started a second broadcast—from the KVOO studios, not from the Cain's—around the time "San Antonio Rose" hit. "There was so much fuss from the old fans about the music," White told Brett Bingham. "They didn't like the horns." In order to appease that segment of his audience, Wills began an early-morning show, airing thrice weekly, called *Bob Wills Fiddling Time,* in which he, Eldon Shamblin, and Tommy Duncan offered up tunes the old pared-down way, using only fiddle, guitar, and vocals. The program didn't last long, though, leaving the air in mid-'42. Even though other bandmates would often fill in for members of that trio, doing another regular broadcast would have been a grueling chore for anyone in that outfit, which played the Cain's twice weekly and headed out for engagements in other venues just about every other night of the week. Plus, there was the lunchtime show, airing every day but Sunday.

"From what I could see," noted White, "they just had too many commitments."

And if all that playing wasn't enough, Hollywood got into the mix. Bob and a hand-picked aggregation had been making trips to Tinseltown off and on since 1940, where they'd managed to break into western movies and done some recording as well. During these forays to the West Coast, Bob would leave the daily broadcasts and area dances to Johnnie Lee's band, originally called the Rhythmaires, which featured several players who'd been with the Texas Playboys in Tulsa but hadn't made the trip west.

People had first seen Bob and the boys on screen in a Tex Ritter western, *Take Me Back to Oklahoma*, released in November 1940. They'd then made a bigger-budgeted picture, *Go West, Young Lady*, with mainstream stars Penny Singleton, Glenn Ford, Ann Miller, and Charles Ruggles. Columbia Pictures put it into national release during November, 1941—only a few weeks before the Japanese attack on Pearl Harbor.

Other movies were on the horizon for Bob and the Texas Playboys, and filmmaking would combine with the exigencies of wartime America—and other factors—to keep Wills away from the Cain's. In point of fact, while he would continue to play periodically at the ballroom he'd made famous, he wouldn't return for any length of time for many years. And by then, his glory days would mostly be behind him.

****

Following the President's declaration of war on December 8, 1941, several band members got caught up in the patriotic fervor sweeping across the country and enlisted in one of the branches of the service. Some were drafted. Others took defense-industry jobs that left them no time to play music. According to longtime Wills fan Frank Spess, who talked with Russ Florence at the 1995 Wills birthday get-together, fans could hear the Playboys come apart in real time. "During the war, at noon, I'd always listen to the radio," Spess said, "and when the band was going to war, every time one of them would leave, they'd have a farewell party for them."

Of course, when Bob himself left for the Army, it was an even bigger event. In his interview for this book, Glenn White noted that O. W. Mayo didn't feel that he needed to take out ads for Texas Playboys dances in the Tulsa newspapers, since the group routinely drew such big crowds with only the radio shows (and the Play Boy Flour products) for advertisement. But in the closing days of 1942, when Wills was to play his last dance before leaving for the Army, his business manager "put an ad in saying Bob was getting ready to go into the service and this will be the last dance for Bob for the duration."

The duration, for Bob Wills, turned out to be far shorter than the war itself. But it took him away from the Cain's. And while he would make occasional guest appearances on its stage, the man who'd transformed a Tulsa ballroom into the mother church of western-swing music wouldn't really come home to it for another decade and a half.

Sec. 562, P. L. & R.
U. S. POSTAGE
Paid
Tulsa, Okla.
Permit No. 543

LOCAL SHOW MAKES GOOD!

KVOO'S BOB WILLS WINS MOVIE FAME

By smashing every record with a more than 50% increase in attendance at Tulsa's Rialto Theatre, Bob Wills' first motion picture, "Take Me Back to Oklahoma," proves another tribute to his popularity.

Bob Wills and his Texas Playboys began daily broadcasts over KVOO almost seven years ago and since then have led the station's fan mail every year. Not only does the entire Southwest area of Oklahoma, Missouri, Kansas, and Arkansas comprise Bob's radio audience, but almost every week brings a letter from such distant points as Hawaii, Venezuela, Alaska, or a ship at sea. Bob Wills continues to broadcast every day over KVOO.

Bob Wills'

May 20-24, 1942

4th A

STAMPEDE

OFFICAL SOUVENIR PROGRAM... WITH RULES & DICTION

Johnnie Lee in 1940 formed his own band, at which time he returned to the traditional family instrument—the fiddle. He soon had a regular six dances per week schedule, two of these in Tulsa [at the Cain's], and was playing some KVOO radio shows. In 1942 World War II was taking musicians from both bands. When Bob joined the Army, the bands merged and Johnnie Lee fronted them. By mid 1943 Bob was discharged and took his musicians to California; Johnnie Lee took the KVOO Radio shows, Cain's Ballroom dances, and the annual rodeo—the Tulsa Stampede. On January 1, 1943, Johnnie Lee assumed all responsibilities in the Tulsa region.

Through the years Johnnie Lee played more dances in the region, more noonday radio shows, and more Cain's Ballroom dances than any other band.

— FROM UNPUBLISHED LINER NOTES BY GUY LOGSDON FOR THE
1978 JOHNNIE LEE WILLS LP *REUNION* (FLYING FISH RECORDS)

There are still a few living souls among us who remember fondly their regular nights of dancing at the Cain's in the late 1940s and early to mid-'50s, shuffling around the floor with their partners (as much as the crowd would permit) to the sounds of Bob Wills' Texas Playboys. Many more, no longer with us, passed their cherished memories of Bob and the Playboys down to their children—and beyond.

And while this book is not meant to disparage anyone's recollections of the ballroom—just the opposite, in fact—chances are exceptionally good it wasn't Bob Wills and His Texas Playboys they were dancing to at all. Instead, it was much more likely the band led by his brother, Johnnie Lee, which was called, variously, Johnnie Lee Wills and His Boys or Johnnie Lee Wills and All the Boys. Many of those boys, including Johnnie Lee himself, had spent time in the Texas Playboys, but after Bob left for the service, his days of residency at the Cain's were—except for a brief, unsatisfactory stretch in the late '50s—over.

"Bob was only here permanently from the '30s to the early '40s," O.W. Mayo explained to Wooley during their 1986 interview at the Cain's. "We came here in '34, and in '42 he went into the service, and when he got out of the service in '43, he went out to California and stayed. He came back here for one year in '58, and then he went back.

"Johnnie Lee took over when Bob left, y'see, and as far as the length of time and all our operations here and so forth, Johnnie Lee was involved much longer than Bob. But Bob would come back for anniversaries and this, that, and the other. He was still a part of the family, if you know what I mean."

Bob had been on the West Coast for much of 1942, doing some recording and appearing in eight westerns for Columbia Pictures, he and the Playboys supporting B-western hero Russell Hayden and comedy sidekick Dub "Cannonball" Taylor. (The "B" designation referred, generally, to the resources, stars, and money a studio put into a film; a "B" movie was made on a lower budget than an "A" movie, and often appeared with an "A" picture as the lesser part of a double-feature presentation. During this time, moviegoers usually got two full-length features, along with newsreels, cartoons, and other short subjects, each time they bought a ticket.)

Beginning in the summer and continuing through autumn, Bob Wills and his small, hand-picked string band—a different outfit from the big horn-accented outfit he had on tour—knocked out each of the Hollywood movies in a week or so, while Johnnie Lee held down the bandstand and made the six-days-a-week broadcasts at the Cain's back in Tulsa. According to Townsend's *San Antonio Rose*, Columbia issued a press release with the news that the last four Hayden-Wills pictures would be sped up "to free the Players for service" in the military.

That announcement may have just been a bit of press agentry, since the director, a B-western specialist named William Berke, was used to grinding out product with lightning-like efficiency anyway. But after the last movie wrapped in early December, several of the Playboys who'd been on the coast with Bob did head into various branches of the service—along with Wills himself, who joined the U.S. Army in late December of 1942, following a Christmas Eve dance. (The cost of the dance was a quite reasonable 55 cents, down from previous years.)

"This marked the end of an era," wrote Townsend. "When Wills went into the army in 1942, he disbanded his big orchestra, and he was never able to put another together quite like it. That band was one reason the Tulsa years were the glory years of his musical career. For the rest of his life, he tried to find another Tulsa, but he never did."

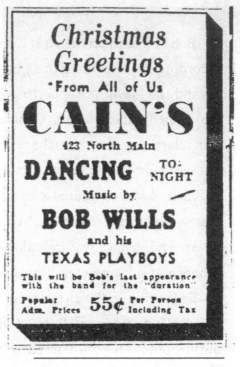

December 24, 1942

He did, however, find that the military life was not for him. It started at the base in Fort Sill, about 200 miles southwest of Tulsa, and continued when he was transferred to Camp Howze in Texas. All sorts of problems arose from the beginning and continued throughout his brief military career. Some had to do with his age—he was almost 38, the cutoff point for draft eligibility, when he went in—and lack of physical conditioning, and others with his celebrity, which brought him far more notice than that accorded the garden-variety raw recruit. Also, as his tenure with W. Lee O'Daniel had shown, Wills was not one to knuckle under to authority figures, especially when he thought they were coming up with bad decisions, and anyone who's ever served in a branch of the service knows that some officers and noncoms make Pappy O'Daniel look like Solomon when it comes to wise choices.

Perhaps Bob's sister Lorene put it the best and most simply in a conversation with John Wooley in the mid-1990s: "Bob and the service," she said, "just didn't get along."

Wills was discharged from Camp Howze in July of 1943, having served for just about seven months. And even though the war had depleted the ranks of working musicians, he was still able to put a new Texas Playboys together in short order and hit the road again, playing, among other things, a series of engagements in support of the government's war bond drives. Instead of returning to Tulsa and the Cain's, however, he opted to go to California.

Why? In *San Antonio Rose*, Charles Townsend offers two reasons. First was the fact that Johnnie Lee had become well-established at the Cain's and KVOO in the preceding seven months, and Bob didn't want to disrupt things by returning. Second, there was the thought that a move might help his marriage to Betty, his fifth wife, because it would get him out from under the responsibilities he felt in Tulsa toward both his family and band members.

(With regard to the first idea, it should be noted that a letter from March 31, 1943, from the collection of Glenn White, features letterhead reading "From the Office of Johnnie Lee Wills and the Texas Playboys," over the Cain's address. So it seems safe to assume that Johnnie Lee—who was apparently 4-F—had actually taken over Bob's band for whatever time Bob might be in the military, returning the Texas Playboys brand-name to Bob upon the latter's discharge.)

Bob also might've figured there were still opportunities for him in the movie business, especially since the Russell Hayden pictures he'd done in a rush before enlisting were still coming out, a new one every few months, which kept his image before filmgoers. And indeed, he and the Playboys made two theatrical shorts and three more features in Hollywood—including two with another sagebrush star, Charles Starrett, in Columbia's popular series of Durango Kid westerns—over the next couple of years. Perhaps he also liked the recording studios in California better than the ones in Texas, where he'd recorded most of his pre-war discs. And it may have been that his proximity to the West Coast entertainment industry helped him better avail himself of the services of the giant Music Corporation of America, the agency that signed him and the Playboys in 1944 and helped them reach a status comparable to, and sometimes exceeding, that of the big touring pop bands. In fact, it was during their days as an MCA act that he and the Playboys became the most popular dance band in the nation.

Whatever the reasons, Bob's decision left Johnnie Lee Wills and His Boys at the Cain's, where the second-oldest Wills brother became nothing short of a local musical icon. As long-time Oklahoma musician and Johnnie Lee Wills bandmate Roy Ferguson told John Wooley for an August '97 *Tulsa World* story, "For Tulsa, Johnnie Lee did more than anyone for western swing."

* * * *

As mentioned earlier, Bob did return from time to time, and when that happened, a lot of fans, friends, and observers—along with Bob himself—acted as though he'd never really gone away. As an unbylined *Tulsa World* story from February 6, 1949, put it, "Bob transferred his headquarters—but not his home, he insists—to California five years ago, because of motion picture and recording contracts."

At the time, he was back in town for a big 15th anniversary celebration, with Bob and the Texas Playboys joining Johnnie Lee and His Boys to play for a special Tuesday night dance as well as for the regular 12:30 broadcast the next day, February 9th. That show was a celebration of the date of the first-ever KVOO broadcast; it was also, according to the *World*, the 6,241st noonday show.

Bob's erstwhile sponsor was still on board, too. General Mills, the company Bob had brought in to take over sponsorship of the noontime show after the Crazy Water Crystals contract ran out in 1935, was now using Johnnie Lee's band to hype its products, including both the Play Boy and Red Star Flour brands.

Another longtime Cain's fixture still hung in there as well. Nine years after Daddy Cain's death, his protégé Howard Turner was continuing to teach folks how to twirl confidently around a dance floor, often starting his classes just after the end of the 12:30 broadcasts. A newspaper ad for the Cain's Dancing Academy appeared—along with similar congratulatory notices from General Mills, MCA, and KVOO —as part of a full-page spread on the 15th anniversary in the Sunday, February 6, *World*. The Cain's portion featured photos of Turner and Ada Perry, wife of Cain's concessionaire Alvin Perry; her title was given as "Secretary-Cashier." In addition to offering kudos to Bob and Johnnie Lee, it hyped the Cain's as "Tulsa's Finest Dance Floor... Where people LEARN to Dance—Where People LOVE to Dance—and Where BOB and His TEXAS PLAYBOYS Will Play for the ANNIVERSARY DANCE Next Tuesday Night."

That full newspaper page also offered up a narrative reinforcing the idea that Bob was only in California for an extended visit. The copy read, in part:

> *Bob still calls Tulsa home, despite the "Texas" tag on his "Playboys," and the fact that motion picture, recording and Music Corporation of America contracts and commitments compel him to commute between the Oil Capital and his temporary homes in Hollywood and California's state capital city, Sacramento.*

Still, those who read between the lines of the copy, and noted the "Johnnie Lee Wills and His Boys" logo at the bottom of the ad, had to know that the change at the Cain's was permanent—or, at least, as permanent as anything involving bands and musicians can be. The text noted that Bob had "turned over" to O.W. Mayo and Johnnie Lee the annual Tulsa Stampede rodeo as well as the daily broadcasts and Cain's dances, adding:

> *For nearly five years Bob's "San Antonio Rose" has given way to a signature song without a name—other than Johnnie Lee's "Thank You" song.*
>
> *For from 416 to 832 times each year at either end of Johnnie Lee's noon-day and night-time broadcasts, listeners on the powerful 50,000-watt KVOO have heard:*
>
> *"How do you do, friends. We're here to play for you. And sing the songs you want to hear, before we are through. It's Johnnie Lee and all the boys sending thanks to you, for your support and loyalty, and your friendship true..."*

Or that closing refrain: "So long friends. We've got to go. We bid you all adieu. Tune us in again sometime and let us hear from you. It's Johnnie Lee and all the boys sending thanks to you..."

In his 2009 interview with the authors, longtime Johnnie Lee Wills band member Curly Lewis recalled that the "Thank You Song" utilized a sped-up version of the dance standard "Wednesday Night Waltz" for its melody.

"I'm pretty sure [Wills guitarist-vocalist] Harley Huggins and Mr. Mayo had a hand in [writing] that," he said. "I know they both had something to do with it."

The great fiddler and vocalist Lewis was one of several musicians who spent time with the bands of both Bob and Johnnie Lee, putting him in a good position to contrast the bandleader who'd left the Cain's with the brother who stayed.

CHUCK ADAMS   FRANK SIMMS   JOHNNIE LEE WILLS   DON HARLAN   **CURLY LEWIS**   CLARENCE CAGLE   EBB GRAY

"I think it was just charisma, more than anything else," Lewis said. "Bob had it and Johnnie Lee really didn't. He was the best bandleader [of the two], though. He knew whoever was on a chorus, and he knew when the next chorus was going to start. Bob, half the time he'd wait until you were 12 bars into the next chorus, and then he'd turn around and point, and you'd better get it. It was just like jumping for a lamb and getting hold of half of it.

"Johnnie Lee, he could read a dance crowd just as good as Bob could," Lewis added. "He could durn sure look out there, and he could tell the next tune to play to keep those people dancing."

Stories persist about Bob Wills being the Elvis of his day, a man who radiated so much personal charm that he could turn a group of mediocre players into a great band simply by stepping onto the bandstand. Johnnie Lee, on the other hand, as Lewis implied, has often been characterized as simply one of the "boys," a good guy who knew what it took to lead a band but didn't have the love affair with the spotlight that his older brother did. Whichever one they were playing for, the members of the group tended to take their cue from their leader.

In a 2008 conversation with the authors, western-swing great Tommy Allsup recalled joining Johnnie Lee's band in 1952, when the primary competition for Johnnie Lee and the Cain's was Bob's former steel player Leon McAuliffe, now ensconced with his band at his own Tulsa dancehall, the Cimarron Ballroom.

"He told me, 'Leon McAuliffe plays over at the Cimarron, and he's got [fiddler] Bouncin' Bobby Bruce, and they all kind of jump around,'" Allsup recalled with a chuckle. "He said, 'We don't do that. We're more of a *solemn* band.'"

Johnnie Lee also reinforced his low-key, one-of-the-boys approach to bandleading in a couple of newspaper stories that ran during the last year or so of his life. In an August 1, 1984 *Tulsa Tribune* piece, he told the uncredited reporter, "I had never even talked into a microphone when Bob pushed me in front of a band. Then he left for California. I was scared to death when he told me to take over the rodeo, the radio show and the dances."

And in another unbylined story, this one from the October 19, 1983 *Tulsa World*, he recalled his uneasiness about fronting a band when Bob and Mayo first hit him with the idea.

I argued against it. I didn't want a band. I told 'em I'd buy me a fillin' station or go back to choppin' fence rows.

I was real shy and, to be honest, afraid. I didn't know if I could meet the public on a one-to-one basis. But we had two brothers who were old enough to work [in the band] and there were some boys around town who were out of work, so I finally gave in....

I was very proud of Bob and I knew how hard he worked. Bob was a showman, but I wasn't that type. I was quiet. I would get excited about something the band was doing, but I was always afraid if I moved around too much people would think I was trying to copy Bob.

At the time, many other bandleaders showed no such restraint, lavishly aping Bob's style of verbal asides. But Johnnie Lee chose to take the stage persona that fit his personality, rather than trying to be a Bob Wills imitator on the bandstand.

The fans didn't seem to mind. During Johnnie Lee's tenure, at least into the '50s, the Cain's continued to pack 'em in at noontime and on Thursday and Saturday nights, utilizing pretty much the same musical approach that Bob had begun in the '30s. Curly Lewis remembered that Johnnie Lee continued the practice of including numbers in his Thursday night repertoire that appealed to a more traditional crowd.

> *We were still doing square dances on Thursday nights. Two*
> *square dances a night and a couple or three schottisches*
> *and some old-time waltzes.*
>
> *When I joined 'em in '45, our lunch crowds would be 100–*
> *150 people or more... and if we had less than 1600 people*
> *[at a dance] on Saturday night, that was a bad crowd. It was*
> *usually 1700 or 1800 on Saturday, and if we got less than*
> *1200 on Thursday, it was bad.*

Of course, as the folks continued to stream into the Cain's, the same old behaviors continued at the dancehall, including fights and consumption of illicit alcoholic beverages, two practices that have long gone hand in hand. Even beer had become taboo in the Cain's in 1944, when the Oklahoma legislature passed a bill that made it unlawful to serve that beverage, or any other with the slightest alcohol content, within 100 feet of where people were dancing. Just about the only effect the law had on the Cain's, however, was to take money out of Alvin Perry's pocket. As the man with the ballroom's concessions business, he'd been able to sell beer—always a profitable item—along with his pop, milk, coffee, sandwiches, chips, cigarettes, and handkerchiefs.

The net effect of the law, as far as Perry and the Cain's were concerned, was to line the pockets of the owner of "a little beer joint across the street," Lewis remembered. "Man, you talk about a busy place on Thursday and Saturday."

The thirst conjured up by a night of dancing could also be slaked by the bootleggers who still hung out around the Cain's, offering their illicit selections of hard stuff. It was the beer and the liquor, said Lewis, "that started a lot of the fights."

Then he laughed, recalling another byproduct of all the alcohol consumption on those frenetic nights. "You remember that bandleader, Sammy Kaye? His motto was 'Swing and sway with Sammy Kaye.' We used to say that *our* motto was, 'Dance and pee with Johnnie Lee.'"

(On the same general topic: For many decades, there was a large metal urinal trough in the men's room of the Cain's. It's been said that if you struck it with a tuning fork, you'd get a perfect C note.)

****

O.W. Mayo, 1940s

According to O.W. Mayo's 1986 interview, he bought out Bob's part of the Cain's lease after Wills entered the service, which may be another reason the bandleader decided to head to California instead of returning to Tulsa. After Bob left, Mayo took over as Johnnie Lee's business manager, and then in 1944 Mayo bought the property from the administrators of the Tate Brady estate.

He continued as Johnnie Lee's business manager for many more years, but once Bob left the Cain's and Mayo bought out his part of the lease, Bob and Mayo had no formal business relationship. Correspondence from the Cain's shows Mayo negotiating to hire Bob and his band for Cain's dates from a variety of managers and booking agents, including MCA. During the mid-'40s, these homecoming dates would generally be around the holidays—there was, for instance, a Cain's dance on Tuesday, November 26, 1946, with the $1.25 admission fee getting patrons in to see, "Direct from Hollywood," the man and the group that had once headquartered in that ballroom, now billed as "America's Most Versatile Dance Band" and "Stars of

Stage Screen and Radio." A little less than four years earlier, admission had been 55 cents for Bob's last Cain's show before he headed off for the Army. And in between, a January 7, 1945 Cain's dance had cost 98 cents plus tax. A $1,570.00 check written to Bob and the Playboys as payment for that engagement indicated that Bob could still pack 'em in; the contracts he got for his occasional Cain's shows gave him 70 percent of the gate receipts against a guarantee.

"The only thing I didn't like about Mr. Mayo was that he told somebody there [at the Cain's] one time, 'There ain't no musician worth over $50 a week,'" recalled Curly Lewis, laughing. "Johnnie Lee was trying to give everybody a raise, and that pissed me off."

To hear Lewis—who was with Johnnie Lee for about a decade—tell it, O. W. Mayo was a man who explored every financial opportunity that ownership of the Cain's offered.

"Johnnie Lee played the Cain's on a percentage with Mr. Mayo," he explained. "Alvin Perry rented the concession stand on a percentage with Mr. Mayo. Mr. Mayo was strictly a businessman."

Of course, Mayo also wrote the occasional song (notably the standard "Blues for Dixie," with a significant assist from an uncredited Cindy Walker) and otherwise involved him-

Mr. Mayo, late 1960s

self with the entertainment end of the business, although hardly to the extent that, say, W. Lee O'Daniel had insinuated himself into the broadcasts and careers of the Light Crust Doughboys.

"He'd announce a lot of times whenever our regular announcer [Frank Sims] would have something else to do, and on those night broadcasts, he'd always say, 'from the Cain's Academy of Dancing,'" Lewis recalled. "It was always the Cain's Academy then. It was never known as [just] the Cain's."

During those Johnnie Lee Wills years, head dance instructor Howard Turner was also "the caretaker or whatever, taking care of the floor and everything and giving dance lessons after the broadcasts," noted Lewis.

"Howard was the instructor, the manager, the bottle washer, the janitor, the sign man," added Don Mayes, Turner's stepson. "Howard just stayed on after Daddy Cain died and managed the property and taught ballroom dancing. He had no ownership; nothing like that.

"I used to go down to the broadcasts at noon, and on the weekends I would clean for the dances," Mayes added. "Oh, man, I used to clean that floor. It was my Saturday morning job, getting ready for the Saturday night dances. It ran right from wood to concrete. I could throw in lubricated sawdust to pick up the dust out of the concrete, but you didn't use sawdust on the wood. I ran dust mops over that."

In addition to Turner—and, on occasion, his young stepson— the Perrys were a major part of the Cain's crew, with Ada serving as secretary for Turner, Wills, and Mayo.

O.W. Mayo received money from the Wills concerts and Turner's dance lessons. He'd also occasionally rent the hall for other functions when Johnnie Lee and the Boys were away. A number of African-American jazz and dance outfits played one-night stands at the ballroom, which was only a few blocks away from the Greenwood district, a mecca for black groups and their fans (as well as the scene of the infamous 1921 race massacre).

"Count Basie worked Cain's one night," Glenn White said. "I'm sure Mr. Mayo turned that whole thing over to somebody he trusted, although he may have sent Alvin Perry down. But it was an all-black thing. The ad was in the black paper in Tulsa, so white folks didn't know Count Basie was in there. Only the black folks knew it."

As the '40s ended, however, and the twice-weekly dances with Johnnie Lee and His Boys began slowly losing their patrons, Mayo began booking more and more outside acts into the ballroom. This gradual but unmistakable shift in Cain's policy was telegraphed to its patrons in 1950, when Mayo began assembling the pictures for the gallery of giant photographs that adorn the walls of the Cain's Ballroom to this day.

Cains Academy

Home of
Johnnie Lee Wills and his Boys *of Dancing*

TULSA, OKLA.

BEVERAGES

Evervess (Mixer)	15c	Orange	10c
Pepsi-Cola	10c	Grapette	10c
7-Up	10c	Ice Water	10c
Coke	10c	Milk	15c
Dr. Pepper	10c	Coffee	10c

Ice Set-up, 25c (With Lemon, 35c)
(Tub Ice, 4 Cups, Spoon)

Extra Cups (each)	05c
Extra Cups (with Ice)	10c

SANDWICHES

Dainty Maid—25c and 30c

Fritos—Potato Chips—Cheetos	10c
All Popular Brands of Cigarettes	25c
Handkerchiefs	25c

Please Pay When Served
CHECK BILL PRESENTED BY WAITER
WITH PRICES ON MENU
DO NOT PAY MORE

YOU LIKE IT
IT LIKES YOU

Prices the Same
at Table or Bar

EVERVESS
SPARKLING
WATER

We didn't have tables and chairs in here. We had these benches, right around in a circle, all around. Then in 1950, I bought those tables and chairs and put 'em in here, and put these pictures on the wall at that time—those artists [in the pictures] were the hot artists of the day.

I wanted to change the image of the place, if you know what I mean.

— O.W. Mayo, in a July 1986 interview with John Wooley conducted at the Cain's Ballroom

Ernest Tubb. T. Texas Tyler. Gene Autry. Pat Breene. Cindy Walker. Pee Wee King. Red Foley. Eddy Arnold. Floyd Tillman. Roy Acuff. Al Clauser. Tennessee Ernie Ford. Spade Cooley. Hank Thompson. These names and others tag the giant photos that have hung from the juncture of wall and ceiling around the Cain's dance floor since the early '50s, the faces gazing benignly down at generations of patrons. Like the stars on the Hollywood Walk of Fame, some names are familiar and even iconic; others are obscure or simply forgotten. At the time Mayo began putting them up, however, the majority of them depicted artists who comprised the current heart and soul of a big musical tent that included styles then called country & western, cowboy/western, hillbilly, and folk—along with western swing, of course. Many of the artists depicted in those larger-than-life pictures had played or would play the Cain's during Mayo's ownership, as he began booking more touring acts on the nights that Johnnie Lee and His Boys were playing elsewhere. Others, like Autry, would occasionally drop by a noonday broadcast to plug personal appearances in the area, and maybe sing a song or two with the band.

It's long been assumed that Mayo hung all of the photos at once, but the gallery was actually an ongoing work that began in 1950 and continued at least through 1951. The Glenn White collection includes a letter from Autry to Mayo, dated February 24, 1951, which had accompanied a publicity photo from Autry, along with a Mayo acknowledgement from March 7, in which he told Autry, "I appreciate receiving this picture very much and as stated in my previous letter it will be blown up to 3'x4' in size and placed in our ballroom along with many of the other artists in the field of Western and Folk music."

As the sole owner of the Cain's, Mayo did all the booking, sometimes bringing in package shows to play Tulsa's Convention Hall along with the acts he bought for the ballroom. As White noted, "Mayo kept up with who was current and who wasn't," and his business instincts led him to turn down a lot of acts for the Cain's, from Merle Travis and the Nashville-based Cousin Jody to performers who simply weren't suited for the venue, like Ray Stolzenberg and the Northern Playboys, a polka band from Minnesota. In response to a January 18, 1954 query from Stolzenberg, Mayo wrote, "There is not much demand for a Polka band in this part of the country" before giving the bandleader a couple of leads for possible bookings in Kansas.

"When he'd write those letters [turning down acts], sometimes he'd go into a lot of detail, and sometimes he wouldn't," said

Gene Autry
HOLLYWOOD, CALIFORNIA

February 24, 1951

Mr. O. W. Mayo
Cain's Academy of Dancing
423 North Main
Tulsa 3, Oklahoma

Dear Mr. Mayo:

Thanks for your letter of February 21st. The other letter you mention must have been lost between New York and here.

I'm enclosing a picture in accordance with your request. Glad to hear you are getting along so well.

Best wishes and kindest regards.

Sincerely,

Gene Autry

GA:l

March 7th, 1951

Mr. Gene Autry,
6520 Selma Avenue,
Hollywood, 28, California.

Dear Gene:

This will acknowledge receipt of your letter and the photograph which I requested in my letter of February 21st.

I appreciate receiving this picture very much and as stated in my previous letter it will be blown up to 3'x4' in size and placed in our ballroom along with many of the other artists in the field of Western and Folk music.

Kindest personal regards.

Yours truly,

OWM/ap   O. W. Mayo

White. "He said, 'I don't think Cousin Jody's known well enough here in Tulsa for me to take a chance on bringing him in. Thank you. O.W. Mayo.' That was it."

He also turned down one of the most popular entertainers ever to step up to a Cain's microphone. On February 29, 1952, Michael F. Kennedy, the acting manager of the Oklahoma City-based Merl Lindsay and His Oklahoma Nite Riders, wrote Mayo to let him know that Tommy Duncan, Bob Wills' longtime vocalist, was appearing as a special guest performer with Lindsay for a few weeks. Unfortunately, the three dates Kennedy wanted at the Cain's were all Thursday nights—one of the two evenings that a Wills band had been playing there weekly since 1934.

"I will be unable to make a commitment at this time on either of these dates," Mayo wrote back on March 3, "as you know that is Johnnie's regular date here in Tulsa and I would have to book him out on one of these dates."

In addition to the regular Thursday and Saturday night airings and the daily noontime broadcasts, Johnnie Lee and the band recorded a syndicated show for General Mills. The 15-minute program aired over scores of stations—including, at one point in the mid-'50s, affiliates of NBC's West Coast Network.

Over the years, there's been a tendency to confuse the noonday broadcasts from the Cain's with the syndicated transcriptions. While both were sponsored by General Mills, there were differences, according to Curly Lewis, who said the band recorded its syndicated material in the KVOO studios, then located in the Philtower Building, with "no rehearsals, no nothing."

*We did about 25 of 'em at a time, and it took about three
days to make them there at the Philtower. We'd just get
up there a day or two before we'd have to do 'em and
everybody would get a songbook or something, and if
somebody ran across a song they knew we'd write 'er down
for a program. We couldn't do more than one BMI tune on a
program because they cost more to do. And we had to use
all the P.D. tunes. You know, if you knew a tune, whether the
others guys did or not, why you'd just put it on there. It was
strictly ad lib.*

BMI refers to Broadcast Music, Inc., a company that collected
royalties for songwriters (and still does) whenever a song was performed. P.D. songs, or songs in the public domain, had fallen out of
copyright or never been copyrighted, so they weren't represented
by a performing-rights organization like BMI or ASCAP and no
royalties had to be paid for their use.

In addition to BMI, there were—and are—other organiza-
tions looking out for the rights of the writers. In the liner notes for
the 1978 album *Tulsa Swing* (Rounder Records), a collection of the
General Mills transcriptions from 1950-51, producer Charles Wolfe
quoted Johnnie Lee, whose remembrances of finding material for
the transcribed shows dovetails neatly with Lewis's:

*We'd have to dig back in those old Stephen Foster books and
get old tunes, 'cause ASCAP was charging 50 cents a tune
and Hill & Range [a music publisher] was 25 cents. We had
a $1.00 per show limit. So we could use one ASCAP, two*

Hill & Range, and then we had to dig up others that was public domain or some of our own. We composed a lot of songs when we were working on a session.

According to Lewis, the band members were far more conversant with the material they did on the noonday broadcasts from the Cain's. "Of course," he pointed out, "they were tunes we were used to doing all the time."

The syndicated shows and the daily broadcasts had at least one thing in common: their regular use of sacred songs. Most of the old Christian hymns were P.D., and therefore free to use, which made them especially attractive for the transcribed shows. Those familiar vintage numbers also had the added advantage of being popular with a big section of the Wills fan base.

One of the many traditions started by Bob and continued by Johnnie Lee was the practice of devoting one broadcast a week to hymns and gospel songs. Fiddler Lewis, who began as a guitarist with Johnnie Lee's Boys, recalled those Thursday shows as the best-sounding things they did.

"On hymn days, we didn't have drums or anything like that, just strings and piano," he explained. "So an acoustic guitar sounded good, the chords and everything."

In late 1952, apparently acting on an idea offered by Mayo, General Mills brought out the *Johnnie Lee Wills Hymn Book*, which was offered on the noon broadcasts as well as on the syndicated transcriptions. It proved to be a popular premium, one now prized by collectors.

But even as the hymnbook was seeing success, western swing was beginning its slow, albeit temporary, fade into the sunset. Rich Kienzle's excellent liner notes for *Johnnie Lee Wills: Rompin' Stompin' Singin' Swingin'* (Bear Family) go a long way towards telling the story. That 1983 album collects 14 songs by Wills and the band, recorded at KVOO and released by RCA Victor in 1952 and '53. During those years, Kienzle wrote, "The western swing market was beginning to erode, partly due to the increasing popularity of television, which cut severely into attendance at the dancehalls.... Also, as Western swing waned the popularity of more conventional country music was on the rise."

That, of course, was something O.W. Mayo knew, as he worked to book top country performers—many of whose photos already adorned the walls of the Cain's—into the ballroom. He even booked Hank Williams into the place on a Friday night, October 17, 1952, only a couple of months before the troubled country icon's death. As legend has it, Williams was too drunk to sing even one song and had to be carried to and from the bandstand by Mayo and Nashville booking agent Lucky Moeller (who also managed Bob Wills for a time in the early '50s, when Moeller was working out of Oklahoma City). Mr. Mayo, always the gentleman, wouldn't confirm that story for publication when Wooley interviewed him in 1986, but he did say he went out to the bandstand that night and spoke to the Western Cherokees, Williams' backing group, after it became clear that Hank wasn't going to be able to perform.

I said, 'Boys, I'm adding a hundred dollars to your contract tonight, but don't have an intermission.' We had a mob, and if you called an intermission, they'd get to talking. And so I said, 'Keep this thing going, one tune after another, even if you have to double back.' So they did, and I gave them an extra hundred dollars.

It had worked for Bob and Johnnie Lee Wills at the Cain's, where the no-intermission policy had done a lot to keep fighting down in the hall. And it apparently worked this time. As long as people were dancing to a live band, their complaints and anger about the non-appearance of the headliner they'd come to see drifted away like smoke, weaving around the persistent beats of the drums and bass and steel guitar. Mayo had learned his dance-hall lessons well.

****

While western swing may have been on the wane in the early '50s, Johnnie Lee and the band cut some terrific numbers for those RCA Victor singles. The problem was that the numbers that counted—the sales figures—didn't add up. According to Kienzle, the biggest mover of them all was one called "The Thingamajig," with a lead vocal by Curly Lewis, which peaked out at somewhere around 10,000 copies. That wasn't a very high number for a major player like RCA Victor, and subsequent discs fell far short in the sales department. Kienzle quotes correspondence (from Glenn White's files) between Mayo and Steve Sholes, Victor's man in charge of country-music records, with Sholes writing that "there is not a Western act in existence today which sells well on records," adding that it was "the real Hillbilly or country acts" that were doing the business.

That letter was written in March of 1953. Seven months later, Sholes pulled the plug, writing Mayo that the contract with Johnnie Lee was terminated, explaining, "We were not making any money from his records, nor was he."

At the same time, even in the cathedral of western swing, fans were beginning—for whatever reasons—to fade away. Lewis noticed it starting about the time the RCA Victor records failed to attract a sizable audience, around '52 and '53. Johnnie Lee and His Boys had picked right up where Bob had left off, with no significant loss in patronage. But now, a decade or so after Bob's departure, the crowds began to thin.

Part of the reason for the drop in attendance may have been competition from his former bandmate, steel-guitarist Leon McAuliffe, with his own western-swing group and his own downtown Tulsa venue, the Cimarron Ballroom. After the war, the man who inspired the phrase "Take it away, Leon" had organized his own outfit and experimented with a more blatantly pop-jazz sound. His fans, however, wanted the kind of stuff he'd done with the Texas Playboys and voted with their feet, so by the late '40s he had righted his ship and begun giving people what they wanted. There's no doubt that he and Wills (along with other Tulsa-based acts like Art Davis, Al Clauser and His Oklahoma Outlaws, and Tex Bynum) were in competition for the same audiences; McAuliffe even had his own noontime broadcast on KVOO rival station KRMG, whose studios were located in the same building as the Cimarron Ballroom.

In a *Tulsa Tribune* story from May 5, 1953, touting Tulsa as "the capital of western swing music," writer Bob Foresman noted that the rival bandleaders—Leon and Johnnie Lee—had both been members of Bob Wills' Texas Playboys, calling them "two worthy successors" to Bob, who was still in California at the time.

"Together they draw about 2,000 dancers on Saturday nights here," he added, "with Leon packing in 1,200 at the Cimarron and Johnnie Lee 800 or so at the smaller Cain's Academy."

Those numbers may be suspect, but they do indicate a downward trend at the Cain's. (Remember Curly Lewis's statement about how "less than 1600 people on a Saturday night was a bad crowd" in the mid-1940s.) Even allowing for some adjustment of the numbers, evidence indicates the attendance had dropped by around half by 1953.

It wasn't just at the Cain's, either. As the RCA Victor sales indicated, the nationwide popularity of western-swing music continued to slump, even in Texas, the place of its birth.

Again, correspondence in the Glenn White collection provides illumination. In a January 16, 1953 letter to Charlie Walker, the Texas-based deejay, recording artist, and promoter, Mayo got a $400 guarantee against 60 percent of the net proceeds for a Friday night Johnnie Lee Wills date in San Antonio. Three years later, in a letter dated January 26, 1956, Johnnie Lee himself asked Texas booking agent (and musician) Bill Mounce for "at least an average of $300 per engagement" to play six dates around Waco. And finally, On March 4, 1957, Mayo requested $850 total for three Johnnie Lee Wills dates in and around Wichita Falls.

By that time, the revenue from the band's Cain's dates had also dropped off precipitously. Ledgers from the ballroom reveal steadily decreasing dance income beginning in the early '50s. In 1952, excluding holiday and other special-event dances, the band was generally earning between $110 and $150 for a Thursday night dance, and regularly hitting around $300 on Saturdays. Two years later, income from the Thursday dances was usually in the double-digits, with Saturdays averaging a little over $200. The broadcasts still went on, along with the Thursday and Saturday dances, but Johnnie Lee scaled down his touring and began figuring out other ways to cut expenses.

Then, in 1955, a major blow came. That's when the General Mills front office decided to stop sponsoring the syndicated shows.

"What kept 'em going every month was this General Mills thing," explained White. "They were getting a $1,000 check each month [from the company]. When that quit, it really hurt 'em. Johnnie Lee told me he had to refinance his house just to hang together."

****

Throughout the early and mid-'50s, Bob continued to return to the Cain's for special occasions, notably the anniversaries of the first Wills radio broadcast on KVOO. Far more peripatetic than his brother, he'd spent a significant amount of time touring the country during the years Johnnie Lee had anchored the Cain's back home in Tulsa. Bob himself had been based in California throughout most of the '40s, then had taken up residence in Oklahoma City for a time before heading to Texas and an ill-fated project known as the Bob Wills Ranch House. A huge dancehall that featured a bar inlaid with silver dollars, it proved to be a money pit that found Bob having to work just to keep its doors open. In 1952, he sold it to local nightclub impresario Jack Ruby (the same Jack Ruby who'd become a key figure in the aftermath of the JFK assassination) and continued to bounce around between California and Texas— when he wasn't somewhere else on the road with his band.

Then, in late '57, he decided to return to the place where he'd launched his national career almost a quarter of a century earlier: Tulsa, and the Cain's Ballroom.

In *San Antonio Rose*, Charles Townsend suggests that Bob's motive for returning was "to help Johnnie Lee Wills rebuild the dance crowds at Cain's." That seems a simple enough explanation, but there's probably more to it than that. Perhaps there was some nostalgia involved—a feeling once described by the novelist John O'Hara as "a kind of homesickness." Maybe it was simply financial—after all, the slump in western swing's popularity had certainly hurt its top name.

Whatever the reason or reasons, the homecoming didn't work out as well as it could have. Here's what Guy Logsdon told Russ Florence in their 1995 conversation:

> *Bob came back to town with a small group and said, "Let's combine bands, stop the radio show, and go on the road again." Bob Wills loved being on the road. For some people, their life is moving from town to town, to show after show. Johnnie Lee was really not quite that way. He had his following in the area.*
>
> *Bob dominated the family. Each and every member of the family fell under Bob's leadership. And so Johnnie Lee said okay, and they went on the road. And that was the end of the Johnnie Lee Wills daily radio show over KVOO, broadcasting live from the Cain's Ballroom.*

"I think some of those band guys thought there would always be a [Johnnie Lee Wills] band," observed Glenn White. "They never thought there'd be a day that Bob and Johnnie Lee would be sitting down together and Bob would take it back over and Johnnie Lee would start playing banjo with him. If they saw that coming, they didn't want to recognize it."

Leon Rausch was making weekend trips to Tulsa from his home in Springfield, Missouri, at the time, in order to sing and play guitar with a western swing band that included players like guitarist Don Tolle and steel player Gene Crownover. They appeared on a local TV show, and when Johnnie Lee had other engagements on a dance night at the ballroom, that band would fill in. As Rausch recalled in an October 11, 2011 interview with Brett Bingham, "I think New Year's Eve 1957 was the last time that Johnnie Lee and Bob had separate bands. They combined and took some members from each band."

Of course, they went out as Bob Wills and His Texas Playboys, even though both Bob and Johnnie Lee were in the group. After a few months, so was Rausch, taking over for Glynn Duncan, Tommy's brother.

There is, however, a bit more to the story than that. A contract from December 31, 1957, calls for a seven-man outfit led by Johnnie Lee's longtime pianist Clarence Cagle to play four Wednesday night dates in January '58 at union scale, plus a 6 percent "contractor's fee." The band's lineup includes such well-known Johnnie Lee Wills bandsmen as Cagle, steel-guitarist Tommy Elliott, and drummer Tommy Perkins, as well as Rausch. Apparently, these were dances that had been added to the regular Thursday and Saturday night events, which the Texas Playboys were coming in off the road to play.

Why did the new group come into being? One reason may be that Cagle was leery of the new Texas Playboys band and chose not to be a part of it.

"They wanted him to go with them, but he wouldn't, because he knew that Bob and Johnnie Lee would not be together very long," explained Cagle's wife, Kathrean, in a 2008 interview with Brett Bingham. "Then, when Bob and Johnnie Lee split, Johnnie Lee came out to our house and took Clarence for a ride in the car and asked him to come back with him."

Another reason may have been that Perkins, Elliott, and Rausch hadn't made the cut for the newly reconstituted Texas Playboys, so their employer gave them, and Cagle, these shows as a kind of compensation. Since their employer was Bob Wills himself, who'd leased the Cain's from O.W. Mayo effective January 1, 1958, that idea seems to make a lot of sense.

So Bob and Johnnie Lee did their touring with the Texas Playboys band, returning to the Cain's on Thursdays and Saturdays for the dances. They were apparently still doing the noon broadcasts at the time as well, although the logistics had to be challenging at that point.

Then, in early March, the Texas Playboys headed out to the West Coast for a series of dates. Since they were too far away to get back for their regular dances, Johnnie Lee stayed home at the Cain's while Bob, with a band that was at least partially assembled just for the tour, headed west.

As Rausch remembered it, Bob Wills had seen him on the Tulsa TV show he was doing with Don Tolle and Gene Crownover and decided to invite him into the band that was going to the West Coast, since Glynn Duncan wanted off the road. Rausch said he and Bob met in Oklahoma City, where they were working separate venues.

"I really didn't know if he was going to do any hiring at that point, but he said he wanted to talk to me, so I suspected that's what it was about," Rausch remembered. "So we met, and he said, 'Did you bring your extra clothes to go with us on this trip?'

"I said, 'Oh, Bob, I'm not situated to be able to leave and go on the road.'

"'Well,' he said, 'I thought you wanted to work.'"

Bob's idea was for Rausch to ride the bus with the band out to California, learning the material as he went, and then, when Duncan was dropped off at his home in Pomona, Rausch would be able to step right in. Since he still had a day job in Springfield and a family to deal with, however, Rausch was unable to drop everything and accede to Wills' wishes.

Luckily for Rausch, however, Glynn Duncan's leaving for the road (and ultimately, leaving the band) meant that there was a place for a vocalist with Johnnie Lee's group in Tulsa. Rausch got that gig. And while it didn't mean that he'd be a Texas Playboy once Bob got back, it certainly helped his chances. Also helping his chances was bandleader Johnnie Lee, who'd mention Leon on many of the broadcasts from the Cain's, talking about how great he was doing and hoping out loud that Bob would feel the same way when he got back.

Rausch's talent, combined with the exposure he was getting with a Wills band, did the trick. As he recalled:

When Bob got off the trip, that job was still open for me; it came up on March 17 [1958]. He had decided, on this trip to California, that he was going to fire Billy Bowman, who was playing steel at the time. And he had looked at Gene Crownover before and liked his work. So he put Gene and me in on the same day.

We went in to rehearsals at Cain's, and I thought, "Man, I've arrived. This is it." You get that surge, you know, when something hits: "This is what I've been waiting on.' And sure enough, we went to work, Gene and I.

****

The contract for the January 1958 dates featuring the Clarence Cagle-led band had been signed by Cain's secretary Ada Perry on behalf of Bob Wills, listed as the band's "employer." As noted earlier, that designation came about because Bob himself had leased the Cain's from O.W. Mayo. A letter supplied to the authors by later Cain's owner Larry Shaeffer affirms the arrangement. Dated November 25, 1957, it was sent by Mayo to Wills, who was then living in Abilene, Texas. Wrote Mayo, in his always-businesslike manner:

In our last telephone conversation you asked that I proceed to have a lease drawn up covering the lease on Cain's to you, effective January 1st. I have asked [their longtime lawyer] Milsten to draw up this lease and since you are going to be in Tulsa next week, I will have it ready and we can sign it at that time.

In the meantime, I thought I would furnish you some information on the items of expense which you asked me to furnish you.

Mayo then goes on to carefully describe each regular outlay of money Wills can expect to have to pay, from the annual city license ($150, payable on January 1), payments to the performing-rights organizations ASCAP ($180/year) and BMI ("based upon the amount of business we do," but lately $90/year), and rental and maintenance of the neon sign outside the building ($20.40/month). He also advises Wills about a Brink's armored-truck service in use at the Cain's for the past several years, at $41.20 a month, public liability insurance ("which is a must anymore in anybody's business") at $9.02 per every thousand dollars of ticket sales, newspaper advertising at $4.50 per column inch (by this time, Mayo was a fan of print ads, telling Wills, "I definitely feel that this newspaper advertising well pays for itself"), and even janitorial supplies "which doesn't amount to much." An illuminating part of the missive comes when Mayo advises his longtime friend on personnel costs.

> *As I believe I explained to you on the telephone, I pay Alvin Perry $40.00 a week as custodian of the building. I have been paying Ada $20.00 a week for selling tickets and doing my office work. I pay a girl to work the check room $5.00 a night and two officers get $7.50 per night and a couple of colored boys who do the cleaning up after the dance each night and shine shoes in the men's rest room, get $19.50 for Thursday and Saturday, one being paid $9.00, the other $10.50, and the colored lady who works in the ladies restroom only, gets $3.50 per night, or $7.00 per week.*

According to the initials at the end of the letter, Mayo dictated it to Ada Perry, showing that she was indeed involved in the Cain's "office work."

O.W. Mayo would continue to own the building until 1972, according to his 1986 interview, but he would not be involved much in its day-to-day operations after leasing it to Bob. (He did, however, continue his involvement with the Johnnie Lee Wills Tulsa Stampede, a long-running and highly successful rodeo Mayo and Bob Wills had started back in 1939.)

Why did Mr. Mayo, who'd owned the building for some two decades, decide to lease it out at this time? Guy Logsdon provided one likely answer.

"He [Mayo] went through a period where he told the dancers they had to wear dress clothes, and that sort of killed it," explained Logsdon. "He was trying to figure out what he could do to upgrade it and bring more people in. So he tried to make it a classy place and it didn't work; some of the old diehards quit coming because they didn't dress up."

Even though his disastrous experience with the Bob Wills Ranch House had shown Wills how tough it was to try to play music and run a dancehall at the same time, he apparently thought he could do it with the Cain's. Even with considerable help from the likes of Turner and Alvin and Ada Perry, he gave up after about a year. According to Mayo, Bob then subleased the place to Perry.

It's reasonable to assume that Perry took over on January 1, 1959, exactly a year after Bob signed the lease with Mayo. A dance schedule for the Cain's in December '58 has Bob Wills and

His Texas Playboys playing the Thursday and Saturday dances (except for one Saturday with Ernie Fields and His Orchestra, a well-known local black dance band) along with the Christmas Eve and New Year's Eve engagements. But then, the first week in January, Jack Arnold and the Flames have the Thursday spot, with Hank Thompson and the Brazos Valley Boys on Saturday.

Of course, this could also mean that the Texas Playboys just hit the road for a week or two and then returned. But there were still the daily radio broadcasts to do—or maybe there weren't. They had stopped sometime in the latter part of 1958 and were just a memory by early '59, when Bob and the Texas Playboys, including Johnnie Lee, accepted an engagement in Las Vegas, which ended up being Bob Wills' base of operations for the next couple of years.

"We worked out of Cain's until Bob got disenchanted, later in '58," explained Leon Rausch. "Bob got upset with KVOO because they started putting baseball games and stuff on the air and it would bust into our radio time. They'd cut us off early on account of a baseball game or something."

There was also, he added, the matter of the red light.

> *Bob didn't like that red light. It was the only communication we had with the station. They had a hookup, and when that red light came on above the microphone, you had to be ready. When it came on, we were on, and when it went off, we were off [the air].*
>
> *I'd get so upset because I could see Bob coming down that aisle with old man Mayo and I'd look at my watch and*

say, "Thirty seconds, and we're on the air." How does he do that? He'd walk up on that [Cain's] stage and pick up that fiddle and that red light would come on. It was magic.

After a few months in Vegas, Johnnie Lee returned to Tulsa and put his own band together again. They'd even perform regularly at the Cain's, although he would never again see the success he'd enjoyed in the '40s and early '50s. Until his 1984 death, however, Johnnie Lee Wills remained a Tulsa fixture, opening a western-wear shop in 1964, continuing to lend his name and energy to the yearly rodeo, and playing the occasional date with sidemen old and new.

Guy Logsdon, Johnnie Lee's friend for many years, offered this assessment of the second Wills brother's impact on Tulsa:

Johnnie Lee Wills gave more entertainment pleasure to the region than Bob ever thought of. But Bob, because of his charisma and because he was the one who forced Johnnie Lee into doing it—Bob is the magic name. And justly so. Johnnie Lee would say the same if he were here. He'd say, "Yeah, Bob is the one who deserves credit."

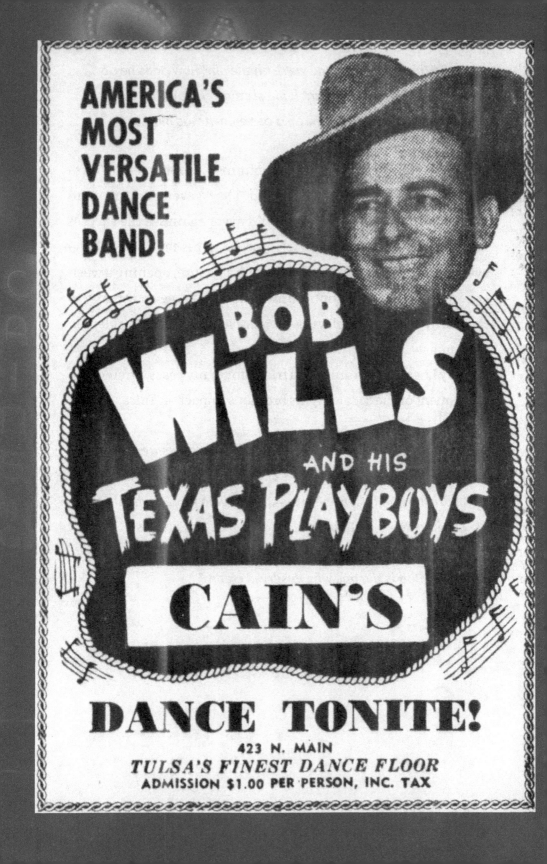

CHAPTER
★★ 08 ★★

Swing was dying, rock 'n' roll was coming on, but we didn't want to lose the people who'd been coming there [to the Cain's] forever. So we played enough stuff that they liked to keep 'em. Then, we played enough rock 'n' roll that we drew new people into it."

— BENNY KETCHUM, QUOTED IN AN ARTICLE BY
JOHN WOOLEY IN THE SEPTEMBER 4, 2005 *TULSA WORLD*

In early October of 2003, Cain's general manager and talent buyer Chad Rodgers received a letter from a man named Benny Ketchum, who was living in Dewey, Oklahoma. Ketchum had seen a *Tulsa World* story about the grand re-opening of the ball-room on October 1, and wrote that the article was "very interesting and informative."

"But," he added, "there was a period in the historic past that seems to always be forgotten or overlooked. It pertains to the years between 1958 and the late 1960s."

He was right. Retrospectives about the Cain's invariably focus on Bob Wills and the ballroom's unshakable place in history as the nexus of western swing, with not much notice given to the years between the end of the combined Bob and Johnnie Lee run and the beginning of the '70s cosmic-cowboy era. Also, there are a lot of people pretty familiar with the history of the Cain's who, if pressed, would say that the only house bands the place ever had were led by men with the last name of Wills.

Although that's not right, it's a perception that can be forgiven. For nearly a quarter of a century, Bob Wills and His Texas Playboys and Johnnie Lee Wills and His Boys held forth on a regular schedule between those walls, adding to their legacy with every live show and KVOO broadcast.

As we've noted in the previous chapter, however, western swing's appeal didn't, and couldn't, last forever, even in the place it called home. The crowds faded away, and at the end of the '50s, the reigns of Bob and Johnnie Lee Wills were over. No more would they broadcast daily over KVOO, throwing open the doors for adoring crowds to come in and watch and listen for free. No more would they do two—and sometimes more—dances there in a week, packing the house so tightly on occasion that the dancers could only sway together in one spot. By early 1959, the famous Wills house bands had left the building, and that was that. (According to Don Mayes, after teaching dancing at the Cain's for more than two decades, Howard Turner also left in the late '50s, taking a job with the Tulsa State Fairgrounds.)

But that wasn't it for a regular act at the Cain's. In fact, following the exit of Bob and Johnnie Lee Wills for the road and Las

Vegas, a house band remained, playing two and then three nights a week well into the '60s (although it did leave for a while and then come back). Singer-guitarist Benny Ketchum, the author of the letter to Chad Rodgers, was its leader.

"I had a seven-piece band and we played Wednesday, Friday, and Saturday nights for over 5 years," Ketchum wrote. "They took down the banner with the 'Home of Bob Wills' on it and replaced it with 'Home of Benny Ketchum.' There was a marquee over the entrance that read 'Home of Benny Ketchum and the Western Playboys.'"

Ketchum, born and raised on a farm north of Dewey, had begun playing and singing professionally in the early '50s, while he was still a teenager. He worked theaters and clubs around the Coffeyville, Kansas, area, where he also had

Benny Ketchum

a daily noon-hour radio show. By the time he reached his senior year of high school, he'd expanded his territory into Texas and was working so much that he was unable to graduate. (Many years later, he'd pick up his diploma.)

Ketchum first came to the attention of Alvin Perry, the Cain's leaseholder at the time, when he played the ballroom with Bobby Helms, the countrified rock 'n' roller who'd hit big in 1957 with the songs "Fraulein" and "My Special Angel." Ketchum had fronted the band, and, as he recalled in his 2005 conversation with Wooley, "We'd packed Cain's full."

"Some of it was just him," Ketchum added, referring to Helms, "but a lot of it was because there was a lot of advertising done on it. He [Perry] had seen that we could do rock 'n' roll, and that's what was selling at the time."

So, as the 32-date Helms tour was winding up, Ketchum got a call from Alvin Perry. "We'd wound up in California, and he called one day and said, 'You guys could be the house band here if you want this,'" Ketchum recalled. "I had the bug that I wanted to do one-nighters, you know. I didn't want to sit somewhere. But I told him, 'Yeah, we'll come back there if the money's good.' So we came back and worked Fridays and Saturdays when we first started. And he paid us fair."

Ketchum said his band started those dates at Cain's "in the general area" of 1958. "The only thing I've got to go by," he explained, "is we bought a brand-new Ford station wagon in 1958. It was a '59, so they came out a year early, and we were already there at the Cain's when we bought it."

Like Bob and Johnnie Lee Wills before him, Ketchum and his band hit the road when they weren't on the Cain's stage. An item from Paul Gayton's column, "The Hunch," in the October 19, 1959 issue of *Billboard* magazine reads: "Benny Ketchum and the Western Playboys continue on one-nighters in the Oklahoma, Kansas, and Arkansas sector while appearing as the regular Saturday night feature at Cain's Ballroom, Tulsa, Okla., managed by Alvin Perry."

Alvin's wife, Ada, had a hand in Ketchum's management as well. On September 11, 1959, a little more than a month before the *Billboard* item, she wrote an acquaintance in Krebs, Oklahoma named Lucille Masiano. In the letter, which now resides in the collection of Glenn White, Ms. Perry asks Ms. Masiano for assistance in booking "a band that we have been using here at Cain's and are wanting to help get started around in this territory."

...I don't know whether you are doing anything in the way of promoting dances or not, but am sure you will know whether McAlester, Kiowa, Hartshorne or any of the other towns in that vicinity are having regular dances, who to contact, etc. I've been out of this "booking" business and have lost contact.

Of course, with Johnnie Lee back in the band business, and with Bob and the band playing in this territory at intervals, it is pretty hard to try to get a band they don't know to try them for the first time, but since both Bob and Johnnie Lee are on tours quite a bit, I thought some of these places might be interested in the band and once they play them I am sure they will want them back.

This band is Benny Ketchum and the Western Playboys. At the present time they have seven pieces and may add another a little later on. They are a real fine bunch of boys and have a good band. We have been using them here at Cain's a lot...

Having grown up well within the range of clear-channel flamethrower KVOO, Ketchum arrived for the new gig very aware of the Cain's and its western-swing heritage.

"When I was a little boy, my uncle lived in Tulsa, and we would come down on a Saturday afternoon once a year, and I'd sit on the bench and watch," he remembered. "So, yes, I knew what Cain's was."

He also knew, however, that it had changed. By the time Benny Ketchum and the Western Playboys debuted as a house act, Bob Wills was gone, the merger with his brother's band proving to be only temporary. Johnnie Lee and His Boys were still playing the Cain's, but in a diminished role. (Johnnie Lee had temporarily left Bob and the road, although he'd rejoin his older brother for the 1959 Las Vegas engagements.) According to Ketchum, Johnnie Lee and his band were working only once a week during that late '50s period—playing Wednesday night dances.

"We'd sometimes be down there rehearsing in the afternoons, and they [Johnnie Lee and members of his band] might come in," he remembered. "O.W. Mayo might be there. We met each other that way. They worked the Wednesday nights, as I recall, and then finally that disappeared, and we done Wednesday, Friday, and Saturday."

The name of Ketchum's outfit suggested that it was, like Johnnie Lee and His Boys, a western-swing group. But that was only part of the story. Younger than the Wills brothers, Ketchum was more attuned to rockabilly and rock 'n' roll, as well as straight country music, although he made sure that the Western Playboys could tackle just about any genre. His seven-man band included two fiddlers who could also play saxophones, and a steel-guitarist—Dicky Overbey, who'd go on to considerable fame as a sideman—equally adept on electric guitar. For the Wednesday dances, which had until recently been the province of Johnnie Lee and his band, "we cut back on our rock 'n' roll and done western swing and waltzes," Ketchum said.

In her letter to Lucille Masiano, Ada Perry emphasized the group's versatility, noting, "They have a Western band, with colorful uniforms, but they can also play rock and roll and pop music if desired. They play practically all of the new songs as well as the old favorites...."

Over at the Cimarron Ballroom, Leon McAuliffe had seen the winds of change whipping around his club as well, and he'd begun booking some rock 'n' roll dances there. He'd continue to try and woo the younger patrons attracted by this new sound. A few years after Ada Perry wrote her friend Lucille, Ray Bingham—who'd go on to a career as a nationally known promoter, producer, and booking agent—began a series of Saturday afternoon "sock hops" at the Cimarron Ballroom.

"They didn't last very long, maybe a few months," Bingham (an uncle of this book's co-author) told John Wooley in 2019. "We played what we called rock 'n' roll records, kind of rockabilly, I guess, and broadcast from the Cimarron. It was free for kids to get in. We did it to try and get a younger audience."

Pressing for any advantage, demographic or otherwise, the management of both the Cain's and the Cimarron continued their rivalry for many years. However, for a time beginning in the late '50s, the Cain's apparently seized the upper hand. Here, according to Ketchum, is how it happened:

Friday night we were in competition with the Cimarron,
so there was a lot of head-buttin' going on at that time.
Well, we figured out a way to beat him [McAuliffe]. We
brought in the names on Friday night, packed it full, and
sometimes held 'em over until Saturday night—got two
nights out of 'em. We did this all the time, holding them
over, but it wasn't advertised that way. So Saturday, we'd
work with [rock 'n' roll station] KAKC and just flood that
sucker [with commercials]. We hurt him badly with that;
he finally began booking in names himself.

So our Friday nights were stars [performing] with us,
and Saturday nights we had to ourselves, except when
we held somebody over.

The "names" and "stars" Ketchum referred to were the recording artists who toured on the strength of their radio hits, traveling without a band, at the mercy of whatever outfit backed them in any particular town. When they got to the Cain's, though, they'd always find a quality backing band in Benny Ketchum and the Western Playboys. Ketchum's groups featured crackerjack musicians, including steel-guitarist Overbey; Buddy Jones, a drummer and pioneering figure in what's come to be known as the Tulsa Sound; and vocalist-guitarist Wayne Kemp, who'd go on to become a country-music recording artist. Another musician plucked from the Tulsa club scene would achieve great rock-music fame—and some memorable Cain's appearances as a headliner—years later.

Jimmy Markham, Leon Russell—Russell Bridges at the
time— David Gates and those people were playing at the
Paradise Club then. They were just kids, and I was a young
man. I was 20. We had rhinestone suits, we were making
money, and I'd take the stars out there with me.

Boy, they just ate that up, that these big stars were
out there to see 'em. And we'd sit in and play rock 'n' roll
and get free drinks and what have you. I met Johnny Cale
through that.

Johnny—later J.J.—Cale became the Western Playboys' guitarist for their regular Cain's gigs, and Ketchum recalled him as
"a good guitar player."

"But I don't think his heart was ever in country music," added
Ketchum with a laugh. "We had to tie his neckerchiefs on him."

Indeed, Cale's rock 'n' roll demeanor drew the attention
of at least one of the touring country acts appearing for a one-
nighter with Ketchum's group at the Cain's. Ketchum laughingly
remembered Nashville star Little Jimmy Dickens calling Cale a
"Fabian reject."

From there, Cale hit the road for California, joining Russell,
Gates, and many of the other Tulsans who'd invaded on the West
Coast, trying to make their marks in the music business. Several
of them, Cale included, succeeded, if not immediately.

Ketchum made his own foray into the L.A. music scene a little
later, along with band members Kemp and Jones. There, they hung
out with the transplanted Tulsa rockers, helping each other with

gigs and room and board and simple survival. As he recalled it, "We pooled our money and managed to live for a while, but not very well." While Kemp stayed, and Jones would end up alternating between Tulsa and L.A., Ketchum left after a while for Nashville, where he and his band toured with country-music package shows until Ketchum "got into it with some of the booking agents that I didn't think were treating us right." The band returned to the Cain's and resumed a Friday and Saturday night schedule, but before long they got a better offer from a Kansas City clubowner. "We went to Kansas City and worked for 10 years," he noted. "We worked five nights a week. But during that time, we still worked Cain's. We'd come back and work Saturday nights at Cain's."

In the time following his return from Nashville, he recalled, "You couldn't sell western swing anymore. Swing had disappeared." So country music, along with touring country-music recording artists, began making up a bigger portion of the Western Playboys' repertoire.

"We had turned country," Ketchum said. "We were still doing rock 'n' roll, because it was still big, but we had almost completely dropped our swing music by that time.

"The second time we came back, it was with a smaller group," he added, "because I couldn't afford that [seven-piece band] anymore."

From there, Ketchum remembered his remaining tenure at the Cain's as an on-and-off thing that lingered for years, always fitted in around his other gigs, thanks to an arrangement he had with leaseholder Perry.

I had a terrible agreement with Alvin: Whenever he needed somebody, I would work. Well, he'd call me at the last minute and say, "[George] Jones didn't show up, man! Can you get down here?" I might have a job in Wichita, and I'd have to leave that band there to work our contract. I'd come to Tulsa, pick up people from bands I used to have, put 'em together, and we'd work whatever we needed to work.

The musicians had to know what I was doing. We didn't do any rehearsing to speak of. They were capable of knowing that when I moved my head, this had to happen, and when I moved my foot in a certain way, this had to happen. They thought like I thought. I was fortunate to have excellent musicians.

In his letter to Chad Rodgers, Ketchum indicated that the Western Playboys' days as the Cain's house band effectively ended when "the overpass took over the parking lot," although Ketchum and his band still returned and played "on many occasions until Alvin Perry was no longer there."

Ketchum and the Western Playboys, as we shall see, ended up as the ballroom's penultimate house band. And even though the stage banner that had once touted Bob and then Johnnie Lee Wills was changed to read "Home of Benny Ketchum," this important bandleader—the link between western swing and rock 'n' roll at the Cain's—has been a forgotten figure in the venue's history. In his interview with Wooley, Ketchum not only acknowledged his relative obscurity, but gave a couple of possible reasons for it.

When the highway [Interstate 244] came through there, it took the parking lot, and at that time we quit. That just killed it, so that was when we began to branch out somewhere else.

And then, a lot of it was due to the fact that Cain's was well-known for Bob Wills, and anybody else who went there [to play], the people didn't know who you were. You might've gotten lots of people, and got plenty of advertisement, but it was still the home of Bob Wills.

If Alvin Perry had followed through with something he wanted to do in the early '60s, Ketchum might've gotten a little more of the cachet he rightfully deserves. Western-swing music's biggest scandal occurred in 1961, when West Coast bandleader Spade Cooley—who'd seen his own fortunes take a tumble because of the diminished popularity of the kind of music he played—beat his wife to death in a drunken rage. (Cooley had played the Cain's on his way back to California following a mostly unsuccessful Eastern tour in the late 1940s.) Bob Wills' chief rival for the King of Western Swing title, Cooley was one of the major artists represented by a poster-sized photograph on the Cain's wall of fame. Following the murder, however, Cooley's stock fell drastically, and Perry decided the bandleader no longer deserved his place on the wall.

"They'd been wanting to put my picture up, but there was no space," remembered Ketchum. "So Alvin said, 'Well, we'll take down Cooley and put your picture up there.' But they never did. Back then, it was expensive to make those big posters. Now, it doesn't cost anything."

Cooley stayed on the wall. He's still there, in fact. And Benny Ketchum, who returned to Tulsa in 1974 and settled into a regular gig at the local Danceland club for the next dozen years, never saw his own photo join the gallery of greats—a fact that should in no way diminish his stature as the last successful Cain's house act to date.

****

Interstate 244 is a nearly 16-mile stretch of road that runs through the heart of downtown Tulsa. Built in the late '60s and opened over Labor Day Weekend in 1970, its construction eliminated the once-ample parking lot that lay north of the Cain's. O.W. Mayo, who was nothing if not a perceptive businessman, undoubtedly knew the loss of the lot would take a big chunk out of his business. There was, however, little he could do about it except take whatever money the government handed him for the property and try to soldier on.

That didn't mean he was happy about it.

"I sold the lot in 1965," O.W. Mayo explained to Wooley. "They took it away from me when they run the expressway through."

The disappearance of ample, easy-access parking did indeed pose a problem—not only to Cain's attendees, but to the performers as well. In a 2009 interview, legendary country star Ray Price remembered playing the place during the Alvin Perry days, telling Brett Bingham that he and his band members parked their vehicles in front of the Cain's, "and when you was introduced, you came right through the audience."

"They didn't have that damn highway then," he added. "That's what really hurt 'em."

Like Bob and Johnnie Lee Wills, Price played music for dancing, and some pop-culture observers believe that the enormously popular 4/4-time country-shuffle beat that became associated with his name through such late 1950s' hits as "Crazy Arms" and "City Lights" supplanted the 2/4-beat western swing as the dominant Southwestern dancehall sound. Certainly, Price and his Cherokee Cowboys performed on many of the same stages as Bob and Johnnie Lee Wills—including the Cain's, which Price said he's played "a million times."

"It was strictly a western-swing place," he explained. "And that's the kind of band I had."

Johnny Bush, who'd go on to achieve fame as a honky-tonk singer and songwriter, was Price's drummer in those days. "When I was with Ray in the '60s," he recalled in a 2005 interview with Wooley, "we'd play the Cain's every New Year's Eve."

Price and the Cherokee Cowboys played their first dates in the Cain's in the late '50s, during Alvin Perry's tenure as lessee and Ketchum's days as the house act. Often, Price told Bingham, he'd sit with Perry in the Cain's office until it was time to go on. One time, fellow country star Faron Young happened to be in the area, and dropped by to see his friend. Recalled Price:

He came into the office, and there was an officer in there, a policeman. Faron said, "That's a fine-looking pistol there. Could I see it?" The policeman handed him his gun, which he should've never done, and boy, when he did, Faron cracked

down on the wall with that pistol. Bam! I guess the hole's
probably still in the wall.

Another time, Price and Cherokee Cowboy Donny Young—
who'd later, as Johnny Paycheck, become a well-known country
artist—engaged in a bit of tomfoolery that led to an excruciating
Cain's performance for the star:

He was horsin' around and I was doing some lift-ups, lying
on my back. He said, "Let's see if you can lift me up," and
he laid down on my hands. I started to push him up, and he
moved and slipped and fell onto my chest. He had a damn
pistol in his pocket, and he broke four of my ribs.

That was just about an hour before I had to go on, so I
went to an emergency clinic and they put tape on me. I got
over to Cain's, and it was hurting so damn bad that I ripped
that tape off. In 15 more minutes I went back over and had
'em put on more tape.

It was hurtin' bad. *But I did the show. Man, that was one*
night to remember.

Despite these sorts of antics, Alvin Perry continued to welcome
Price and his boys back to the venue. "He always treated me real
nice," Price recalled. "I guess he treated everybody real nice."

Price, of course, was a moneymaking act, and that undoubtedly had something to do with the welcome he got from the Cain's
proprietor. Others, however, weren't treated with the same amount
of warmth.

Take, for instance, the former Cherokee Cowboys' bassist and front man, a Texas singer-songwriter named Willie Nelson.

In a 2008 interview with Brett Bingham, Willie called the Cain's "one of the better beer joints" he'd played in his career.

"What I really enjoyed about that place was the pictures on the wall," he said. "That made it different from the other places that I'd been playing. You could look around the walls and see that before you got there they'd really had some hot acts—Johnnie Lee Wills, Bob Wills. All those huge pictures were very impressive."

Nelson first visited the Cain's in the late 1950s with Price's band. As the Cherokee Cowboys' front man, he was responsible for warming up the crowd before the star took the stage.

"Those were good days, when I fronted for Ray and did about 45 minutes," he recalled. "I didn't have any records out at that time, so I sang a lot of Hank Williams songs and told Little Jimmy Dickens jokes."

Nelson left Price for a solo career in 1961 and was booked at the Cain's soon afterward by Ray Bingham, a couple of years before Bingham began working for the Cain's competing venue, the Cimarron Ballroom. "I'd had a hell of a time booking Willie in there to start with, because Alvin Perry only wanted people who made him money," remembered Bingham in a 2002 interview with John Wooley for the Tulsa World's Spot magazine.

Unfortunately, Nelson didn't exactly make the turnstiles spin for Perry.

"We only had about 30 or 40 people that night," Bingham said. "I remember that Willie had on his little green business suit, probably a J.C. Penney suit, and a little skinny tie. He was neat and polished, but even then his phrasing wasn't like anyone else's. People criticized him a lot for that.

"He started his show, and my wife and [Tulsa performer] Frances Self and I went out and stood in front of the stage and watched him, trying to get some people to stand with us. But no one cared."

According to Larry Shaeffer, who not only owned the Cain's for more than two decades, but also, later, became a booking agent for Nelson, Willie knew he'd flopped and was depressed about it for days afterward.

Shaeffer found all of this out in February of 1999, when he had to move a Nelson show from the Cain's to Tulsa's Brady Theater because of heavier than anticipated ticket sales. The promoter visited Nelson in his tour bus after the show, and instead of being happy about the great reception he'd gotten in the sold-out larger venue, Nelson seemed upset.

"I asked him why, and here's what he told me," remembered Shaeffer in his interview for Wooley's 2002 *Spot* story. "'Larry, you know that I grew up in Texas listening to Bob Wills playing from the Cain's Ballroom over KVOO, and besides the Grand Ole Opry, the Cain's is the place I most wanted to play.'"

After his first performance on that stage, Nelson said, he wrote a letter to Alvin Perry, talking about what an honor it had been to play the Cain's and adding that he'd love to play there again anytime. Within a few days, according to Shaeffer, Nelson received a reply that read: "Thank you for your recent letter. But please be advised that the management of the Cain's Ballroom doesn't intend to ever bring you back."

The Cain's had gone through nearly 40 years and several changes in management when Nelson and Shaeffer met on that bus, but in all that time Nelson had never made an encore appearance at the Cain's Ballroom. Several years after he'd struggled to get a few dozen people through the doors of the dancehall, he'd gotten so big that he'd had to be booked in arenas, huge halls, and on outdoor-festival stages; the Cain's couldn't have begun to hold the people who wanted to see him. In the late 1990s, however, as more modest-sized venues became a part of his booking strategy, he longed to return triumphantly to the stage where he'd failed decades earlier, to finally drive a stake in the heart of the rejection he'd gotten from Alvin Perry and the Cain's.

"I remember what he told me at the end of the story about Alvin Perry," Shaeffer said. "He told me, 'You know what, Larry? I've still got that damn letter.'"

Willie Nelson finally returned to the venue for two shows on March 13 and 14, 2001. Appearing on a Tuesday night and a Wednesday night, he was greeted the first evening—according to *Tulsa World* reviewer Andrea Eger—by "a Cain's Ballroom so packed that representatives of the Fire Marshal's office were said to have shown up."

So his second go-round as a Cain's headliner couldn't have been more different from his first. That inauspicious debut had happened four decades earlier, an obscure appearance by a struggling young country-music singer witnessed by very few and remembered by even fewer, a performance by a man who would nonetheless go on to become one of those superstars so well-known that they're universally recognized by their first names. And, even though he had been *Willie* for many years, it still had to feel pretty good for Nelson to gaze out over that wall-to-wall shouting and sweating Cain's Ballroom crowd, the classic photos of the old-time stars looking down at him like effigies of ancient gods, and, maybe, say to himself: *finally!*

In the 1960s, country-western music declined in general. Some of the old stars died, others faded from the spotlight. Across the nation, rock and roll overshadowed country music. Many thought the time had come for country music to die a merciful death.

But country music refused to die. It merely slipped into a coma.

During the comatose years, 1960-1970, Cain's changed from a frenetic ballroom to an echo of the past....

— WRITER DOUG DARROCH, IN HIS ARTICLE FROM
THE DECEMBER 10, 1975 *TULSA TRIBUNE*

The decade-plus between the end of the Cain's classic western-swing era and the cosmic-cowboy years of the mid-'70s have been the least-written about in the ballroom's long history. Part of the reason, as Benny Ketchum, Ray Price, and O.W. Mayo all pointed out last chapter, was the I-244 expressway, which eliminated the venue's parking lot. The ballroom's "wrong side of the tracks" location would be exploited in a successful ad campaign later on, but in the mid-'60s, the fact that the Cain's no longer had an adjacent lot meant that attendees had to find their own sometimes remote parking places in a part of town many Tulsans considered unsafe. A sizable number of patrons and would-be patrons became unwilling to do that, especially as they aged. It was one thing to park right across the street from the door; it was another to navigate several blocks of dark sidewalks that might hold unwelcome surprises in their shadows.

Still, the Cain's was hardly moribund during those years, as later reports like Darroch's would make it out to be. Alvin Perry, with his wife Ada (like her husband, a familiar figure at Cain's since the Bob Wills days) selling tickets and keeping books, brought in some of the top country acts of the time throughout most of the 1960s. Country music may have been off some people's radar then, but it thrived in Tulsa.

"I remember one weekend in the '60s when Hank Thompson was at the Cain's, Jim Reeves was at the Cimarron, and Conway Twitty was at the Caravan—and all of 'em had good crowds," said Ray Bingham in an interview for this book. Bingham, as noted in the last chapter, was the man responsible for Willie Nelson's first Cain's appearance; he also booked many other country performers into the Cain's during Perry's tenure as proprietor.

"I never knew of him bringing in anything else but country," Bingham said of Perry. "My deals were all on Saturday night, because [country artist and deejay] Billy Parker was nice enough to have me on a little show on KFMJ radio Saturday afternoons, where we could talk about the artists I had coming in. I booked acts like the Louvin Brothers, Little Jimmy Dickens, Jimmy C. Newman, and Frances Self and her Playmates, who were local but had played all over—they'd been at the Golden Nugget in Las Vegas."

Bingham was also responsible for booking those Ray Price New Year's Eve dances. And, Bingham recalled, until the very end of Price's life, every time they got together, the veteran star would say, "You know, we ought to play that New Year's thing at the Cain's again." Bingham also engineered a Cain's appearance by big-name star Ernest Tubb that was intended as a live recording session for Tubb's next LP. But, as Ronnie Pugh noted in his book *Ernest Tubb: The Texas Troubadour* (Duke University Press, 1996), things didn't quite work out that way.

"Tubb and the boys played Cain's December 16, 1961, and Decca [Tubb's record label] made a genuine attempt to record their show for a live album," wrote Pugh. "Band members recall that too much crowd noise ruined those recordings, so it was back into the Nashville studios in March and April to recut the songs."

In the book, Pugh quoted Tubb's steel guitarist at the time, Buddy Charleton: "We cut it live, but the crowd was so noisy and rowdy we couldn't use it. Decca was there and everything, but they were just wild—they always were at Cain's when Ernest was there."

Tubb and his Texas Troubadours band nonetheless returned to the ballroom a couple of months later in order to pose for album-jacket photos. Released in October 1962 under the title *On Tour*, the subsequent LP featured liner notes touting the fact that it had been "recorded live at the famous Cain's Ballroom in Tulsa, Oklahoma." One of the tracks, Leon McAuliffe's "Steel Guitar Rag," had been performed (and later re-recorded in the studio) as a tribute to Take It Away Leon's days on the Cain's bandstand with Bob Wills.

By the time *On Tour* came out, however, McAuliffe had long owned his own Tulsa nightspot, the Cimarron Ballroom, which—as mentioned earlier—was the Cain's biggest competitor, especially for weekend dances. Ray Bingham had gone from booking acts for the Cain's to a similar job at the Cimarron—after McAuliffe, who was on the road a lot at the time, personally asked Bingham to take over that part of the operation.

"We started doing a Saturday afternoon radio show live from the Cimarron Ballroom, and that's when Alvin Perry kicked us out of the Cain's," recalled Bingham, laughing at the memory. "They had someone there—Billy [Parker] says it was Buck Owens—and we cruised over to see how big their crowd was. We walked through and had almost got to the bandstand when [steel-guitarist] Gene Crownover's brother, who was the bouncer and a really big guy, stopped us. He said, 'I'm sorry, but I have to take you guys out of here,' and he ran us back through the crowd. He was nice to us— we knew him, of course—but he was big enough to do it.

"As we got to the door, we passed Alvin Perry, and he said, 'You both are barred from here. You're never coming into Cain's again.'"

Bingham recalls getting tossed out in 1964. But Perry must've softened after a couple of years; for the big Saturday night Cain's dance held in conjunction with the 1966 Johnnie Lee Wills Tulsa Stampede rodeo (which Johnnie Lee and O. W. Mayo continued for years after Bob and Johnnie Lee stopped their broadcasts and regular dances from the ballroom), the entertainment was provided by Johnnie Lee himself, along with Billy Parker and his Western Band.

****

Both Bob and Johnnie Lee Wills continued to play the Cain's on an intermittent basis during the '60s, although they both stopped touring with their own groups during the early '60s. In 1964, Johnnie Lee opened his Johnnie Lee Wills Western Shop at 2128 S. Memorial Drive, in Tulsa's Memorial Shopping Center. His wife, Irene, and his son, John Thomas, joined him at the western-wear store, and it was a success; by 1968, it had expanded to three times its original size.

As noted earlier, after leaving the Cain's to go with Bob and the band to Las Vegas, Johnnie Lee had returned, reformed his band, and continued to play and tour. However, according to guitarist and vocalist Roy Ferguson, by the time the doors of the Johnnie Lee Wills Western Shop opened, Johnnie Lee had let his Boys go. Whenever he was booked—and Ray Bingham did a lot of his booking in those days—Johnnie Lee would contact Ferguson, who had his own group, Roy Ferguson and the Royals.

LEFT TO RIGHT: *Glenn "Blub" Rhees, Johnnie Lee Wills, Alvin Crow, and Roy Ferguson*

"Johnnie Lee got rid of his band sometime in the early '60s," said Ferguson in an interview for this book. "He'd slowed down a little; he had some heart problems, and problems with his intestines. So if John needed a band, he'd ask me to put one together. Sometimes it'd just be my band, and sometimes we'd add people he'd played with, like Blub [saxophonist Glenn 'Blub' Rhees] and [pianist] Clarence Cagle."

Ferguson had toured with Johnnie Lee Wills and the Boys in 1960, and longtime Wills band member Curly Lewis was a member of Ferguson's Royals at the time, so Johnnie Lee knew what he was getting with the group.

"When we'd go play these deals with Johnnie Lee," Ferguson recalled, "I'd always tell him it was his band, and he could run it the way he wanted to."

"When Johnnie Lee played with the Royals, he'd always refer to them as the Boys and the Girl, because [vocalist and Ferguson's wife] Candy Noe was with the band," added Bingham. Of course, the Boys—sometimes known as All the Boys—had been the name of Johnnie Lee's band during all his years at the Cain's.

Roy Ferguson and the Royals continued to perform on their own as well as with Johnnie Lee—and other stars—on an *ad hoc* basis until Johnnie Lee Wills' 1984 death. During that stretch, they backed Johnnie Lee for several Cain's engagements.

Bob Wills, on the other hand, had been dealing with his own health problems in the early '60s, suffering his first heart attack in 1963. The next year, he sold his band and the Texas Playboys name to a fan in Fort Worth named Carl Johnson, who had provided Wills with financial and other incentives to move his base of operations to Johnson's hometown. According to the Charles Townsend book *San Antonio Rose*, "[Wills'] arrangement with Johnson made possible what he had wanted to do for the past few years, but never could actually bring himself to do—give up his band and work alone. He had had the responsibility of a band since 1929 and wanted to be relieved of the burden."

Bob Wills continued to work for Johnson until a second heart attack later in 1964, which required him to leave Johnson's organization—and the Texas Playboys—for a period of recuperation. From that point on until the end of his career, Wills toured as a solo performer, traveling across the country and fronting local bands. Of course, the quality of the musicians he found backing him on the road varied widely, so he often ensured a certain level of professionalism by bringing proven performers like vocalist Joe Andrews—later replaced by Tag Lambert—and Gene Crownover along for the ride.

And while the days of the daily broadcasts and twice-weekly dances at the Cain's were long gone, Bob still managed to get to his old honky-tonk hacienda on a regular basis. Townsend wrote that Wills returned to the Cain's in March of 1969, the week of his sixty-fourth birthday, and "Ada and Alvin Perry provided a three-tiered cake that would serve 750 guests. Bob symbolically cut the cake with his fiddle bow and told the audience, 'I'm on a diet, so all of you folks just come up and help yourselves to a piece of the cake.'"

A couple of months later, he came back for another go-round. This engagement, however, would turn out to be a far less joyous occasion.

* * * *

In late May, 1969, Bob returned to Tulsa, with Crownover and Lambert in tow, to play a dance at the Cain's. The authors have not been able to unearth the name of the band that backed him that night—some have contended it was Johnnie Lee's outfit, but Ferguson said it wasn't. Bob had at least one familiar face waiting for him, however. According to Townsend, Wills' longtime guitarist and arranger Eldon Shamblin showed up, plugged in, and played as a surprise to the bandleader he always called "the old man."

"Whenever Bob would play Tulsa in those days, Tag would come stay with Gene and me, and Bob would stay at the Downtowner Motel," recalled Margaret Riley, who was then married to Crownover, in a 2007 interview with John Wooley. "So that night, we went to pick him up, and when we got there he was just getting dressed. Bob's hat was sitting on a chair by his bed, so Gene picked it up and put it on the bed so he could sit down.

"Well, when Bob came in, he really got after Gene. He said, 'You know how I feel about a hat on the bed!' He was very superstitious in that way."

The idea of a hat on a bed being bad luck had been around for a very long time by then. But this time, those who believed in such things could've found all the proof they needed. The hat incident, in fact, directly preceded the end of the great Bob Wills' days as a bandleader and performer.

That night at the Cain's, Wills hit the stage at the appropriate time. However, as Shamblin later told Townsend, "Bob came out to play, but he couldn't play. I knew something was wrong. He had lost his coordination."

Wills had likely suffered a small stroke. A couple of days later, after receiving an award at the Texas Governor's Mansion, he was hit with another, more massive one. It paralyzed his right side, effectively ending his career. He never fronted a band again.

****

It's impossible to know what effect Bob Wills' last Cain's performance had on Alvin Perry. It may have had nothing whatsoever to do with Perry's leaving the Cain's. But, for whatever reason, he did, later that same year. By deciding not to renew his lease, Perry and his wife ended a relationship with the ballroom and O.W. Mayo that stretched back decades, to the halcyon days of Bob Wills and the Texas Playboys. From the late '30s forward, prior to their taking over the whole operation themselves, Perry and his wife had been integral cogs in the ballroom's machinery, with Ada functioning as the ballroom's secretary for many years, and Alvin running the concessions and functioning as O.W. Mayo's trusted right-hand man.

By the time Perry left, the Cimarron Ballroom—his main competitor for many years—had shut down for good. In 1968, the Tulsa phone book listed only two entries under "ballrooms"—the Cain's and a place called Dutsch's Party Barn in Broken Arrow. Leon McAuliffe's Cimarron had been included in those listings only a year earlier; now, it was gone.

Mayo, in his 1986 interview with Wooley, said that Perry subleased the Cain's from Bob Wills in 1959, after Wills himself had leased it from Mayo in '58. But when music-store owner Jim

Hardcastle picked up the lease later in '69—ten years after Bob Wills had allegedly taken control—he made his deal with Mayo, who had continued to own the property.

A little mystery, however, exists between the end of the Perry era and the beginning of Hardcastle's tenure as lessee. According to both Hardcastle and Benny Ketchum, a man leased the Cain's for a few months in 1969 with the idea of turning the place into a ballroom, where people could dance to a big pop group as they had in the golden days of the big bands.

The problem is, Hardcastle and Ketchum didn't jibe on the guy's name.

"A fellow by the name of Young had it," Hardcastle told Brett Bingham in an interview for this book. "He just couldn't maintain it with what he was doing. It was more or less a ballroom deal; he wanted more of a ballroom deal than he wanted a country joint."

Ketchum's memories of the man reinforce Hardcastle's words. "He was trying to put an orchestra together, to combine swing and rock 'n' roll," explained Ketchum to John Wooley in a 2010 conversation. "He was crazy about swing music. He and his wife and their friends usually came to our Wednesday night dances.

"I was out in California at the time, and he called and told me if I'd come back and front the band, he'd pay me whatever I wanted. But that wasn't the kind of music I wanted to do then, so I didn't go."

Ketchum, however, said that the man who contacted him was not a Mr. Young but Bill Fanning, a well-known Tulsa antique dealer. By the time Ketchum became acquainted with Fanning and his wife, Min, Fanning was an older man—"I'd say in his seventies or even eighties," Ketchum speculated.

The Fannings had been a familiar sight at the Cain's even before the Ketchum era. Curly Lewis recalled them from his days with the Johnnie Lee Wills band. "I knew him and his wife; she was a real tall lady, and he was kind of short," said Lewis. "They were big fans of country music and western swing, and they hardly ever missed a Thursday night or a Saturday night dance. I remember one time when we were out on the road, probably in the mid-'50s or a little earlier, Mr. Mayo rented the whole hall to 'em for several days, and they put on an antique show and had all these booths set up in the Cain's, with dealers and people from all over."

Lewis remembered hearing about an attempt to launch a big pop band on the Cain's stage in the late '60s, but he believed it might not have actually come to fruition. Benny Ketchum had his doubts, too, saying, "Possibly he was speculating when he called me, trying to get it together."

Their recollections were reinforced by saxophonist Jim Fanning, who played for decades in Tulsa-based jazz and swing bands. He was Bill Fanning's second cousin, although Bill was much older.

"It never did get off the floor," Jim Fanning told Wooley in an interview for this book. "They got it going to a certain degree, but then they both got sick and died, so it fell through."

Perhaps the Cain's was dark for a while in 1969, during the time the Fannings were trying to convert the ballroom to a big-band venue. Given the time frame, that period couldn't have lasted more than a few months—at the outside. Jim Hardcastle assumed the lease in the latter part of '69, and Perry had it until at least May. Still, Hardcastle was adamant that he assumed the lease from Mayo only after Mr. Young failed to make a go of it.

And to further complicate matters, a listing in the 1970 program book for the Johnnie Lee Wills Tulsa Stampede rodeo, advertising a May 9 dance at the Cain's with Conway Twitty and the Twitty Birds, lists a man named Leon Clark as proprietor. When Hardcastle was contacted by Brett Bingham in 2019, he did not recall Clark, so the two were probably not connected. Hardcastle, however, was sure he took over the lease in 1969 and continued with it for a couple of years straight. Could it be that O.W. Mayo was renting out the building on a piecemeal basis to anyone who wanted to book it for a dance (or even an antique show), and Hardcastle began as only one of the promoters doing business at the Cain's before leasing it for a longer stretch? Billy Parker, whom Brett Bingham also contacted re: Leon Clark, vaguely recalled the name and thought he had a daughter who sang. Could Clark have booked the Cain's on a few different dates so that his daughter could open for some nationally known bands? Had he even been involved in the attempt to bring the big-band style of music into the Cain's?

With the passage of time and the passing of people who might've been able to clear things up, it's doubtful that these questions will ever be fully answered. So that's where we'll have to leave it, one more little mystery around a ballroom that's never been lacking for secrets.

****

Jim Hardcastle was selling pianos and organs out of a Tulsa business simply and aptly named the Music Store when he heard that the man he remembers as Mr. Young was giving up on his plans for the Cain's and getting out of his lease because he was losing so much money. Not only was Hardcastle a longtime patron of the Cain's and a fan of country music; he was also a business neighbor of Johnnie Lee Wills, with the Music Store located only a couple of buildings away from the Johnnie Lee Wills Western Shop on Memorial Drive.

Hardcastle went down and struck a deal with Mr. Mayo, and soon he was opening up the Cain's every Saturday night, running local bands along with the occasional touring country act. The place was dark the rest of the week, except when he got the opportunity to book a major act on an off-night at a reduced rate. "I couldn't afford [Merle] Haggard or some of the others, but they'd come in if they had a cancellation," he said. "Jack Greene and a bunch of the others like that, they'd come in if they'd have a cancellation. That was the way I did it—I'd catch a cancellation or something like that."

He also booked nationally known recording artists with area connections, including Billy Parker—who'd left town in 1968 to front Ernest Tubb's Texas Troubadours, returning in 1971 to take a deejay job at Bob Wills' former station KVOO and continue to perform and record—Wanda Jackson, and Stoney Edwards, all Oklahoma natives. Most of the time, however, Hardcastle's weekly Cain's dances featured well-known local country acts, including Benny Ketchum and Roy Ferguson and the Royals.

When Hardcastle threw open the Cain's doors every Saturday night, patrons were likely not only to see him, but many of his family members as well.

"My wife took the tickets, and my daughter and my mother ran the popcorn machine," he explained. "My son and I worked the concession stand. All we were selling back then was Coke and 7 Up and ice, cigarettes, stuff like that. They'd bring their own booze and I'd sell 'em the setups. We had three porters, and when we'd bring a star in, we had a little maid down in the women's restroom. That was about it."

Work on the I-244 expressway was in full swing at the time, which not only limited the parking for Hardcastle's patrons but, on one occasion not long after he'd taken over, also caused a major problem.

One night it came a whale of a rain, and all that dirt was loose, with no grass. Water and mud started coming in the doors on a Friday night and kept up until about 1 a.m. on Saturday. We had probably two inches of mud from the state's highway in Cain's Ballroom, and we had to take big crews there to get it all cleaned up and get it ready for dancing. The state brought people there; everybody was really trying to help us get it back.

The floor wasn't good and dry, but we had a dance that night.

We sure did.

The first major star Hardcastle remembered bringing in was Jeannie C. Riley, whose Tom T. Hall-penned tune "Harper Valley P.T.A." had been a No. 1 country-to-pop crossover hit in late 1968. At seven dollars a ticket, she attracted a wall-to-wall crowd.

"She was the first one that really filled the house for us," he said. "We went on from there. We had a bunch of big stars come in, and we set a record New Year's Eve—it had to be in 1970—with Billy Parker and Cal Smith. We had fire marshals down there. We'd let two out and they'd let two in. We set the record with 1567 people, and we had people standing outside waiting to get in the whole time."

The aforementioned Stoney Edwards turned out to be a solid attraction for Hardcastle as well. When bands took breaks at his Saturday night dances, Hardcastle would play records for the crowd. One of the discs he started spinning was a lachrymose number called "A Two Dollar Toy," about a man who trips over his daughter's toy as he's abandoning his family and decides to stay. Reportedly based on an incident from Edwards' own life, the recording made a big impression on the Cain's crowd. Remembered Hardcastle:

I'd play it and everybody would come up and say, "When did Haggard come out with that?"'On that song, he really does sound a lot like Merle Haggard. And I'd say, "That's not Haggard. That's a new guy called Stoney Edwards."

I kept getting quite a few inquiries, so I thought, "I'll just bring him in and see what happens." I was the first to bring him into the Cain's, and I started bringing him in all the time.

As it turned out, Edwards was a Seminole, Oklahoma native, although he'd migrated to California years earlier. And when he hit the Cain's for the first time, he did it with a band that would become, on its own, the best-known western-swing revivalist group in the world, and a favorite Cain's act for decades. Fans know the band as Asleep at the Wheel; when that aggregation saw the Cain's for the first time, however, its members were collectively known as the Poor Folks, the name derived from one of Edwards' 1971 releases on Capitol Records, "Poor Folks Stick Together."

"We backed up Stoney, but we were always working on our own stuff," founding Wheel member and front man Ray Benson told Brett Bingham in 2010. "We were Asleep at the Wheel, but they [Capitol Records] just wouldn't let us call ourselves that. They thought that was too weird a name. So we were called Stoney Edwards and the Poor Folks, which we were."

As Benson recalled it, Edwards and the band first hit the Cain's while working their way from California to Nashville, where they were to play at the Capitol Records showcase for the annual country-music disc jockey convention. The band members were already performing western swing and were well aware of the ballroom's history. Also, remembered Benson, "We all had that Texas Troubadours live at Cain's Ballroom record and copped licks off it. So we knew all about Cain's before we'd ever set foot in it."

Fortified by a half-pint of corn whiskey they'd purchased at a nearby liquor store, the band members went in to set up. Said Benson:

> At that time, there was just the original round backdrop with the big red musical notes on it, and there was a microphone that came down from the ceiling and ran into this little closet on the side. It had a Bogen P.A. in it, I'd say from the '50s. On either side of the stage were these big circular horns instead of speakers.
>
> I said, "Let's try this thing," and cranked it up. When I touched it, I got a 110-volt shock!
>
> We had a little column P.A. we used for the club gigs, so we started setting it up. The old lady who ran the place [probably Hardcastle's mother] came in and I said, "We're going to use ours."
>
> She said, "Why don't you use ours? It was good enough for Bob Wills."

Later, Benson said, when the band stepped out on the Cain's stage and hit its first lick that night, "I just got chills down my spine. You know, I was 20 years old, and it gave me the chills to be on that stage, playing for the folks. I was exhilarated."

The Cain's audience had heard Edwards' "A Two Dollar Toy," but they hadn't actually seen the performer himself, whose heritage was African-American, American Indian, and Irish. Although Charley Pride had shown that black artists could become country music stars, there weren't any others at the time. According to Hardcastle, however, the inadvertent experiment in integration turned out fine. "That evening," Hardcastle recalled, "all of his folks showed up. They got there before he did, and the only colored people we'd had in there before were the porters and the waiters. And man, here come all these people in and I thought, 'Well, what in the world is going on here?'

"Then his dad and mother came in. It was like Charley Pride. They [Edwards' record label people] were trying to keep it quiet until he caught on."

* * * *

In his own words, Hardcastle had just "wanted a shot at Cain's." And for a little more than two years—from late '69 to Valentine's Day, 1972, he had it.

That's not quite true. By the time of Hardcastle's final event, the Cain's had a new owner. O.W. Mayo, who'd been forced to sell the parking lot back in 1965 because it was needed for construction of the new expressway, had finally decided to divest himself of the building as well. The improbable new owner was an octogenarian named Marie L. Myers, who made the deal with the intention of installing a band fronted by her friend, a local country singer named Gene Mooney. She'd officially taken ownership earlier in February. Hardcastle, however, had one more major act booked into the venue—Freddie Hart, a country star whose "Easy Loving" had been a monster crossover hit a few months earlier.

Hart was coming in as a single, so Hardcastle made a deal with Ms. Myers to have Gene Mooney and his group back the star. In those days, it was common for an artist to send recordings of his or her songs to a house band in advance, so that the local musicians could practice the songs they were to play in the upcoming show, making sure to get them down with the right timing and in the right keys.

Hart sent the recordings to Mooney well in advance. But when the time came for the show, according to Hardcastle, things didn't work out the way the artist planned:

> *Freddie Hart sings about a quarter to a half-key off, so you don't just throw a band out there with him. They've got to work on the songs. Every Saturday night after Mrs. Myers bought the thing, they were there [at the Cain's], and I'd say, "Gene, did you practice those records?"*
>
> *"Yep, yep," he'd say. "Getting his songs down pat."*
>
> *So the night came for the dance and, man, I mean we had a packed house. They get up there and Gene does his thing and then brings Freddie up. I don't remember what*

the first song he sang was, but he kept turning around and looking back at the band, like, "What the hell is going on?" Then he sang "Easy Loving." Well, that one went over pretty good so he tried a song, and he was looking back at the band, back at the band, until it progressed to halftime.

I don't know if you know much about Freddie Hart, but he's a black-belt, and he's a tall sucker. And he comes off that stage mad. I started up to play a record and he said, "No you don't, Jim. Come with me."

I thought, "My God, what have I done now?"

He took me back in that office, and I never thought I was gonna get my butt whipped any more in my life. He was going at me: "I sent you those records, told you to practice my songs, and the only damn song of mine that band knows is 'Easy Loving.'"

I said, "Freddie, wait a minute. Wait a minute. Let me go get Gene." I went out there and hunted old Mooney down and I said, "You tell him I gave you those records and I asked you every night if you was practicing and you told me yes. Now he's about to whip my ass!"

So Gene said, "We done 'Easy Loving' and I thought we could handle the rest of it." But man, you can't do that with Freddie Hart.

Freddie came back after the show and apologized, and I told him I thought I'd had it.

That was my last dance at Cain's. I moved my stuff out of there and it was done.

Why did she buy the ballroom in 1972?

"I bet I've had a thousand people ask me that," she says.

"I just wanted it. That's all I can tell you.

"Well, I was going to build a big boat down on my land at home (on the Grand River). It was going to be a showboat.

"But I couldn't get the ground zoned, so I came up here and bought this."

> — Marie Myers, quoted in a story by Joy Hart in the July 14, 1975. *Tulsa Tribune*

After nearly three decades as the sole owner of the Cain's Ballroom, O.W. Mayo was ready to divest himself of the property. So, toward the end of Jim Hardcastle's time as lessee, Mayo approached him about buying the ballroom.

Hardcastle, however, passed. Although he'd found out that he enjoyed the country-music business and wanted to continue in it, he was looking well beyond downtown Tulsa for a new

169

venue. Eventually, he'd open the Big Country Corner Ballroom in nearby Coweta.

One day while Hardcastle was still at the Cain's, an 83-year-old woman with a bent right leg showed up to visit with him. As it turned out, she was seriously thinking about buying the place outright; as Hardcastle recalled it, she told him, "I'm going to get it for Gene. I'm going to make Gene my house band."

Her name was Marie Myers, and "Gene" was the singer and bandleader mentioned in the last chapter, Gene Mooney. A cousin of famed steel guitarist and Oklahoma native Ralph Mooney—who was at this time at the beginning of a long stint with Waylon Jennings' Waylors—Gene fronted a local band called the Westernaires. Hardcastle had booked the group several times during his tenure at the Cain's, although, he said, "It was one of the least-drawing bands around this area because he sang a different type of country song, and he wouldn't let anybody else in his band sing. It was all Gene. I liked his singing, but it was like listening to bluegrass all night long. It gets to sounding the same, and that's the way he was."

Ms. Myers, however, apparently could have listened to Mooney all night, and then some. Certainly, she was convinced of his talent. But several people interviewed for this book, including Jim Hardcastle, indicated that the relationship between the two was more than strictly business. Asked about how Myers and Mooney met, he chuckled and said, "She went down there [to the Cain's] one night and asked him to sing 'Hello Darlin' to her. That was it."

The adjective "colorful" seems an appropriate description of the octogenarian who officially took over the Cain's following

Hardcastle's Valentine's Day '72 date with Freddie Hart. Born in Dublin, Arkansas, Myers had lost both her parents before the age of 10 and, for the *Tribune* piece excerpted at the beginning of this chapter, told interviewer Joy Hart that she was running a boardinghouse at 12.

(The term "boardinghouse" may have been a euphemism, at least later on in her life. In a 2019 interview with Brett Bingham, western-swing and cowboy-music star Red Steagall, who worked the Cain's several times during Ms. Myers' tenure, remembered her relating a story about "staffing" a brothel in Fort Smith, Arkansas. She told Steagall she would ride a horse back and forth from Fort Smith to Tulsa to "recruit new talent," sending the girls to Arkansas via the railroad. When Steagall asked her why she didn't ride the train herself, she said, "I couldn't be seen with women like that.")

Ms. Myers told the *Tulsa Tribune* writer that she disguised herself as a man in order to mine gold in Colorado, and had run all kinds of enterprises, including "a gold mine down in Arkansas... a cattle business, a sawmill, vegetables, and a ballroom." Her first husband, George McFadden, as she recalled it, was a singer who'd worked the vaudeville circuit and recorded some discs for Edison. Her other experience with the entertainment business, she said, included a stretch as the lessee of Tulsa's Majestic Theater, booking "wrestling matches, boxing, and shows"—at the age of 16.

"I just got it leased," she noted, "and there was nothing they could do about it after I got it leased."

In another piece, published in the May 19, 1973 *Tulsa World*, writer Tom Wood explained the circumstances that ended up propelling her toward the Cain's:

Her husband, Charles Elmo Myers, died four years ago
at the age of 91.... For two years after her husband died,
Mrs. Myers stayed in her house close to the banks of the
Grand River and grew lonelier and lonelier.

"I wanted to throw myself into the river. I had two
dogs, but they died. I don't have any close relatives. I
don't have anybody. I don't have anything but a rooster
and 10 hens."

After her idea for the Grand River showboat didn't materialize, Wood added, "a friend told her that the Cain's was on sale."

"I bought it after seeing only the outside," she told Wood. "I wanted a dance hall. Days get long when you're sitting on the banks of a river. I got tired of that."

Wood noted the participation of Mooney, with whom she had "worked out an agreement and a plan to try to revive the dance emporium." However, he added, "The results have been from poor to mediocre to good, depending on who the attraction is. Each Saturday night they offer dancing from 9 p.m. to 1 a.m., but, according to Mrs. Myers, the crowds usually run between 80 and 100."

She told him she had lost $19,000 in the past year, which was her first as the ballroom's owner. (According to future owner Larry Shaeffer, she had paid O.W. Mayo $40,000 for the Cain's building.)

"She was an Indian from Muskogee, had a lot of that Indian money," Hardcastle said. "But she didn't have no business being in the music business."

He told this story to illustrate his point:

When she came down and talked to me, she asked me, "Who are the top people you bring in who make you the most money?"

I said, "Stoney Edwards, Cal Smith, Wanda Jackson. Those three can come in single or you can bring 'em in with a band. They're reasonable and you can make some good money on 'em."

So I sold out, and about a month or a month and a half later, one of the old regulars who used to go down there when I had it called me up and said, "Are you coming down tonight?"

I said no, and he said, "Well, Stoney's here."

I said, "Do what?"

He said, "Stoney's in. Miz Myers brought Stoney in."

So I went down there, and there probably weren't 35 or 40 people in the place. She was sitting back on one of the long benches that sat right against the wall where you came in, and she saw me come in and said, "Come over here. Come over here. I thought you told me you made money on this guy."

I said, "Man, you've got to let people know he's here. You did no advertising whatsoever on the radio or in the paper. How do you expect people to know he's here?"

"Well," she said, "Gene's running this, and Gene's running that...."

After a while, Gene Mooney would run away from the Cain's completely, leaving Myers to take care of the ballroom by herself. But before that, he would audition a young steel guitarist, just out of the Army, who would figure greatly in the history of the Cain's. Here's how the guy who auditioned remembered it:

> *Gene Mooney called me out at my parents' house and said, "I hear you can play steel guitar. We need a steel-guitar player. Come in here tonight. Please."*
>
> *I said, "I can't play well enough."*
>
> *He said, "Just come down and try it."*
>
> *I was afraid I'd embarrass myself, but I went anyway and tried out one Saturday afternoon, and afterward he said, "You're right. You can't play well enough."*
>
> *But he was nice about it, and I was relieved, because it scared me to death to go try to do a four-hour set with a bunch of guys.*

Within a few years, however, that man would own the stage he auditioned on, along with every bit of the ballroom that surrounded it. His name was Larry Shaeffer, and under his long-term ownership, the Cain's would once again take its place as one of Tulsa's top live-music venues.

At the time of his audition, though, it was still Mrs. Myers' baby. The thing was, she didn't quite know what to do with it—especially after Gene Mooney's exit.

****

After taking over the ballroom, Myers doggedly kept opening up every Saturday night with Gene Mooney and His Westernaires as the house band, continuing to draw very small crowds and lose money. Despite the advice she got from Hardcastle at the Stoney Edwards show, there's little evidence to indicate that she did much, if any, advertising in the local papers and on radio, so most of Tulsa and the surrounding area stayed unaware of the dances.

Sometime around late 1973, Gene Mooney left the building. The details of his departure are lost to time, but several people indicate that a serious disagreement between him and Myers led to his exit. Perhaps he was tired of playing to crowds of a few dozen every weekend. Maybe it was something more. For whatever reason, he and the Westernaires ended their tenure as the Cain's house band. That mantle then fell, for a time, to Bob Cobb and His Oklahoma Playboys, after Myers contacted Cobb about coming in to run the Cain's for her. (A western-swing group led by Gene Crownover, Bob Wills' former steel guitarist, and featuring players from the Bob and Johnnie Lee Wills bands, would become the house band during the final days of Myers' ownership.)

By the time Mooney left, problems had begun to arise. Myers, who was by this time in her mid-eighties, was simply overwhelmed by the day-to-day business of running a ballroom. One day, following Mooney's departure, Glenn White came down from Oklahoma City to pick up some memorabilia from the ballroom that Johnnie Lee Wills wanted him to have. White recalled what he found:

She had on her desk there at the Cain's office two stacks of records, and she said, "See those records? They cost me three thousand dollars. They're Gene Mooney records, and I'm trying to get the disc jockeys to play 'em."

"Well," I said, "that might be impossible, Miz Myers, because the disc jockeys are pretty independent. They don't listen to anybody from the outside."

She had letters on her desk from the state of Oklahoma, the Oklahoma Tax Commission, and they'd be demanding this and that, and she didn't have the foggiest idea. She'd say, "Would you read that letter and tell me what you think about it?"

I'd look at it and I'd tell her, "Apparently there are some back taxes on this or something. I don't know, Miz Myer, maybe you could call up there to the state capitol and talk to someone about it."

She had those letters stacked up, those records stacked up, and she'd just gotten stuck with all of it.

A measure of relief came in the form of Cobb, who'd worked the Cain's, and many other area venues, with his Oklahoma Playboys. "She'd been around where my band had been playing, and she just got in touch with me," he recalled in an interview for this book. "She called me and said, 'Say, I need somebody to run Cain's,' and I said, 'Well, I'm busy working, but I guess we can find time to do it.' Of course, me being a musician, I was really interested.

"My whole family went in there and cleaned it up and straight-ened it up. We cleaned the gum off the bottom of the tables, painted the tables, sanded the floor and varnished it, and dusted off the pictures [on the wall]. Then Benny, my son, worked the bar, and my wife helped on the ticket counter."

As Cobb recalled it, the Cain's was open every Saturday night during his tenure there, with his Oklahoma Playboys featured as the house band. As had been the case before, sometimes a touring act would play on a weekday, and, he said, "We might've been open on Friday nights."

"We had some pretty fair crowds," he added, "but at that particular time, they'd started to dwindle for western swing. Television had come in. The hippies came in. And so western swing kind of tapered off."

Occasionally, a "hippie" or two could be found in the crowd at the Cain's, which led to at least one humorous situation. Once, Cobb remembered, a kid came up and asked if the band could do any heavy-metal songs.

"I said, 'I don't think so,'" remembered Cobb with a laugh. "'About the closest thing we've got is "Take These Chains from My Heart and Set Me Free".'"

Cobb, who had a day job with a pipeline supply company, also did Myers' paperwork, but only "took care of what happened after I got there."

"I didn't sign any checks," he added, "but I turned everything in to her."

The work of running both a band and a ballroom, coupled with the substantial demands of his day job, led Cobb to leave the Cain's after several months. "I don't think I was there a year," he said. "The company I was working for wanted to send me out on service calls—in some cases, overseas." So he left Myers' employ, and she was back to where she'd been after Mooney's departure.

Sort of, anyway. According to Cobb, Gene Mooney actually returned to the Cain's after Cobb's own exit. If that's true, his second go-round couldn't have lasted for very long. For one thing, Mooney would've quickly found that Mrs. Myers was disenchanted with the whole ballroom business, disinclined to continue as the Cain's owner, and more than ready to shuck the whole deal.

In fact, she'd been ready for a while.

"At one time, she offered me Cain's Ballroom for $65,000. The problem was the $65,000," Cobb said with a laugh. "As a guy raising five kids, I didn't want to step out on a limb, so I just didn't pursue it."

Myers, however, did. She apparently wanted out from under the responsibility of the Cain's pretty badly, so perhaps it was something of a godsend the day a young man named Jim Edwards showed up at the door of the Cain's, offering her an opportunity to get out from something that hadn't turned out the way she planned.

Then again, it didn't exactly turn out the way Jim Edwards planned, either.

****

"I had visions of a San Francisco music-listening room," Jim Edwards told John Wooley in an interview for this book. "When we opened the doors, we had checkered tablecloths and health food."

He and the other young promoters who made a deal to lease the place from Myers would quickly find out, however, that the

Cain's wasn't going to be drawing a checkered-tablecloth crowd. Had he known its long history as a working-class honky-tonk, Edwards might have realized that a listening-room vibe had never existed there. But he didn't. In fact, when he came upon the place during an aimless drive around downtown Tulsa one late summer day in 1974, he had never seen the place before. "I just came around this corner," he recalled, "and there was the Cain's Ballroom in all its splendor."

As it turned out, he and a friend named Robert C. Bradley had been looking for a venue to stage some live-music events. Both were graduates of the Tulsa private school Holland Hall, but Bradley was four years older than Edwards.

"I met him through some mutual friend," remembered Edwards. "It was like, 'Oh, if you want to do music, you guys ought to get together.' So we just got to know each other, started hanging out. He had been a concert promoter at Duke University, which had a real sophisticated program. They were doing the Grateful Dead and all those bands, so he had those kinds of connections."

Edwards, on the other hand, had begun promoting local shows when he was in high school—staging, among other things, a Renaissance fair in Tulsa for a couple of summers.

Even though he knew absolutely nothing about the Cain's, Edwards was intrigued enough to stop by and knock on the door. After a while, he said, "This tiny wrinkled lady opens the door and it's Mrs. Myers. I went in, and the fondest memory I have is that the whole place had this *horrible* smell."

It took him a couple more visits to realize that the smell came from chamber pots set out by Mrs. Myers, who was living in the ballroom's office. "It was cold, and she didn't like to walk across the ballroom all the way to the bathroom, so she was using these like bedpans," he explained.

"I asked, 'Well, what do you do with this place?' And she said, 'Well, Gene Mooney, you know, talked me into buying it, and then he split town.'

"So we worked out a deal. I took Brad down there, and somewhere in the mix was our friend Ed Thornton, who had a little bit of trust-fund money."

In a 1995 interview with Russ Florence, Bradley—who would die of brain cancer the next year —remembered their discovery of the Cain's a bit differently. In his version, "on a real cold, blustery day in October of '74," he and Edwards were looking at the old Union Depot in downtown Tulsa as a possible place to rent for shows.

"Unfortunately," he said, "it was condemned at the time and the city wasn't allowing anything to go on in there."

But we looked down—actually, it would be to the north— and saw the old Cain's Ballroom down there, and said, "I wonder what that place is?"

We went down, knocked for a long time on the door, and finally Mrs. Myers came out. We thought she'd been sleeping. Later, we figured out that she'd probably been trying to put her wig on. She had this big red fright-wig that she always wore.

She said, "What do you want?"

She had a "for sale" sign on the door, so we said, "We want to talk to you about buying the place."

And she said, "Oh. Okay." That was the line that got us in.
As soon as I walked into the front door of the place, I said
to Jim Edwards, "This is where we need to do shows in Tulsa."

Both versions of the story jibe on at least one point: Neither Bradley nor Edwards had ever set foot in the Cain's before. According to Bradley, "I just felt like that was the place where I wanted to center an energy for music in Tulsa," and Edwards agreed on the spot. To hear Bradley tell it, if the two of them hadn't come along when they did, the Cain's long life as a dancehall might've been over, and maybe for good. "Financially, at that time, she was struggling," Bradley said, referring to Myers, "and considering another offer, to turn Cain's Ballroom into a boat warehouse. She had a friend who was building boats and needed a place to store them."

Before that could happen, Bradley and Edwards—with the help of Thornton, whom Bradley described as "our first benefactor"—decided to negotiate a one-night lease with Ms. Myers for Halloween, which was coming up in only a few weeks. Then, using the booking and promotion skills he'd learned as an undergraduate at Duke, Bradley began making calls. By the time the doors opened for the show, three Tulsa acts were on the bill. Two of them, vocalists Jim Sweney and his Cream Cheese & Jive band and the country-rock act Tweed, were local favorites. The headline group, the GAP Band (an R&B act named after the Greenwood, Archer, and Pine streets that run in close proximity to the Cain's), was at the time working closely with rock star Leon Russell, who had recently returned to Tulsa from Los Angeles. Earlier in the year, Shelter Records, headed by Russell and British producer Denny Cordell, had released the GAP Band's first album.

Bradley remembered the evening this way:

We called the dance the Magician's Holiday because that was the name of the GAP Band's first record...and we turned people away. Unfortunately, we didn't happen to count our money very well. We enlisted the help of our parents as doormen, and they thought it was such a wonderful party that they pretty much just let people come in. So some people had tickets and some didn't.

Really, what we proved that first night was that people would indeed come to Cain's Ballroom. And the audience was an interesting mix of rock and rhythm & blues [fans] as the GAP Band at that time was not just playing rock 'n' roll music, but was playing more of an R&B type sound.

While that event would become the prototype for many years of frequently outrageous Halloween nights at the Cain's, it apparently wasn't the first one of its kind held in the dancehall. Edwards said that a year earlier, in October of 1973, a young man "we just barely knew" had rented the ballroom from Ms. Myers and put together a one-off Halloween show dubbed the Freakers' Ball. (From the 1972 Shel Silverstein-penned song by Dr. Hook, "Freakin' at the Freaker's Ball.") Although the details of that night have been lost to history, Bradley appropriated the "Freakers' Ball" title for future Halloween blowouts, with Larry Shaeffer

Freaker's Ball 1975

continuing the name and the tradition after he took over ownership of the Cain's later in the decade.

More important than all that, though, was what Halloween
night, 1974, showed the young Tulsans who'd leased the 50-year-
old ballroom for the evening, unsure of what might happen. To
their joy and surprise, so many fun-seekers had arrived at their
doorstep that they'd had to turn some away to stay within the
boundaries dictated by the fire marshal. This wasn't the sad
sprinkling of people Mrs. Myers had too often been drawing with
her country and swing dances; it was a huge and boisterous crowd
that threatened to burst the place at its seams—not unlike the
crowds that had greeted Bob Wills in the glory days of the Cain's.

It would take work and some savvy promotion to start getting people through those doors on a regular basis, but Bradley, Edwards, and Thornton, energized by their Magician's Holiday turnout, were more than ready to get in there and make a serious commitment to firing the place back up for a whole new audience.

Only one thing stood in their way. The owner insisted that they buy the Cain's from her before they did anything else, and even with all of their resources pooled, they simply didn't have the money.

Mrs. Myers was a really fun lady. Of course, we spent a lot of time with her down at Cain's. I emceed all the shows I did at Cain's, and from the stage I would always acknowledge Mrs. Myers, and I would always ask the crowd to thank her for letting us use the building. She would receive rousing applause, and she would just beam, and would always say to me, "You know, Mr. Bradley, if you would just marry me, I'd give you this place."

Of course, that was a little awkward. I didn't take her up on the offer. But you know, I considered it.

— R.C. BRADLEY, IN A MAY 21, 1995 INTERVIEW WITH RUSS FLORENCE

Bradley and Edwards knew that the "for sale" sign they'd seen on their early visits to the Cain's Ballroom didn't have an "or rent" attached to it. The octogenarian owner was really looking to get out from under the responsibilities that came with possessing that piece of property, and she had little interest in becoming a landlord. At an asking price of $60,000 (she'd apparently dropped it by $5,000 since offering it to Bob Cobb a year or two earlier), the cost of the place was reasonable enough, but it still lay well beyond the means of the young men who wanted to run it.

So they assured Mrs. Myers that, yes indeed, they intended to buy the Cain's, but maybe she could rent it to them first and let them get started with the kind of entertainment they wanted to bring in. Then, they told her, once they got the ballroom re-established and generating a good income, they'd be happy to purchase it outright.

Myers was unsure about that kind of arrangement. As much as she liked being in the entertainment business, selling the venue was uppermost in her mind. Plus, she wasn't particularly crazy about the kinds of acts these youngsters wanted to put on her stage. As Bradley noted, after seeing the crowds and hearing the acts on the Halloween night extravaganza, "Mrs. Myers was excited but perplexed. She really wanted to see Cain's more as a country dancehall."

Perhaps the deal-maker was their offer to retain Gene Crownover and his western-swing band as a regular part of the entertainment lineup, with Bradley and Edwards assuring Myers that the Tulsa steel-guitarist and his outfit would be on the bill every Thursday night. Maybe she was persuaded to give them a shot because they only asked for a three-month lease. Whatever the reason or reasons, Myers finally relented and rented them the place for three months, still insisting that they needed to buy it, and soon.

Tulsa attorney Jeff Nix, who would shortly become a member of the group leasing the Cain's, told John Wooley that the rent "might've been as little as 500 a month, or it could've been as much as a grand—I just don't remember." Larry Shaeffer, who began his involvement with the ballroom a little later on, recalled the amount of the group's monthly lease as $600. In his interview with Florence, Bradley didn't name a figure but said Myers "raised my rent three times" that first year.

Whatever they ended up paying, they started forking over the cash in early 1975, when they began operating the ballroom. True to their word, they retained Crownover's western-swing group, hoping to figure out a way that those older guys might somehow fit into their new plans. "We tried to do a little crossover with Gene Crownover," said Edwards with a chuckle. "We'd try to book him with other acts—I think I have a poster of Gene Crownover with El Roacho—and it just wasn't happening."

According to Bradley, however, it happened pretty well the first time they tried it:

> *The first show we ever did on our lease was a band out of Norman that Kevin Welch had called New Rodeo. They headlined for us on a Thursday night. The stipulation with Mrs. Myers was that we would indeed include western swing, so the first band we put on stage was Gene Crownover's Western Swing All-Stars. And they tore up the house. The young crowd really enjoyed them....*
>
> *The second night was Leon Russell's wife, Mary McCreary, who had a record out on Shelter. We just*

assumed that Leon would come to perform, but Leon was
nowhere to be seen. However, Mary's band acquitted them-
selves very nicely.

Then that Saturday night, our first Saturday night at
Cain's, we did a sellout crowd with Michael Martin Murphey,
who had a hit single at the time. We paid him seven hundred
and fifty dollars flat and grossed three thousand dollars on
tickets alone. Right out of the box, people flocked to Cain's.

That first weekend was indicative of the direction Bradley
intended to go with the Cain's—rock 'n' roll, R&B, and especially
the new rock-influenced hip-country acts, mostly coming out
of Texas, who were known informally as cosmic cowboys. This
group included the likes of Murphey, Jerry Jeff Walker, Ray Wylie
Hubbard, Rusty Weir, Asleep at the Wheel, and Alvin Crow, with all
of them becoming regular visitors to the Cain's stage. As Edwards
remembered:

The first really big night, when I knew what we had and what
we were up against, we had Jerry Jeff Walker. We had 1400
people twice, for two shows, in one night.

The first crowd comes in, and Jerry Jeff's backstage,
half-drunk, and the place is packed out. People are throw-
ing beer bottles against the wall, just to see what it sounds
like. When Jerry Jeff comes on, a guy stands up on a table,
ten feet away from the stage, arms up, and Ed Thornton and
I look at each other and say, "Oh, my God. We've got a tiger
by the tail."

That metaphorical tiger was hardly the checkered-tablecloth and health-food venue that Edwards had hoped for. "Jimmy was always wanting to do the artsy-fartsy stuff—and I say that with respect," Jeff Nix told Wooley. "It was just turning into a honky-tonk, and he didn't care for it."

Nix had become a part of the group when Edwards, Thornton, and Bradley had sought his legal advice about incorporating their Cain's management team. Nix agreed to do that work in exchange for what Bradley called "a small percentage of the business."

After a few months, it had become clear that the business, true to the roots of the Cain's, was going to attract a clientele far rowdier than those who might be interested in patronizing the kind of "San Francisco high-end music listening room" that Edwards envisioned. (Much later, in March 1992, former cosmic cowboy Willis Alan Ramsey, opening for Lyle Lovett, would cut his set short and walk off the stage because of the boisterous crowd—indicating that things hadn't changed much at the Cain's since the mid-'70s.) Still, Edwards, with Thornton's support, clung to a higher-minded ideal.

"Brad was in a different state of mind than Ed and me," Edwards explained. "He was, 'Yeah! Party! Hang on for the ride!' So we had *that* dynamic tension going on."

All of that leads up to the night we had Hot Tuna. So here we've got half of the Jefferson Airplane – Jorma Kaukonen, playing like four men, and [bassist Jack] Casady up there, and this was basically the fulfillment of the vision. This was as close as we were going to get in Tulsa, Oklahoma, to the Fillmore.

So, while the band's playing, somebody throws up on my back. I thought, "Okay. That's it. This isn't what I signed up for."

Bradley and I had been fighting quite a bit about this tension, and the next day we had this sort of pow-wow, and it was determined that because Bradley was the guy who had the connections in the music business, it should go in that direction. So I was kicked off the island, basically. But it was one of those things in life where you know you're supposed to go a different direction, and I may have made my decision that night.

Thornton, whose contributions had included building the Cain's first walk-in beer cooler and rebuilding its bathrooms, "stuck it out for the remainder of the first season," Nix recalled, before taking off himself. By the time summer hit, Bradley and Nix were the only two left.

Meanwhile, Mrs. Myers had become increasingly antsy about selling the ballroom instead of renting it, and decided not to let them renew their lease. She talked about her decision in the July 14, 1975, *Tulsa Tribune* piece. "I had it leased out to some people," she told interviewer Joy Hart. "They were going to buy it, but they said they didn't have enough money—so I said I wouldn't lease it any more.

"It was all hippies, you know. I'll tell you they had 2,700 people in here one night," she added. "That's what hippie bands will bring in. Country and western bands won't do it any more."

Hart reported that Crownover was scheduled to play at the Cain's on August 2. "Then," she wrote, "Mrs. Myers plans to book other national country and western acts every Saturday night. Well-known rock groups will be booked during the week."

While Myers' motive for dropping the lease seemed to be her desire to sell the place (along with, maybe, an aversion to "hippies"), the idea of this lady in her mid-eighties taking over and booking rock acts along with country seems a little curious.

In his conversation with Russ Florence, Nix offered one possible explanation:

> *The place was just ridiculously full in April, May, and June. We were just knocking 'em dead. Not much of the money was staying home, but we were turning over a bunch of it.*
>
> *Mrs. Myers would come down there and sit back in the back and drink a beer. She had this gold-handled cane, and when she talked about money, her hands would just twist over it. She was just crazy about money, and every time you saw her, boy, her hands were just twitching because she wanted to hear the cash register ring.*

Nix said he was convinced that Myers and a Muskogee lawyer named Bill Smalley had decided they could make those cash registers ring themselves. All they had to do was book the kinds of cosmic-cowboy and rock acts that had done so well for Bradley and the boys. So she forced the issue by giving Bradley and Nix the choice of immediately buying the place outright or leaving.

Although the two had been doing well with the acts they brought in, they didn't have anywhere near the $60,000 asking price, so the decision to stay or go was out of their hands. The season-ending show they'd planned in June turned out to be what they thought would be their final Cain's hurrah; after it was over, Nix and Bradley reluctantly packed up, figuring they'd be gone forever. Nix told Florence about their early-morning exit from the building:

I'll never forget the night we finished the season. It was after a show, three o'clock in the morning, and we were bringing the stuff out of the office as slowly as we could. She's sitting there on the bench, tears in her eyes.

We're all, "Oh, Mrs. Myers, we just wish we could've worked something out," and she's saying, "Well, I know, boys, but you just need to buy the building."

"Well, we just don't have the money."

Finally, there was nothing else to carry out. It was all gone, and we had no choice but to walk out the door. We put our arms around each other, the three of us [Bradley, Nix, and Myers], and we're walking out slowly.

Then, Mrs. Myers says, "Boys?"

We turned around hopefully.

"Come back," she said, "if you get any money."

＊＊＊＊

As Nix remembered it, after he and Bradley left the Cain's, the first act Myers and Smalley booked was Red Steagall and his Coleman County Cowboys. In many ways, Steagall looked like the kind of act the previous promoters had been having such success with. He was from Texas, and he wrote a lot of his own material. He'd even had several hits on the radio—interestingly enough, his tribute to the Cain's former occupant, "Lone Star Beer and Bob Wills Music," was climbing the country charts around the same time he played the ballroom.

The problem was, Mrs. Myers had gotten it only half right. Steagall was a cowboy entertainer, to be sure—one of the all-time great ones. He just didn't happen to be a *cosmic* cowboy. Red Steagall's following came (and still comes) much more from aficionados of western and traditional country music than from the young rowdies with rock roots who made up much of the Cain's clientele in 1975. Nix recalled that the show was not a success for Mrs. Myers, and after another try or two, she had second thoughts about being back in the band-booking business and decided that renewing their lease might not be all that bad an idea.

"So in September," Nix said, "we were back in. We leased it then, but she needed a way to save face, so she and I cooked up a deal where we had a right of first refusal. If anyone made an offer to buy it, she had to let us know, and we'd have 30 or 60 days to match the offer."

As it turned out, someone did make an offer to buy it—and, in fact, ended up owning it for more than two decades. But that wouldn't happen until the next year, and not without a considerable amount of legal and financial wrangling.

Meanwhile, Bradley and Nix made plans for a grand September re-opening, booking vocalist Marcy Levy and her band for both Friday and Saturday night. Levy was best known at the time for her work both in the studio and on the road as a vocalist with

Eric Clapton. During the early '70s, after Leon Russell had moved back to Tulsa and established his Shelter Records recording studio, the city had become something of an international crossroads for rock musicians, and Clapton had come in and picked up some players for his new band. Their collaborative disc, *461 Ocean Boulevard*, rocketed to the top of the *Billboard* charts in late 1974. With Clapton off the road for a time, Levy brought a group to the Cain's that, Nix recalled, included drummer Jamie Oldaker, bassist Carl Radle, and organist Dickie Sims, all members of Clapton's band.

Because of the Clapton connection, and the fact that the band was mostly made up of Tulsans, Nix and Bradley expected to start the new season off with a bang. What they didn't expect was the A-bomb that exploded when Clapton himself unexpectedly made the scene.

★★★★

The story is one of the most famous ones in Cain's history. At the time it happened, Nix had just left a law firm and opened his own practice. "I had a wife and a six-year-old and an eight-year-old and exactly three thousand damn dollars to my name," he recalled. "We kept thinking we would get an investor. But as it came closer and closer to [the September] opening, I'd put every dime of that three thousand dollars into the ballroom—booking, paying the water bill, all that. I had zero money in the world." A couple of hours before the doors opened for the first show of the new season, Nix added, he was sitting at the Cain's thinking "I can't believe I've done this" when he got a phone call from the police reporter at the Tulsa World.

> *He says, "Clapton's in jail. Was he on his way to play the Cains?"*
>
> *And I go, thinking fast, "Yes, he was. You mean they've got our Eric? My, how could they?"*
>
> *"Are you going to get him out?"*
>
> *"Yeah," I said. "Who else?"*
>
> *About this time a guy comes up, and it turns out to be Willie Spears. He's Clapton's roadie, and he says, "We've gotta get Clapton out of jail."*
>
> *I was in a state of shock. "What's he doing here?" I asked.*
>
> *"He thought he'd surprise Marcy and all of 'em, and join them on stage."*
>
> *And I thought, "Well, they're certainly going to be surprised. I know I am."*

As it turned out, Clapton, who'd been living down in the Bahamas on a place called Paradise Island, had heard about the grand re-opening and flown in, making arrangements with the Tulsa-based Spears to meet him at the airport. In his 2008 book, *Clapton: The Autobiography*, the rock-guitar great wrote that he was drinking heavily and "had got in some kind of altercation on the plane and they had called ahead to the Tulsa police, who were waiting for me when the plane landed, and I was arrested."

After getting belligerent with an officer, Clapton—one of rock music's top stars at the time—had been tossed into the drunk tank. "I kept trying to tell them who I was, but they refused to believe me," he wrote, "so I said go and find a guitar and I would prove who I was by playing. They did this, and then they let me out."

Nix, however, said that Clapton wasn't arrested for what he did on the airliner, but for his behavior after he arrived at the Tulsa airport.

> *When Clapton got off the plane, he was carrying his luggage. That was back when the ticket counters were down below and the arriving passengers were up above, and there was a handrail. Spears, who'd come in to pick him up, was down below, and as Clapton's tottering down the hallway, two of Tulsa's finest are walking the other way.*
>
> *Clapton is just reeling, and then he sees Spears and he shouts, "Hey, Willie!" and throws his bag over the rail.*
>
> *That's what the cops see. They didn't see Spears. They just see a drunk throw his bag over the handrail. And they busted him for public drunk.*

Nix also said there was a bit more to getting Clapton out of jail than simply proving he was who he said he was.

> *Spears and I get into this two-seat Triumph Spitfire I had at the time, and we go down to the jail. And I go in and say, "I want to O.R. Clapton." Lawyers can get someone [booked on public drunkenness] out of jail on their own*

*recognizance, instead of having to put up bond, because it's
a misdemeanor.*

*But they had a rule to keep public drunks for six hours,
and Eric wasn't quite done yet. So the guy said, "I can't let
him out."*

*I said, "Well, okay, let me get your name, because there
are over 1,000 Clapton fans over on the north side of town,
and when he doesn't show up, there's going to be a riot.
People are going to say, 'Who in the world is responsible for
that riot?' and I want to be able to give 'em your name."*

*The guy goes, "All right. I'll let him out. Is he a resident
of Tulsa County?"*

*In those days, you could only O.R. Tulsa County resi-
dents, so I said, "Oh, of course he is."*

*Clapton comes reeling in with this thick British accent,
and the cop looks at me like, "Tulsa County?"*

*"He's got a Jenks address, okay?" I said [naming a Tulsa
suburb]. "It's for tax purposes." And the cop winks at me
and says, "Okay. I gotcha."*

Squeezing a still-woozy Clapton into the two-seat sports car,
Spears and Nix raced off for the Cain's, after getting assurances
from Clapton that he wanted to go directly to the ballroom and
play guitar with the band. When they pulled up, recalled Nix,
"There's a line of people, because it's now nine o'clock, and we
open the doors at nine. There were probably 500 people waiting to
get in as we come squealing up and jump through the crowd and
everyone's saying, 'Oh, it's Clapton!' A shock just goes through

the people. They're using our phone, calling other people, and there's just a *buzz*."

As Doug Darroch put it in his December 10, 1975 *Tulsa Tribune* article about the Cain's renaissance, "...[W]hen the man described by many as the greatest living guitarist jammed with his band at Cain's, the audience exploded with delight.... Although somewhat inebriated (he spent a few hours in the city jail drunk tank prior to the concert) the mere presence of the rock superstar thrilled the Cain's crowd."

After the show, in the early morning hours, a call came to the ballroom from a writer from the *London Daily Observer*, wanting to know all about what had happened. It was the first of many calls Bradley and Nix would field in the subsequent hours. Spurred by the appearance of a photo of a jailed Clapton on the front page of the *Tulsa World*—carrying the wry caption "E.C. Was Here," which was the name of Clapton's just-released live disc—people began flooding the office with calls. (In *Clapton: The Autobiography*, published in 2007, the rock icon writes that the photo appeared in the morning's *Tulsa Tribune*, which was actually the city's afternoon paper.)

"I go down to the ballroom about eleven in the morning, to clean up the place, and the phone's ringing every few seconds, it seems like," Nix remembers. "The [*World*] story had said he was on his way to play the Cain's, and people are asking, 'Is Clapton going to be there tonight?' At first, I'm saying, 'I don't know. This is his attorney and I'm not a hundred percent sure.' Finally, I'm saying, 'Oh yeah. He's right here, right now!'

"That night, we had twelve hundred people."

"The next night, Clapton played again," Darroch wrote of the encore show. "He was stupendous. Not only did the legendary superstar play for a couple of hours, he also chatted with the patrons, answered the Cain's phone, and endeared himself to Tulsa fans."

"And so," concluded Nix, "we made enough money to stay open week in and week out for the rest of the year."

****

Bradley and Nix ran shows, mostly on Thursdays, Fridays, and Saturdays, into June of 1976, with Mrs. Myers continuing to let them lease the space. In addition to the structural work Ed Thornton had done that first year, Bradley's friend from their junior-high-school days, Peter Mayo, came aboard to serve as sound engineer and supervise the reconfiguration of the Cain's stage.

"The old bandshell that they had used just really didn't accommodate the size of amps and the size of drum kits the bands were using," explained Bradley. "Peter invested thousands and thousands of dollars in the actual sound configuration of the stage. At one time, he brought in Santana's sound engineer. At another time, he brought in the Doobie Brothers' sound engineer. He was always working to upgrade the equipment."

He also provided the Cain's with a new sound system, which had come from the Doobie Brothers as well. "As a matter of fact," said Bradley, "at one time the cabinets actually had 'DOOBROS' on them."

The acts that played through that system were a varied bunch. There were the cosmic cowboys, of course, most of them returning for repeat engagements. There were blues and R&B greats like B.B. King, Lightnin' Hopkins, Freddie King, Bobby "Blue" Bland, and Sonny Terry & Brownie McGhee; contemporary bluegrass and folk acts including John Hartford, Vassar Clements, and the New Grass Revival; hippified country-rockers like the Flying Burrito Brothers and Commander Cody and His Lost Planet Airmen; and even country-radio favorites Waylon Jennings and Ronnie Milsap. Local bands, led by the Turkey Mountain Troubadours, began to pick up their own followings through Cain's appearances.

Freddie King

IMAGE COURTESY SCOTT MUNZ

And, of course, there were the rockers. In his interview with Russ Florence, Bradley remembered one such group, a Florida-based outfit called Mudcrutch, that happened to be in town doing some recording with Leon Russell and his Shelter Records partner Denny Cordell.

"Denny Cordell paid me three hundred dollars to put that show on," Bradley said. "Mudcrutch ended up being Tom Petty and the Heartbreakers, and I always felt like that was the best buy I ever made at the Cain's. Tom Petty—and I got paid to do it."

Those who were around R.C. Bradley at the time know that making good buys was one of his hallmarks. Nix saw early on, he said, that "Brad was one of those rare people who knew what they were doing." So instead of trying to get involved in the booking, Nix took care of much of the day-to-day business, letting Bradley find the talent and make the deals.

To hear his partner tell it, Bradley was a master of a certain kind of negotiating style that Nix still sometimes employs to this day:

He had a way of talking on and talking on. He'd talk to agents and say, "Life is just terrible and I'm not making any money, but, hey, you know, if your act doesn't want to play here, I can't force you to. If instead of playing Tulsa you want to go from Kansas City to Dallas and spend Saturday night in a motel, I can understand that. Why play in our dinky little old ballroom, you know, for seven hundred and fifty bucks? Just tell Michael Murphey, 'Michael, here's where Hank Williams played and here's where all these people played, but I don't want you to play there because it just isn't enough money, Michael, so you're just going to sit in a Holiday Inn instead of playing Cain's.' And tell him hi for us; we've got his album."

Even with Bradley's considerable negotiating and promotional skills—he originated the phrase "Tulsa's timeless honky-tonk on the wrong side of the tracks," for instance—the pair continued to operate on the thinnest of margins. "We never had a dime," Nix said, "and we never had a moment's rest. One bad week would wipe out three good weeks. The strain was just unbelievable."

Still, the partners continued to ride the tiger. In 1976, Nix said, they brought Tulsa TV news reporter Dino Economos in. He put up some money for future shows, which took a little of the stress away. But then a new development came along, something that had certainly loomed in the back of their minds as they paid Mrs. Myers off month by month.

What they'd feared from the beginning appeared to be finally happening.

Someone was buying the Cain's.

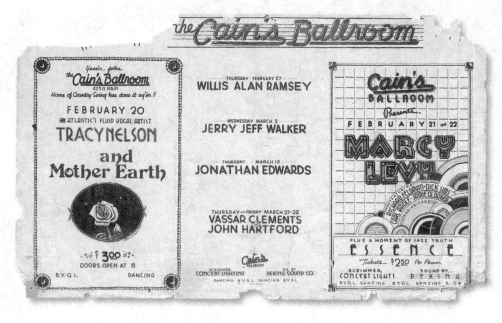

OUTLAW
MEMBERSHIP CARD

MEMBER'S SIGNATURE
IS A MEMBER IN GOOD STANDING OF THE
CAIN'S BALLROOM
OUTLAW CLUB
423 No. MAIN · TULSA, OKLAHOMA

AUTHORIZED SIGNATURE   1110
                           CARD NO.

CHAPTER 12

I grew up west of Tulsa, and my grandfather's brothers and my uncles all went to Cain's in the '30s and '40s. I would overhear these wild stories about this or that girl, or this or that bootlegger, or this or that fistfight, or this great music and this guy named Bob Wills. I heard that background talk over every canasta party at my house for 20 years, before I was old enough to see the place.

The first night I saw Cain's was when I tried out in '71 for Gene Mooney. I walked into the place and actually got a shiver down my back, because it was almost like walking back into time.

— LARRY SHAEFFER, IN A MARCH 12, 2009 INTERVIEW WITH BRETT BINGHAM

A University of Tulsa graduate and Army veteran, Larry Shaeffer hadn't been mustered out long when he got the call to audition on steel guitar with Gene Mooney's band at the Cain's. Although that didn't work out, Shaeffer stayed in the music business as a promoter, taking his first steps not long after his encounter with Mooney. "By 1972, I did just enough shows to rent a cheap apartment," he remembered during one of a series of interviews for this book. "Then, after I started doing fairly well by landing a couple of good shows here and there, I was notified by my attorney that Cain's was for sale.

"The day I found out it was available, I just started running it through my mind: 'Man, that's where I'd like to be.' I was officing at Skyline East, and it was like working in a doctor's office. It was sterile, awful, and it smelled like bleach. I hated it and wanted something downtown."

Shaeffer had been "really affected" by his first actual visit to the ballroom, where Mooney had given him a couple of original posters of Tommy Duncan and Bob Wills. A few years later, in September of 1975, he'd been at the hall for the surprise Eric Clapton appearance described in the last chapter. "I'd just stumbled in to watch Marcy Levy, without knowing that Clapton was going to come through the door," he said. "When Clapton came in, I decided right then and there, 'I'm going to buy this place.' It was something neat and for some reason I wanted to own it. I didn't have a thought past that."

Even though he was making his living promoting shows, the idea of bringing acts into the Cain's on a regular basis didn't really cross his mind then, he said. Instead, he simply had the idea that this funky old historic place would make a great home base. "In those days, if I could do eight or 10 shows a year I thought I was busy; if I made 10 grand, I could live for a year off of it. So I really wasn't considering going into the Cain's Ballroom business. I was not thinking about running it on a full-time basis," he explained. "I just wanted to own the building and have an office there."

So he and his attorney, Jack Maner, contacted the real-estate agency that was handling the property for Marie Myers, found out what she wanted, and made a deal.

"I can't remember if it was $58,000 or $60,000, but in 1976, that was the price of a normal home," recalled Shaeffer. "So I went to the realtor, which was Town & Country, agreed to the terms, and gave them a $3,000 check, earnest money, which is what she was asking. I figured I had it bought. I was prepping myself to make the transition—and then it comes out in the paper that another group had bought it."

Marie Myers, perhaps conveniently, had apparently forgotten about the right-of-first-refusal clause in her contract with Bradley and Nix.

They, however, hadn't. According to Jeff Nix, when word got out that Shaeffer was buying the Cain's, Nix contacted Myers and then speedily recruited four Tulsans to invest in the ballroom. They were Ainsley Perrault, Jr., Tim Smith, Rick Loewenherz, and Dick Walker.

"I'd grown up with Tim Smith, and Loewenherz was friends with my brother in college," said Nix. "He had a company called Giant Petroleum; and he and Pinky Perrault were partners in it. Loewenherz was a lawyer. He had a duplex, and his next-door neighbor was an insurance guy, Dickie Walker, and they knew Tim Smith, who was an investment broker. Then there was Brad and me. So that made six of us, although Brad and I didn't put up any money. They bought it, and Brad and I had a corporation, and we leased it [from them]."

"Basically, Ainsley Perrault gave us a blank check, literally, at lunch over several cocktails at the Ramican Restaurant downtown," Bradley told Russ Florence in their 1995 conversation. "He handed Nix and myself a blank check and said, 'Just go buy the place.' And indeed we did. We immediately called Mrs. Myers. Nix drove me out there in his little Triumph Spitfire. And we cut a deal with Mrs. Myers on the spot."

Myers, as noted earlier, had been wanting out from under the Cain's for quite some time, with zero interest in functioning as a landlord. She was simply interested in selling the place, and the sooner the better. So when that pair of hippie boys flashed a check for tens of thousands of dollars at her, it's little wonder that she grabbed it. That unbylined story in the April 30, 1976 *Tulsa Tribune* made the transaction official:

> *A group of Tulsa investors announced today the purchase of Cain's Ballroom, 423 N. Main St., for an undisclosed price. [A Tulsa World story from the next day quoted property manager Scott Munz as saying the selling price was "pretty close" to $55,000.]*
>
> *Promoter Robert Bradley and attorney Jeff Nix, who have jointly operated the historic dance hall since January 1975, head the list of purchasers which also includes Ainsley Perrault Jr., Rick Loewenherz, Timothy Smith and Dick Walker.*
>
> *Cain's had been owned since 1972 by Marie Myers....*
>
> *"We still are supporting the basic country music traditions espoused by the history of the Cain's," Bradley said*

today. "And our philosophy is one of supporting Tulsa tal-
ent—groups either from Tulsa or who have ties here."

The ballroom will continue to be open weekend nights
and on announced weekdays, Bradley said. "And this sum-
mer we hope to keep it open on a more regular basis during
the week."

As things turned out, however, the ownership was anything but settled. Shaeffer, feeling strongly that he'd had the place unfairly snatched out from under him, filed suit in Tulsa court against the partnership. "My investor group didn't think much of this lawsuit," Bradley remembered, "and basically told myself and Jeff Nix that they wanted us to negotiate a settlement with Shaeffer."

"We'd filed the lawsuit, and we were ready to ride it out," Shaeffer recalled. "My attorney felt there was no way I could be kept from winning."

So the legal wrangling began, continuing over the next several weeks. Finally, an agreement was reached. Under its terms, Shaeffer would buy out the ownership group and take over the Cain's. However, there was a stipulation that Nix and Bradley could lease it from him and continue to put on shows there. "I bought it in about October of 1976, when I closed the deal; I actually reimbursed that partnership of guys," recalled Shaeffer. "I didn't pay Marie Myers. She'd already been bought out by them, even though I was getting ready to turn the deal over in the courtroom.

"They were able to lease it from me at a negotiated price. I think it was $1,250 a month," said Shaeffer. "It was enough to make it worthwhile. It was also worthwhile to me because any dates they weren't playing a show I had access to, to do my rock 'n' roll shows there. It was the deal I wanted. Their lease paid my payments [on the ballroom], made me about $400 a month, and gave me a free office — and I'd have free [venue] rent on any of my shows, with them keeping the bar."

It was, in fact, a rock 'n' roll concert that had allowed Shaeffer to pay off the investor group. On July 25, 1976, he'd cashed in big with an outdoor show at the Tulsa Fairgrounds Speedway. With the fast-rising Peter Frampton as headliner, and popular acts Santana and Gary Wright in support, the event drew more than 30,000 attendees. "All of a sudden, I had an extra $40,000," said Shaeffer, "and I had a partner on that show. That was just my half. So, having Frampton allowed me to close the deal without having to scramble for money."

Once negotiated, the agreement seemed to benefit everyone involved. But, according to Shaeffer, the lease payments dried up after only a couple of months. Although Bradley and Nix continued booking acts in the Cain's for a while longer, ultimately, Shaeffer said, "I was so thinly financed that I had to evict them and come in and run the place myself. On that day was when I had to decide how I could get that thing [the Cain's] to make some money to support itself."

While all of this activity was beginning to play out in the ballroom she'd formerly owned, Marie Myers had taken herself and her money back to Muskogee. But she didn't have much time to savor her newfound freedom from the pressures that had come with being a honky-tonk landlord. On November 24, just a few months after she'd taken that check from Nix and Bradley, she died. She was, according to her obituary, 90 years old.

****

Why did Bradley and Nix not fight their eviction? Bradley offered a couple of possibilities when he told Russ Florence that "Nix and myself and Dino [Economos] were pretty much at odds on how to operate the building," and further claimed that their efforts were hampered because "Larry started putting on shows at the Cain's twice a month. So basically our lease meant nothing, because Larry was booking shows in there on top of us.... [He] would bring in popular attractions twice a month, particularly on payday weekends."

(As noted earlier, their agreement gave Shaeffer the right to book Cain's shows on the nights his lessees didn't have any of their own concerts scheduled. However, when interviewed for this book, Shaeffer didn't remember bringing any acts at all into the ballroom during the time Bradley and Nix were there.)

Perhaps the toughest thing for them was simply the sheer weight of responsibility for all those shows, the dealing with acts and their entourages, the worry about whether they'd make money or go in the hole, the thousand and one problems that can come up in the club business on any given night, including the challenge of drunken and drugged audience members who never had much restraint—or home training—to start with. Perhaps it's ironic that the same kind of crowd behavior that had driven Jim Edwards away after the first year came back to haunt Nix and Bradley several hundred Cain's shows down the line. Nix remembered the events leading to his personal epiphany this way:

We were probably doing three shows a week, on average, and so we'd done several hundred, and I was really getting tired of seeing the way people were acting. Brad was getting tired of it. We were just beat.

I remember where I was standing and what I was wearing when I said, "That's it for me." We'd had a pretty good show – I don't remember who it was, but it was a good crowd, and I was walking over toward the office when I saw a biker pissing against the wall.

And I said, "That's it."

By that time, Nix added, the Cain's clientele—most of them older teens and young adults—had figured out that "once you got in the door, there just weren't any rules."

"We couldn't sell drinks," he said. "We could sell setups, so people brought their bottles, and they were just drinking enormous amounts of liquor."

Other behaviors involving substances far less legal than whiskey were also rumored to be going on at the Cain's during those years. Put all of that together, add in the relentless pressure of keeping the place booked and running, and it becomes easy to empathize with something Bradley said about Shaeffer's evicting him from the Cain's: "Looking back in retrospect, I'm really grateful for that," he told Florence. "It could indeed have saved my life, because of the excess activities that we'd undertaken when we were there."

In that interview, however, Bradley also said that he and the people who'd joined him in the venture "knew we were onto something big," and that while they had come along to save a Tulsa landmark, their pioneering efforts were, he believed, "forgotten."

As we'll see, Larry Shaeffer owned the ballroom for a quarter of a century, while Bradley and Nix leased it for three, a fact that may have something to do with their relative places in Cain's history. But the latter two are hardly forgotten, and certainly not by the man who took the ancient building over and steered it through the rest of the '70s into the '80s and to the very end of the 1900s.

"R.C. Bradley was a bright, belligerent, loud, talented promoter...[who] came in and quickly started doing some pretty neat music," Shaeffer said. "He did David Allan Coe, he did Michael Martin Murphey, he did Hot Tuna, he did Emmylou Harris, and for the first time ever, Cain's was being filled with people like me who didn't know it even sat down there. R.C. Bradley was the brilliance that made that happen."

****

It took Larry Shaeffer a while to assume full control of the Cain's—ten months, by most accounts. But it took no time at all for the enormity of his new job as a ballroom owner and operator to sink in. "After I acquired it," he said, "the responsibility hit me in the face. Honestly, I was real comfortable having someone lease it. Then, I owned it without really having to hump it. But those guys, I don't know if they just lost interest or ran out of money or what, but the magic left them, and I went in there and had to do something quick. It was on me then to keep the lights on, and the building was in terrible disrepair."

Fortunately, thanks to his Frampton payday, Shaeffer had a bit of money left over for repairs and upgrades. He got his mother and father and some neighbors to come in and paint the ceiling; the fact that the elder Shaeffer was a plumber by trade made him especially valuable to his son's efforts to fix the place up. He also enlisted the help of the aforementioned Scott Munz, a New York native who'd started working on shows and concerts as a college student. Now the marketing and public relations director for the Oklahoma State Fair in Oklahoma City, Munz admitted to having a tough time getting established in his new home state all those years ago.

"My roommate, a guy named Bob Burwell, and I came out to Oklahoma [in 1976] to do shows because our college advisor was brought to Tulsa to be the architectural consultant and managing director of the new Performing Arts Center," he recalled in a November 13, 2019 interview with Brett Bingham. "We came out, and we were under-financed. We did a few shows, but that kind of didn't happen, so I went off and got a regular job and he [Burwell] worked for the [Tulsa-based] Jim Halsey Company, which, in its time, was the quintessential country agency."

It may have looked to Munz like his idea of a show-business career was over. But by complete chance, he was soon back on the path he'd hoped to take when he'd moved to the heartland. "Living next to me was R.C. Bradley, and we got to be friends," said Munz. "I forget what he was actually doing at that time, if he was doing anything, but he was the consummate pitchman and promoter, and he decided he wanted to resurrect Cain's Ballroom."

And once the resurrection happened, Bradley put Munz on the staff. And even though the *Tulsa Tribune* article excerpted earlier in this chapter identified him as the ballroom's "property manager," he felt that his status was something less.

"I was really just the bartender," he noted. "I don't know if they even considered me the bar manager. R.C. basically did that. I scheduled the bar staff and worked behind the bar."

In those pre-liquor-by-the-drink days, the Cain's was only allowed to sell beer and setups. If patrons wanted to consume the hard stuff, they had to bring it in themselves—which, of course, they did. "To me, coming from New York, it was like the wild wild West," recalled Munz. "We were selling this thing called the Big Jug, which was basically a wax milk carton that you filled with beer. They'd come in with their Wild Turkey or beverage of choice, and we wouldn't check the bottle in. So they'd be sitting at the table with a bottle and a jug of beer, taking shots out of the bottle, not using any glass—we didn't have shot glasses or anything fancy like that. We did sell setups, but very few people used them. If they were drinking something straight, they'd drink it right out of the bottle and chase it with their beer."

Once Shaeffer took over the booking of the room, Munz added, "The prominence of that [bartender] position increased, and he knew that I had concert experience, so the fit was good."

In fact, Munz would indeed become the property manager of the Cain's, and, for several years, one of the most valuable parts of Shaeffer's management team.

"I gained a tremendous amount of experience working with Larry," said Munz. "He was the guy booking the bands. He'd buy the acts, and he'd buy the advertising, and I'd pay the bill when they came around to collect for the advertising.

"Once the bands were booked," he added, "I basically took over. We had a guy named Clint Doolittle who was doing sound at the time, and I'd turn the advance for the audio over to him. And I'd schedule what time we would be in, to make sure the stagehands were there."

But before all of that happened, Munz showed his willingness to be a part of the Cain's team by joining Shaeffer and Shaeffer's dad, Cecil, for that manual-labor cosmetic work on the venerable building.

"We went in there and we got sanding machines, redid the floor, replaced ceiling tiles, threw sparkle back up on the walls," Munz remembered. "We made sure everything was as good as it could be, just restoring but not making any wholesale changes to the look of the building. The only thing we did that actually changed the look was build a small dressing room back behind the stage. We came in 10 feet off the back wall and cut it abruptly short, so the stage was no longer a full clamshell. It went to a back wall and there was a door with a dressing room behind it."

Soon, there were also doors with new staff members behind them. "Jan Adams was the office manager or secretary or whatever you want to call it; she would do the catering because back then it was simple: You'd get them [the acts] a few burgers or some donuts in the morning and some drinks and call it good. There was a door on the outside that led to an office that had knotty pine on the walls, and all the pictures [of performers]; that was Jan's office. Larry had one in the middle, and it had knotty pine on the outside. I had the room with the box office, an old cubbyhole from when it was a hat-check room.

"A lady named Estelle Epperson sat in the little box office that opened onto the lobby. She'd sit there at the window. She must've been 75 if she was a day. She'd be all dolled up, her face made up, lipstick on—and she ran that thing with an iron fist. If you came there [to try to get in without a ticket] and you weren't on the comp list, you didn't get in. You couldn't talk your way in. She was just phenomenal.

"We had some solid people," he added. "We had some good people. Jerry Bockman was there; I still have tremendous respect for Jerry."

With those people and others working out of those offices, Shaeffer not only ran the Cain's, but also his Little Wing Productions, which brought acts to both the Cain's and other venues, as well as a staging company, Little Wing Staging. (Both named after a song on Jimi Hendrix's 1967 LP, *Axis: Bold as Love*.)

"When I came on, Dino [Economos] tried to stay on with me, but I couldn't make a place for him," remembered Shaeffer. "It was me and Jan Adams and Jerry Bockman, and a guy named R.G. Pyle. My staging company was very successful, and a lot of that was Jerry Bockman. I had semi-trucks full of scaffolding and I-beams and base plates and screw jacks. There weren't any legit staging companies [in the area] except for Teri [Productions] out of Knoxville, and I pretty much copied what they did.

"We went coast to coast. We'd load up two semis with forklifts, and I might charge 12 or 15 thousand dollars to take the stage out. Each guy would have a driver and would be capable of supervising the stage. If I needed [staging for] my own outdoor shows, I didn't have to spend the 12 grand. So when you see photographs of my outdoor shows, it's my staging."

"When we worked outside the ballroom—we did Wichita and we did Little Rock and we did Tulsa and Oklahoma City—I'd be babysitting," added Munz. "I'd be the promoter's representative there at six or seven in the morning, and I'd be there all day. I'd settle with the buildings and, generally, I'd pay the bands. We had that typical deal that a lot of businesses have, where if the train ever stopped, the money flow would stop. So we were using the money from this show that was on sale to pay for the show that just ended, to keep the books open."

****

The "wild wild West" atmosphere that had struck Scott Munz when he'd signed on as a member of the Cain's staff stuck with the ballroom long after R.C. Bradley, Jeff Nix, and the rest of the "hippie" management team had left. There may be no better example of that than something that happened within the first few years of the Shaeffer era.

"We had these little swamp-cooler things on the roof," recalled Munz. "They were just big fans. You'd run cold water across them and that was the only cooling ventilation we had. So, one night, somebody dropped a Molotov cocktail down one of them."

Nobody knew about it, according to Shaeffer, until the next day, when he arrived at his office and "kept smelling petroleum." Finally, he said, "I walked out into the ballroom and there was a pool, probably 30 feet wide, of kerosene. It had been poured up in the opening of one of the coolers and had gone all the way to the floor, where it had made that big puddle."

"Fortunately," Munz added, "the rag had fallen out of the bottle, so the burnt rag was there on the floor, and the bottle was there."

Shaeffer remembered the rag being on the roof, along with the box of matches that the perpetrators had used to ignite it. "It had burned a big circle on the roof, but it never went down into the attic and took off," he said.

The Cain's owner felt sure that the arson attempt had been made by someone from a rival club, but when the local fire marshal came to investigate, Shaeffer kept his suspicions to himself. "At that point, I wasn't ready to point fingers," he explained. "What I *was* ready to do was buy some camouflage clothes and an AR-15. So for weeks I would park my car three blocks away, walk down behind Cain's, where there were a bunch of hedge-apple trees. I made myself a little sniper's nest."

Again, Scott Munz's telling of the story differed slightly. He remembered that he and sound man Clint Doolittle donned camouflage, took up weapons, and joined Shaeffer in the vigil. However, he believed that they staked themselves out on the roof rather than in the hedge-apple trees. "We did that more than one night," he said. "I think it was in the winter, and it was pretty cold up there, and we decided we weren't that tough."

Looking back on those evenings, both he and Shaeffer agreed that they're glad the alleged perpetrator, or perpetrators, failed to return to the scene of the crime.

"Larry had his weapons, and Clint was a former military man, and I'm just damn glad the guy didn't show up,' said Munz, "because if he had, we probably would've killed him—and we would have been in some deep shit."

CAIN'S BALLROOM

423 N. MAIN ST.   (918) 584-23

CALENDER 1977

FRIDAY SEPTEMBER 23
LARRY RASPBERRY *and the* HIGHSTEP

SATURDAY SEPTEMBER 24
DOUG KERSHAW

SUNDAY SEPTEMBER 25
Rock N Roll Night ## ANDY PRATT *and* BLISS

SATURDAY OCTOBER 1
JOHN MAYALL

FRIDAY OCTOBER 7
RUSTY WEIR *and the* MISSION MTN. WOOD

SATURDAY OCTOBER 8
STOMU YAMASHTA *and* GO!

FRIDAY OCTOBER 14
JOHN HARTFORD *and the* DILLARDS

SATURDAY OCTOBER 15
VASSAR CLEMENTS

TICKETS WILL BE AVAILABLE AT HONEST JOHN'S   OZ   ODYSSEY MALL   AND   SOUND WA

CHAPTER

★★ 13 ★★

Cain's is wide open to all musical styles. I present a lot of new acts here. I want to offer Tulsa a variety of music.

Last season, 100 of my shows featured acts that had albums out. They were nationally known acts. Locally, we have presented Bob Welch, Patti Smith, Sex Pistols, Elvis Costello, Stanley Clarke, Al Di Meola, Jean Luc Ponty and Eddie Money.

— LARRY SHAEFFER, QUOTED IN A STORY BY ELLIS WIDNER
IN THE SEPTEMBER 1, 1978. *TULSA TRIBUNE*

When Shaeffer began booking acts for the place, he stayed with the cosmic-cowboy element that had been a major part of the previous regime's booking. But he also looked well beyond that musical subgenre to many other kinds of acts.

"The first shows, I believe, were on a weekend, and I think it was Elvin Bishop Friday and Pure Prairie League Saturday," Shaeffer said. "A couple of years ago, Vince Gill told me that was

Vassar Clements on stage at Cain's. On the left is longtime Tulsa favorite Debbie Campbell

the first date he ever played with Pure Prairie League."

"Larry opened up with Elvin Bishop, because Elvin Bishop was a Tulsa boy," added Munz. "We were flying by the seat of our pants. Larry really didn't have any bar experience, and I didn't have any real bar experience. It was kind of the learn-while-you-earn plan. Since I'd been doing it a little bit with the facility with R.C. and Jeff, I had a little knowledge of the walk-ins and the tap lines and all that stuff; I'd worked in bars before, but I'd never run one."

It was indeed, as the cliché goes, a learning experience for them both. So were Shaeffer's early attempts at filling the Cain's stage.

I was fairly connected with a few of the major rock agencies then. I wasn't connected with Willie Nelson, or David Allan Coe, or Michael Martin Murphey, or Commander Cody or Dr. Hook. But I quickly started making phone calls.

It was kind of a hard sell. Most agencies said, "Who? Where?" They didn't know what it was. But by 1978, it was beginning to be a stop. In that era, record labels were rich and powerful and they had people out scouting to sign new talent seven days a week. All of a sudden, my ownership of the Cain's became their connection, giving [their acts] a stop off I-40 [highway]. That wasn't going on in Oklahoma City. It wasn't going on in Wichita. It wasn't going on in Little Rock. It was going on here in Tulsa. These pretty cool agents were thinking I was pretty cool, and they were feeding me one after the other. "Do you wanna book Van Halen? Do you wanna book Edgar Winter? Do you wanna book Johnny Winter? Do you wanna book U2, the Eurythmics—Freddie King, B.B. King?"

I paid U2 five hundred bucks. The Police were $1500, and "Roxanne" was already pushing No. 1. It was such a new frontier.

Press Kit for The Police

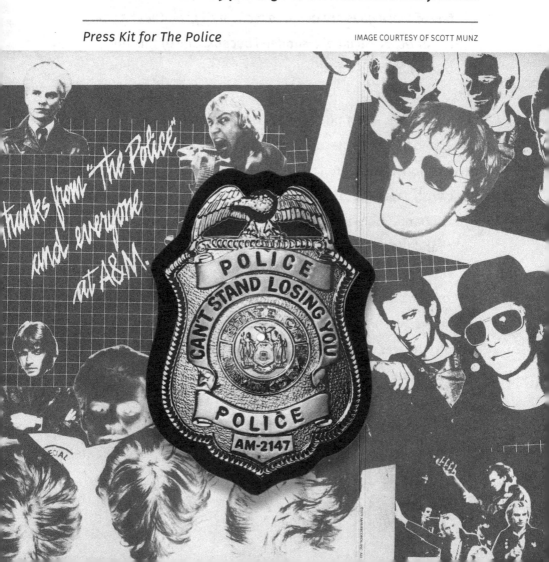

The reason the Cain's became a hotspot for new and emerging national talent, he added, had a lot to do with the fact that he'd book just about anyone he was pitched.

They just kept coming, and I realized the importance of doing a dollar [ticket] for some baby band that was playing for $300 for me, trying to build an audience. That was called showcasing, and a lot of it was just dumb luck. Remember, the labels were choking in money, and with that money they were gobbling up every act they could get, knowing that a few of these guys are going to make it big and they're going to get richer. So all of a sudden I become one of the guys that'll just take 'em all.

It was that exact philosophy that led him to book an act early on named Stomu Yamashta, a percussionist, keyboardist, and composer whose avant-garde music blended elements of contemporary rock with Japanese percussion. "Larry didn't shy away from any type of band," noted Munz. "And I hate to single them out, but the only band [booked into the Cain's] I didn't care for was that one."

He wasn't alone. The show did not do well for Shaeffer. However, it brought him and his ballroom to the attention of a young and energetic Warner Brothers Records representative named Noel Monk, who was on the road with Yamashta and his group.

"He came in with Stomu Yamashta, and he and I got on good," Shaeffer recalled. "We spent that night in my office. Shortly after that, I booked [the rock band] Montrose, and Noel suggested that Van Halen get on that tour, opening for Montrose. Sammy Hagar was in the Montrose band. So that's how Van Halen came in; I had them opening for Montrose."

Monk is probably best-known to rock aficionados for his years as Van Halen's manager, but his résumé is studded with other notable work. He was, for instance, the tour manager for the Sex Pistols' only American tour, which happened in January of 1978—and included a stop at the Cain's Ballroom. "That was the third time Noel Monk influenced our lives," Shaeffer said. "He chose Cain's as a Sex Pistols stop."

Of the thousands of concerts staged at the Cain's during Shaeffer's 24 years of ownership, none is more famous than the one that took place on the night of January 11, 1978, a Wednesday, when a crowd estimated at between seven and eight hundred braved snowy weather to catch the notorious—and trailblazing—British punk rockers at the Cain's. It would turn out to be one of only seven shows the band played on its American tour, which began in Atlanta and worked through the South and Southwest until the final stop at San Francisco's Winterland Ballroom. The Cain's show was not only the penultimate date on the tour, but also the next-to-last concert the band would ever perform. The Sex Pistols broke up a few days after the Winterland engagement.

Interestingly, the punk-rockers had performed the previous night at Dewey Groom's Longhorn Ballroom in Dallas, which had formerly been the Bob Wills Ranch House, a later headquarters of the man who'd initially made the Cain's famous. The Sex Pistols members, said Shaeffer, had "shown up on my doorstep at 10 a.m. the day of the show, ready to get off the bus," after having ridden all night instead of staying in Dallas. The reason, he said, was

Item from the Sex Pistols Press Kit in 1978

IMAGE COURTESY OF SCOTT MUNZ

that they were trying to avoid a fight with some Texas boys over a camera lead singer Johnny Rotten had smashed. (Other sources indicate that lead guitarist Sid Vicious had kicked a female photographer and picked a fight with a security guard at the Longhorn, so there was no shortage of possible reasons for the lads to hightail it out of Texas.)

"Their manager, Malcolm McLaren, was brilliant," Shaeffer noted. "He put them on tour in America after they're huge in London as the bad boys of rock. Smartly, he doesn't play them in New York, Detroit, Chicago, or L.A. He puts them down South where there's probably going to be some redneck and Southern Baptist resistance.

"It was seven dates, and it had to be in the South," added Shaeffer. "They wanted trouble. They wanted publicity. Malcolm had to approve [the ballroom], but he had never heard of Cain's. And Noel Monk stood up and said, 'You've got to play this place.' That's how the Sex Pistols ended up there."

The Cain's indeed saw a bit of the resistance Shaeffer mentioned, as reported by the *Tulsa World*'s Vern Stefanic. In his January 12 review of the show, Stefanic mentioned that the "vomiting on stage, spitting and violence" that had marked other Sex Pistols concerts seemed to be absent at the band's Cain's appearance. "In fact," he added, "the most intense emotional display came from about 30 'Jesus People' outside Cain's before the show. The youngsters greeted Cain's customers with sermonettes, reading material and a ten-foot-long sign which read 'Jesus Loves You.'"

"I had every undercover cop in Tulsa County in there," Shaeffer said, "with their trench coats and their white socks and loafers.

They were thinking they were going to arrest these guys for doing something crazy onstage. There were dozens and dozens of people with cameras. Maybe thirty or forty percent were people from Tulsa, most of whom didn't know who the Sex Pistols were, but they were curious.

SEX PISTOLS   JOHNNY ROTTEN   WARNER/REPRISE

"You had to be a person somewhat informed to know who they were," he added. "There wasn't a single bit of airplay [in Tulsa]. You had to be reading *Rolling Stone* or something."

Two young men who fit Shaeffer's latter description were a pair of roommates from the University of Oklahoma named Johnny Ray Vanderveer and Chris Tyler. After articles about the band in *Rolling Stone* had piqued their curiosity, the two had gone out and bought a cassette tape of the band's debut release, *Never Mind the Bollocks, Here's the Sex Pistols.* "We both got a kick out of 'em," Tyler recalled in a 2010 interview for this book. "We thought they were real irreverent. We played their music everywhere we went."

So when Tyler and Vanderveer found out the Sex Pistols were stopping off at the Cain's, they knew they had to make that scene. At the time of the show, they were both in their shared hometown of Chelsea, about 50 miles northeast of Tulsa, waiting for OU's

SEX PISTOLS

WARNER/REPRISE

spring semester to start. "Before the show, it was snowing quite a bit, as I recall," said Tyler. "Johnny had a pickup truck, and we had a bottle of vodka and a couple of plastic cups. We'd stop every few miles, scrape some snow out of the bed of the pickup, and make us kind of a little vodka slushie —so we'd be ready for the concert," he added with a laugh.

Thus fortified, they arrived at the Cain's, only to find "three or four news trucks and klieg lights and reporters and stuff out there," Tyler remembered. "I thought, 'Is something else happening here? Are they opening for somebody else?' But it was all for the Sex Pistols."

Once they'd gotten through the door, the two decided that nothing would do but for them to sit as close as possible to the stage—so, said Tyler, they decided on a bit of subterfuge: "When we got in, we pulled out all our various forms of University of Oklahoma student ID, chemistry department voucher slips, whatever we had. Johnny had a little Instamatic camera, and I think I was pretending my checkbook was a notebook or something, and we convinced 'em we were with the student newspaper. They sat us right up front."

Following the opening set by a Bartlesville, Oklahoma-based hard-rock band called Bliss, which Shaeffer was managing at the time, the Sex Pistols came out, beginning their set with the anthematic "God Save the Queen."

"Then," remembered Tyler, "they had an electronic problem, or one of the guys walked offstage; there was some kind of a pause or break, and people started yelling stuff out. Somebody yelled to Johnny Rotten, 'How do you like Oklahoma?' and he shouted back, 'I effin'—expletive deleted—*hate* it!' And then Johnny Ray shouted, 'Well, I hate England!'"

Vanderveer, who died in 2004, had been born a Thalidomide baby. Each of his arms was truncated, ending in two fingers—a physical imperfection Rotten immediately seized upon.

Johnny Rotten and Sid Vicious on stage at Cain's

"Johnny Rotten looked down at Johnny and said, 'You don't even have any effin' arms!' and Johnny Ray said, 'You don't have any effin' *talent!*' Then Vandeveer tore his shirt off. I don't know if it was Johnny Rotten or Sid Vicious, but one of 'em was shirtless, and he'd painted something on his chest. So Johnny started spitting beer at him. And Johnny Rotten started spitting beer at *him*. These guys made fun of each others' physical infirmities throughout the evening."

Added Tyler:

We were sitting down there so close that we were all lit up. There was a lot of light on us, from the backlighting behind the guys, and I can just see those punks looking down and seeing Vanderveer swigging beer with no hands and thinking, 'This is great. Who is this freak?'

I don't care who it was—if someone started popping off, Vanderveer was going to pop right back. Johnny Rotten called him a crippled American, and a freak, and Johnny called him a dopehead and a British fag. And the people around us were going, 'This is interesting. Here's a guy on stage making fun of a guy with no arms. That's not something you see all the time."

But Vanderveer got the last word in. I will go to my grave with that. The boy from Chelsea got in the last word on the boy from England.

According to Ellis Widner's *Tulsa Tribune* review, which ran (under the headline "Pistols' music mostly noise") the same day as Stefanic's *Tulsa World* story, about 15 minutes after the Sex Pistols set began, "a steady flow of people began filing out until Cain's was more than half empty by the time the group completed its performance." They also both reported that the Tulsa police got a call about a bomb in the women's restroom, which proved to be a hoax. Each reviewer dismissed the show and the notion of punk-rock in general, with Widner writing that "American rock 'n' roll fans are the subjects of an attempted seduction by overblown media hype." For his part, Stefanic called the band "simply a novelty, not a trend-setting act," and added his belief that "it's doubtful punk rock is here to stay."

"I've read reviews where people said [the show] was sloppy and it wasn't much," said Tyler. "But I remember the music being very much like what I thought it would be like. And the sense I had was, 'These guys are truly rebellious.' I was thinking, 'Is this what another generation saw in the Beatles, or the Stones, or Jim Morrison?' We knew this could be something special."

Oddly enough, he added, the band apparently had no merchandise table. "Every concert I'd ever been to, they were selling music or shirts or something—but not these guys. So when it was over, we went out to the truck, and Johnny turned on [the Sex Pistols tape]. We ended up with a crowd of about 30 or 35 people, standing around that truck, bopping and banging into each other, sipping vodka and snowballs and listening to the Sex Pistols, because they didn't get a chance to buy their music inside."

Shaeffer paid the band $1,500 for its appearance, although he recalled the original amount as being an even $1,000. "For most of the super-legendary shows that happened at the Cain's, the tickets were under $10," he said. "I think the Sex Pistols' were $2.50. Then I marked them up to $3.50 because they didn't have enough money for the road and needed an extra $500 bucks. I've got some of those tickets still. I sell 'em on eBay for $300 to $500 apiece."

The night of that notorious show, Scott Munz added, "I was paying the band, and Sid Vicious and Johnny Rotten were sitting in that office of mine with the hat-check things and Estelle sitting in the box office, and they were laughing and joking and putting cigarettes out on their arms. They thought that was funny."

At this writing, in late 2019, the Longhorn Ballroom in Dallas had recently reopened as a private-event venue. Otherwise, the Cain's Ballroom is the only venue on that notorious tour that's still standing today.

Sex Pistols Press Kit

CHAPTER 14

There was something almost every weekend, even if it was not a national touring act—and, periodically, during the week...if that was the only day [the act] could come in. The New Wave was hitting about that time, but we had the outlaw-country thing, too. Jerry Jeff Walker was there a bunch. Ray Wylie Hubbard and the Cowboy Twinkies, whom I absolutely loved. And then Kinky Friedman and David Allan Coe.

— LISA LYONS, FREQUENT CAIN'S PATRON IN THE LATE '70S,
IN A SEPTEMBER 6, 2008 INTERVIEW WITH BRETT BINGHAM

The Larry Shaeffer era of the Cain's Ballroom had begun in the late '70s, when he booked his first weekend of acts at the venerable hall. As noted in the last chapter, they were blues-rocker Elvin Bishop on Friday and country-rock band Pure Prairie League on Saturday. Maybe, if one or both had flopped, Shaeffer would've rethought the idea of bringing shows into the Cain's. But they each made money, and the die was cast.

"Yeah, I hit that first weekend," Shaeffer said. "I might have made $500 or $1,500. I can't remember. But it gave me a little confidence and I said, 'Okay, I'm going to get busy now.' I went to the rock 'n' roll agents on both coasts. I didn't want it to be a country place. I didn't want to resurrect Bob Wills. That era was over. So I started making offers for the rock acts."

But while he didn't want to book any pure country-music performers, he did have an interest in the Austin, Texas-based outlaw-country scene, just as his predecessors had. "That consortium of partners had been trying to bring Austin music up here," he explained. "And the Cain's became very much a part of all of that, because it was so in synch with what was happening in Austin. It meant something to people like Michael Martin Murphey and Ray Wylie Hubbard. To Asleep at the Wheel, of course. To Gary P. Nunn, Jerry Jeff Walker. If you were in Austin, you weren't going to go to Springfield, Missouri and play something as historically important as the home of Bob Wills. You weren't going to get that in Oklahoma City, either, or Little Rock. Cain's became a very important thing to those artists. It had all the DNA of what a good musician would want to be part of."

There was, added Scott Munz, another more practical reason that playing the Cain's made sense to those acts. "We were kind of on the circuit with the [famous Austin-based venue] Armadillo World Headquarters and the Longhorn [Ballroom] in Dallas," noted Scott Munz. "So the country artists that came out of there—Jerry Jeff Walker, Alvin Crow, Asleep at the Wheel— were able to route up and down I-35."

In fact, according to Shaeffer, one of the reasons the Cain's began to flourish was because of its desirability as a routing date, and not only just for the Texas acts. "The agents in New York, especially, found a place their bands could play on an off-night. They didn't have to go from Kansas City to Dallas. Now, they had a stop. That's valuable if you're on a 24-date tour, especially if a band's looking at being off that night. All of a sudden, there was this place to stop in Tulsa. And, instead of playing a bar that had

240 seats, if they were playing Cain's, and if they were on, they'd sell 1000 seats. That's heavy. That makes an impact on a record label and on other promoters.

"Were any of those artists enthralled by that old dirty building?' he asked rhetorically. "No. Pat Benatar walked in and said, 'I smell dogs-hit.' It echoed through the whole building— which is why I never booked her again," he added. "But very quickly I started inheriting baby bands, and a lot of them Tulsa had no awareness of."

The term "baby bands," generally speaking, applied to acts that had just recently been signed to a major record label, which would

then start working on getting them national exposure. Naturally, that plan included touring. "At the time, the way the music business was working was that a label—Warner Brothers, primarily —would subsidize a band on the road to the tune of something like $200,000 a month and then charge the clubs to book 'em," explained Munz. "Shaeffer paid $500 for Van Halen. He paid $500 for Pat Benatar. It was pre-MTV, so the labels had to put them on the road, and they obviously couldn't charge $5,000 for Van Halen when [the single] 'Runnin' with the Devil' was first out, because nobody knew Van Halen. That's how they built a band up."

Of course, it was a gamble for the labels to put out that kind of money on performers who had yet to prove themselves on a national level. And on a smaller scale, Shaeffer was rolling the dice as well when he booked one of those baby bands into the Cain's. Many of the acts that a big label had high hopes for, ones that played the Cain's and many other venues across the country in hopes of building a name and career, either never made it or never *quite* made it. Others became some of the biggest names of that era. But there weren't many that Shaeffer wouldn't take a chance on as a Cain's act—especially when they were affiliated not only with major labels, but also with big-time booking agencies. That was especially true for the heavyweight Premier Talent, which Shaeffer called "the Cadillac agency of the world."

They were down on Broadway in New York City. They had Jethro Tull, they had the Who, they had Led Zeppelin. They had most of the stuff I wanted, because that's the kind of music I liked. Those were the albums I was buying.

When I got a call from that agency, luckily, I won them over quickly. That became the first agency to send stuff through Cain's— baby acts like U2, Van Halen, Bon Jovi. On occasion, when I would get a call from them, I would have never heard of the band. But I knew that if I wanted some things I had to take everything.

I had never heard of U2 when I got the phone call. U-what? The danger was that most of the people in the area hadn't heard of U2 either. Very often I would put somebody in the Cain's who was going to be a superstar, and maybe 50 people knew who they were. That didn't mean that 400-500 people didn't come, because people had started realizing that if I did a show there, it was probably a real show and they'd better go check it out. There was a little phenomenon that was happening.

* * * *

Outlaw-country or New Wave, heavy metal or straight-ahead jazz, punk or funk, baby band or veteran act, Larry Shaeffer invariably promoted whomever he brought to the Cain's over the town's top rock radio station, KMOD (97.5 FM). "I would say 95 percent of my advertising in the Cain's era was through KMOD," he told Brett Bingham. "Even if it was David Allan Coe, I was advertising not on [country stations] KVOO or K95 but on KMOD. So I was bringing in all these youthful rockers and these outlaw-country guys were loving it."

One of that ilk who especially dug it was Hank Williams, Jr. In the late '70s and very early '80s, when Hank Jr. was still laboring to escape from his late father's long shadow, Shaeffer booked him in the ballroom. At the time, Hank Jr. was trying mightily to make the transition from, essentially, doing a Hank Sr. tribute show to performing his own outlaw-style material.

"Here's a guy who's frustrated," Shaeffer noted. "People are expecting him to play all his dad's hits and say goodnight. It was killing him. So somehow, I delivered a KMOD crowd to his performance, and he lit up. He sold out the second time I played him there, and the crowd was noisy, drunk, and yelling at the top of their lungs. That was a big payoff for him. He really liked it."

Williams liked it so much, in fact, that when he began to break big in the early '80s, he had his agent, Dan Wojak, ask Shaeffer about becoming part of the Hank Jr. team.

"Hank thought I could get the kids in to see him, not the people who wanted to see his daddy," explained Shaeffer. "Dan Wojak called me in '81 or early '82 and said, 'Larry, Hank Jr. is headed for superstardom. Trust me. He wants you to be a primary promoter.' He hadn't even met me. He just thought I was the guy who could deliver that crowd for him."

Shaeffer remembered there being three primary promoters—"two guys on the East Coast and me"—working with Hank Williams Jr. at that time; and, sure enough, Hank Jr. took off. His country-music ascendency turned out to be an extremely lucrative turn of events for Shaeffer and his company Little Wing Productions, whose prime source of revenue was still arena shows, not the Cain's. Over the next few years, as Williams graduated from clubs to concert halls to arenas, Shaeffer was right there with him, reaping the benefits.

"I don't know anybody who did more dates on Hank when he was selling 10,000 seats. I was making 40 grand a night some nights, making 100 grand on a weekend—and then coming back to Cain's," Shaeffer said with a laugh.

But not always. During this time, he added, "I got so busy with Hank that I would go dark at Cain's for two or three weeks," and he began to talk publicly about wanting to divest himself of the building. As Cathy Milam wrote in the August 12, 1982 *Tulsa World*, "Shaeffer, who has become a nationally prominent concert promoter, said he decided to sell the ballroom because it was no longer his top-priority project."

Making money in big halls with Hank Jr. and others, Shaeffer began to see the Cain's more and more as a kind of burden. He explained his mindset in those days to Brett Bingham:

I always felt like I'd have to pass Cain's off at some point to somebody else because I would literally sit there and imagine that the roof was an inch lower than it was yesterday. It would rain and we'd be mopping for hours because water would just rush through the place. We were getting harassed by the police department. The police would come in and try to arrest people and mess with me and my staff. It was becoming more and more miserable to sustain myself there.

Before I bought the Cain's, where I was headed, I thought, was to be the guy who brought in the arena shows to Tulsa and Oklahoma City—maybe even fanning out to do a couple of other states. That was my mindset. Cain's became a hiccup. I loved the Cain's from the moment I saw it, but to me it was holding me back.

In the *World* article, writer Milam cited "an 'eminent' historian and professor from California who has long been interested in the place" as Shaeffer's potential buyer. The deal never came to pass, though, and while Shaeffer would periodically make public mention of the Cain's being up for sale, he would hold on to it until the final years of the 20th century.

* * * *

Although the Cain's hadn't really had a house band since the Marie Myers days, it came close in the late '70s and early '80s with a country-rock act called the Turkey Mountain Troubadours. Friends who had all attended Tulsa's Webster High, they formed the group after graduation, naming it after a notorious high school makeout spot. The group parlayed its winning of a 1975 KMOD talent contest into a series of gigs at the Cain's, quickly establishing the Troubadours as a local attraction.

"They put on a great show," Shaeffer recalled. "It was comical. It was colorful. I loved 'em."

The group would appear at the Cain's for many years afterwards, with an annual Thanksgiving night bash continuing well into the '90s, after the Troubadours had gotten back together following a five-year breakup.

"I would rate them as one of the primary acts custom-built for the Cain's in my era," Shaeffer added. "They opened a lot of

[national] shows; they even headlined. I'd play 'em once a month or so, and they just really worked well."

But that was as close as the Cain's got to a regular act during those years—unless you want to call ladies mud-wrestling an act.

It's unclear exactly why mud wrestling became a regular happening at the ballroom. Chances are good, though, that its genesis can be traced to an event Shaeffer brought in on March 13, 1981, billed as "The 1981 Professional Hollywood Female Mud Wrestlers

PLUS Preliminaries for Tulsa Ladies All-Star Mud Wrestlers." In booking that special event, and the subsequent regularly scheduled mud-wrestling sessions, Shaeffer acceded to the wishes of his friend Mark Hine, a fellow promoter—and, later, as Mark Mason, a filmmaker (*Party Crasher: My Bloody Birthday* [2000] and *The Prize Fighter* [2003], starring Gary Busey).

"Mark brought me the idea and just pitched me and re-pitched me," Shaffer remembered. "Then all of a sudden our [Cain's] softball team is playing in a league every Thursday night. So I come up with the idea that this will be great for the softball team to have something to do after the games. That was really what it was about.

"But then, all of a sudden, it took hold, and we were packed there for a year or two. We'd be there in our softball uniforms during the season just yukking it up and having a great time. Maybe it wasn't a historically significant event, but I still sell mud-wrestling posters all over the country."

The matches didn't just coincide with the Cain's team's softball season. They extended well into winter; there was even one on Christmas Eve of 1981. The ballroom's antiquated heating system was not known for keeping the venue toasty, so simply trying to get warm was a big challenge for the wrestlers when the temperature dropped off.

Norma Rush was one of the early participants. After seeing a TV news story about the upcoming matches, she headed down to the Cain's and, almost before she knew it, she was grappling before a crowd in the mud pit. Rush recalled the experience in a 2011 interview for this book.

> *I think I wrestled on the very first night, and I think I was in the very first match. It seems to me there were a lot of people there, and they were pretty loud, and the drilling mud we wrestled in was cold. Very cold.*
>
> *I believe it was the chilly time of the year, because I remember having a hard time trying to find a swimsuit. Of course, now you can get them any time, but back then, they were only sold during the season, pretty much. I had the good sense to wear a one-piece swimsuit. It was not unusual for girls to show up and lose part of their [two-piece] swimsuits during the competition.*

Rush, who had decided to participate because "it sounded like an adventure, and I liked adventure," lost the match, but decided to continue to compete, learning some moves from a family friend who was also a high school wrestling coach. "It took me, I think, five times before I won," she said with a laugh. "But after I won, I quit."

Winners, she said, were paid $45, with the losers getting $20 or $25. "A lot of young ladies wanted to participate," she added. "And there were a lot of different kinds of girls, from just plain girls all the way to strippers—an interesting mix of people."

"We did mud wrestling for a long, long time," remembered Scott Munz. "It took us a while to figure out what the exact composition of that drilling mud should be, and how to mix it up. You don't use regular mud, you use drilling mud. It's pretty dense. We'd mix it in a 55-gallon barrel, put a trolling motor over the edge, mix up a batch, and pour it in the ring. Then we'd mix up another batch and pour it in the ring.

"And you talk about a mess. After a while, we got smart and hung Visqueen on the walls, because they'd come in and they'd have mud all over them, and they'd be squeegeeing it off their arms and legs."

For one memorable mud-wrestling evening, the group was made more interesting by Jim Millaway, who was at the time— under his TV and radio persona of Sherman Oaks—a very popular morning-drive personality on KMOD. Shaeffer hired him to emcee one of the bigger matches.

"I was introducing the girls, and I'd meet them and write their names down—and then I'd make up backstories," Millaway recalled in an interview for this book. "'She works with special-ed children. She's a beekeeper in Owasso.' The most popular one was when I introduced 'a little girl from Skiatook, Oklahoma—and folks, she's a Viet Nam veteran!' The crowd liked that. She actually won."

Millaway recalls the dressing room, "wall to wall, ceiling to floor, covered with Visqueen sheeting, something like you would see in [the serial-killer TV series] *Dexter's* kill room. That was done so that they could hose 'em off afterwards, so it had a total abattoir feeling," he said, laughing. "The girls didn't seem particularly nervous. *I* was certainly taken aback."

Since the matches went on for a few years, Millaway and Rush were likely involved at different times, under slightly different circumstances. The only place Rush remembers seeing Visqueen was around the wrestling ring, forming a perimeter for the drilling mud used in the matches. "I don't recall a lot about the dressing room," she added. "My biggest memory is that there was one tiny shower and no hot water. We went through the hot water very quickly."

As Shaeffer indicated earlier, the ladies' mud-wrestling eventually ran its course and appears to have been gone from the Cain's entertainment roster by early 1983. Millaway was kidding when he said, "It was replaced by pig races, but after those were judged too inhumane, I think they went back to mud wrestling."

However, even though Shaeffer can laugh about them now, there indeed *were* pig races at the Cain's Ballroom—for one evening only—and the results were no joke at all for the venue's owner, who'd sunk plenty of his own cash into the event.

****

Shaeffer's sales rep at KMOD was an energetic, obsessive, and off-the-wall-funny guy named Mike Wahl. The two of them had been friends since Shaeffer's pre-Cain's days, when he'd started advertising his arena shows on the station. "He was so close to me that when I bought the Cain's, and my dad and I needed to expand the size of the stage, Mike Wahl was one of the guys with a hammer," Shaeffer said. "It was me and Mike Wahl driving the nails when we built that stage up."

So when Wahl came up with the idea to hold pig races at the ballroom, Shaeffer listened. "I think he'd heard about one somewhere and thought it would work," explained Shaeffer. "He had the stroke to get KMOD to present stuff, and we were pretty much throwing things up against the wall to see if they'd stick.

"But the pig races were...an *ill-conceived* project," he added with a laugh. "Mike presented it to me in a slick way, but I don't think he knew all the grisly details that were going to come with it. Let me say this: It told better than it lived."

Those grisly details, he explained, sort of sneaked up on him:

I was doing something else, and not paying close enough attention to it. Then, all of a sudden, we're building chutes for the race and putting pig wiring outside of Cain's on the side lot, and I've got a pig farm down there. They're running through the building, they're squealing through the neighborhood. We had breakouts.

We had to buy the pigs at a certain age, and they had to reach a certain size just at the time the pig races happened. It was almost like raising baby chicks for Tyson. When the weekend came, it involved two days of intense pig training, so those pigs would know that when they got to the end of the track, there'd be food waiting for them. That's why they ran. No other reason.

I come into the office maybe a day before the races. I can smell the pig shit clear down Main Street, and I walk in the front office and go to open the door to the ballroom— and I can't. There are bodies against it. It's a couple dozen little piglets, all stacked up on one another, sleeping.

Dubbed Pig Time Racing, the event went off as scheduled on April 26, 1985. But despite advertised attractions that included the Hog Bog, Pork Pull, and Hog & Honey Race, and competing pigs named after favorite Tulsa TV and radio personalities (including Billy Porker, a play on Billy Parker's name), "people stayed away by the thousands," Shaeffer said.

"We might've had 150 people show up, and we'd spent a lot of money—a lot of *my* money," he noted. "The races worked. The pigs raced. There was a winner every time. But no one cared to be there."

So Pig Time Racing ended with a single staging at the Cain's, leaving in its wake a sizable dent in Larry Shaeffer's bank account as well as the pungent, pervasive odor of pig manure, which hung around the ballroom for, he estimated, at least six months.

****

Never afraid to try something new at the ballroom, Shaeffer had more hits than misses. But, besides Pig Time Racing, a couple of other ideas for additions to the Cain's Ballroom experience just didn't work out.

One involved a mechanical bull, the barroom attraction that had heated up after the 1980 release of the movie *Urban Cowboy*. Much of the action took place in and around the real-life Pasadena, Texas honky-tonk, Gilley's, which prominently featured one of those bulls; soon, dancehall owners in other parts of the country wanted to get in on the action.

At first, Shaeffer was more bull broker than owner. As he remembered it, "I bought a bucking bull during that time period, and people kept trying to buy it from me, so I started looking for more. Bill Poulos, a champion cowboy back then, was helping me. He'd call me about every two weeks: 'Well, there's one up in Boulder.' So I started buying all these bucking bulls, six or eight of them, when the Gilley's thing was hot. When somebody called, trying to buy my bucking bull, I'd get six or eight or 10 grand out of 'em. I was buying them for $750 or $1,500. These guys in Chicago and Detroit and Philly would pay whatever my price was and come and pick 'em up."

That part of the mechanical-bull business worked well for him. But actually having a bull on the Cain's floor—that was another story.

"People loved seeing it—but here's what happened," he said. "There was this beautiful girl—I mean *beautiful*— and she'd been drinking too much and decided to ride the bull. It bucked up and hit her mouth, and knocked all of her teeth out, right in front of me. It looked like the bottom had fallen out of a box of Chiclets. She was bloody, dripping blood. And I said, 'That's it.'"

Surprisingly, the same sort of thing never happened—at least with that kind of severity—when the Cain's became, at least for several evenings, a roller rink. Looking back, said Scott Munz, "The liability exposure on it was ridiculous. We were selling beer, it was a hardwood floor, and people would spill beer on it. We didn't have any rules or anything. If you wanted to skate around with your cup of beer, you skated with your cup of beer. If you spilled some on the floor, so be it. And when another skater came around and hit that beer on the floor, they'd go flying.

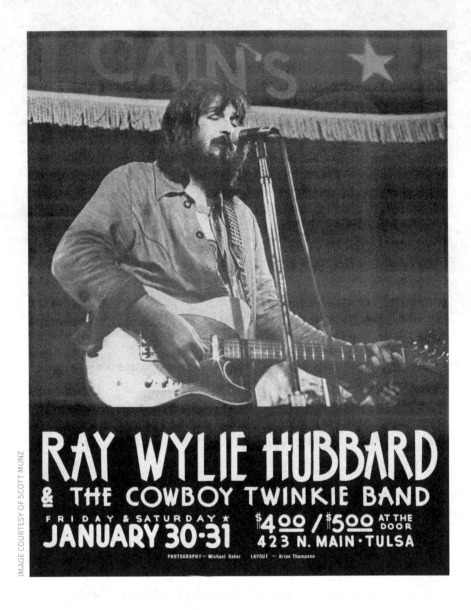

"We'd bought a bunch of pews from a church that was closing in Red Oak, right outside of town, and we'd put tables and chairs in the front. Then those pews would start at the end of the hardwood floor on the carpet before the mix platform. People would go flying into those benches and we'd kind of laugh. We didn't even think about the insurance exposure."

Also, he said, "There were two local girls who would come in during the day and skate around the ballroom floor in their bikinis. We'd be sitting out there in the pews just watching 'em, and that pissed Jan [Adams] off."

But while the bikinied skaters offered a nice diversion, better judgment must've prevailed fairly quickly, perhaps on an evening that Munz and Shaeffer watched as body after body piled into those hard wooden church pews. For whatever reason, Munz said, the Cain's time as a roller rink simply "didn't last long."

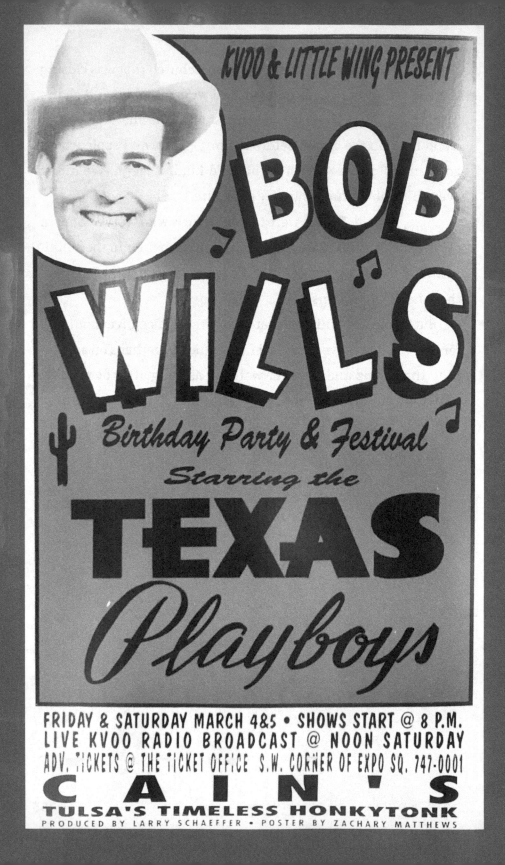

There is no evil entity in Cain's Ballroom. I spent many nights there, and I was so cozy and comfortable and never worried about anything. But on many occasions around 3 a.m.—not two, not four—I'd wake up and hear noise on the stage and equipment being moved around and lots of conversations going on. I could hear them. And I'd go open the door, and there would be nothing but darkness and an empty stage. It would be blank empty. I actually accepted that without getting shivers down my back.

What did I finally decide? It was the Playboys setting their gear up. That's what I chose to think. They were loading in. It was clear as a bell. There was conversation, and bang, boom—and a little laughter.

— Larry Shaeffer, in an August 30, 2019 interview with Brett Bingham and John Wooley

From the time he took over the Cain's, Shaeffer had seemed to possess an almost supernatural kinship with the ghost of Bob Wills. (Johnnie Lee Wills didn't pass away until 1984.) In Cathy Milam's 1982 *Tulsa World* story announcing the proposed sale of the Cain's, for instance, Shaeffer said, "The day I told my employees I was going to sell, one of the ceiling panels in my office slipped down, and out fell three fan letters addressed to Bob Wills." So it was probably inevitable that a regular series of Texas Playboys tribute shows would begin during Shaeffer's tenure as owner.

"I realized after a few years at Cain's what a sentimental journey it was for those who came there," Shaeffer said. "We all know what Bob and Johnnie Lee—mostly Johnnie Lee—did on that stage, but because I was always having an old couple show up, coming in and reminiscing, it became obvious that I should try to offer those guys a place to reunite."

He started doing that in the early '90s, always centering the show around Bob Wills' March 6 birth date. But before those birthday celebrations began, several precursor events found their way to the Cain's stage. Johnnie Lee Wills himself, for instance, headlined his own birthday soiree with a show and dance on September 2, 1982, the exact date of his 70th birthday. The first hour of the Thursday night event was carried over KVOO radio, following the pattern of the Thursday night Wills dance broadcasts in the '30s, '40s, and '50s.

Two years later, KVOO and the Cain's collaborated on another bit of Wills nostalgia, presenting a noonday program in the tradition of Bob and Johnnie Lee. This time around, the man doing the tribute was one of the biggest names ever to grace country music.

In 1970, Merle Haggard—who was by then a huge country star—had recorded *A Tribute to the Best Damn Fiddle Player in the World; Or, My Salute to Bob Wills* for Capitol Records, using several former Texas Playboys in addition to his own band, the Strangers. (Some credit that LP with beginning the '70s western-swing revival.) Then, three years later, he'd participated in the Tommy Allsup-produced *For the Last Time* album, which marked the final recording-session appearance for Wills, suffering from the effects of several strokes. A Bob Wills fan from childhood, Haggard brought his band to the Cain's for a free noontime show on Monday, June 4, 1984, evoking the Wills noon broadcasts right down to the traditional 12:15 starting time. O.W. Mayo introduced the group, KVOO aired the show, Johnnie Lee Wills was in attendance, and Haggard's Strangers included guitarist Eldon Shamblin and mandolinist-fiddler Tiny Moore, both of whom were not only Wills-band alumni but also contributors to *A Tribute to the Best Damn Fiddle Player in the World.*

Playing fiddle himself, a bearded Haggard addressed the packed house before airtime, telling the audience that for the next hour he and the band would, essentially, *be* Bob Wills and the Texas Playboys. As the *Tulsa Tribune*'s Ellis Widner reported in his June 5 story, Haggard said, "If you shout out requests, ask for a Bob Wills song. If you yell out for Merle or one of my songs, that's a sure sign you want to leave." And from the "Texas Playboys Theme" that opened the broadcast to the closing number, "Goodnight, Little Sweetheart," it was all Wills material, played happily and almost reverently, as the giant photo of Wills himself beamed down from the wall.

"It was kind of spooky," Haggard told John Wooley in an interview backstage at the Cain's immediately following the event, "and kind of fun."

Why did Haggard choose to do this show on that particular date? An ancillary reason had to do with the then-Tulsa-based Jim Halsey Company, which at the time was the biggest country music agency in the world, with Merle on its roster of clients.

"Basically, the main reason for the show is that Merle's always wanted to do it," Halsey agent Steve Pritchard told Wooley for a June 5 *Tulsa World* article. "And this was a good time because we wanted to tie it into a show in Muskogee we're doing."

The proposed Muskogee show was to be called American Freedom Day, to be held annually on July 4 starting in 1985, utilizing Haggard and several other big acts on the Halsey roster. But while that proposed event died aborning, Haggard's heartfelt and eerily authentic salute to Bob Wills at the Cain's is still a much-talked-about event in western-swing circles.

What hasn't been talked about nearly as much is exactly how and why he got there. Indeed, as Steve Pritchard said, Haggard had probably long wanted to do a Bob Wills show on the Cain's stage. That, however, is just part of the story. As mentioned earlier, in addition to running the Cain's, Shaeffer was promoting a lot of concerts around the country for Hank Williams, Jr. in the early '80s; he was also working with other big-name country acts, including Haggard.

"I had Haggard out for four or five dates in Tennessee and West Virginia, and we ended up in Knoxville for the next-to-last date," Shaeffer recalled. "I had a friend there named Zane Daniel who was the most powerful attorney, probably, in Tennessee, and he loved to come backstage and see Hank Jr. and pass the flask around. He was there [for the Haggard show] that night, and we went to Asheville, North Carolina, the next morning for the last of my run of Merle dates."

Whiskey manufacturer George Dickel was a backer of the Haggard tour, and usually, at some point in each concert, Haggard would pull out a bottle of his sponsor's product and take a swig or two, along with some of his band members, all of them acting as though they were trying to be surreptitious. As things turned out, it would've been a good idea to actually hide it at the Asheville concert, since there was a city ordinance there prohibiting "the possession and consumption of spiritous liquor at certain locations." That's according to a UPI story from May 21, 1983, archived at www.upi.com.

It's possible that the law wouldn't have been enforced at that particular Haggard show. But it was, thanks to the concert hall's management.

"There was a new building manager [in Asheville]," explained Shaeffer. "He'd been there about a week, and he didn't like being where he was. Everybody was silly and ignorant to him. So he comes up in front of those guys at sound check and says, 'I would appreciate it if you'd tell Mr. Haggard that if he drinks alcohol on the stage tonight, he will be arrested.'"

As it happened, Haggard was in the building at the time and heard the threat. Shaeffer remembered Haggard calling him over and sending him to a liquor store for "the biggest bottle of whiskey they've got."

The show starts, and at about the middle, out comes the bottle, and they take three pulls apiece. Backstage are some good old Asheville cops in uniform, telling me they don't want to arrest Merle Haggard and they're sorry about this new guy [the building manager]. Then, as Haggard comes down the stairs after the show, they arrest him. He goes to jail, and he's strutting around in handcuffs and just loving it.

I had no connections in Asheville, so I called Zane Daniel in Knoxville and told him what had happened. He said, "Don't worry about it. I'll make a call."

About an hour later, he called me back and said, "Go to the jail." I did, and Merle was out—but they did charge him with a misdemeanor.

The UPI story noted that two of Haggard's band members, fiddler Jimmy Belken and horn player Don Markham, were also arrested and released, along with Haggard, "under $500 secured bonds." A story posted by Asheville TV station WLOS (wlos.com) on April 6, 2016, following Haggard's death, noted, "When the officer made the arrest, Haggard told him he'd be a good poker player because he doesn't show whether or not he's bluffing."

After his release, Shaeffer said, "Merle was just pumped up. He'd showed 'em. And he wanted to go out to a Denny's or a Sambo's for breakfast—some 24-hour place, because it's the middle of the night."

Shaeffer remembers Haggard's drummer Biff Adam and manager Fuzzy Owen joining him and Haggard at the restaurant. "And we're sitting in a booth, and I happened to be wearing my Cain's Ballroom softball jersey. Merle looked at me and said, 'Where did you get that?'

"I said, 'Merle, I've owned Cain's Ballroom for eight or 10 years.'

"Well, he just lit up. He started telling stories about Cain's and Bob Wills that I'd never heard. They were riveting. And then he said, 'Here's what we're going to do. We end our tour at Billy Bob's'—I think that's right—'in Fort Worth, and then we're going to come up and play Cain's for a live noon broadcast. We won't charge you anything, but you can't charge at the door. It has to be free like it was when Bob did it.'

"And that," he concluded, "is how the show happened at Cain's."

* * * *

The year of 1984 was an important one for the first family of western swing and its fans. Following Bob's death in 1975, a new group, sanctioned by Bob's widow, Betty, and directed by Leon McAuliffe, had been assembled. Under the name of Bob Wills' Original Texas Playboys, the players—most of them long-time Bob Wills sidemen—had begun recording together for major-label Capitol Records, but they soon moved to the Texas-based Delta Records label, where they proceeded to turn out a number of albums. Then, on August 11, 1984, Delta sponsored a Texas Playboys reunion show, hosted by McAuliffe, at the Tulsa Convention Center, bringing in several dozen former Wills sidemen from all over the country. Shaeffer told Brett Bingham he was never contacted about hosting the show at the Cain's, which may have been for the best, as the event drew more than the 1800 or so that the ballroom could comfortably hold. (The Cain's did, however, host its own two-day event on December 14 and 15th of that year, "Asleep at the Wheel's Tribute to Bob and Johnnie Lee Wills," bringing the Texas-based act back to one of its homes-away-from-home.)

Johnnie Lee Wills, who was not present at the reunion (and not a member of Bob Wills' Original Texas Playboys), passed away a couple of months later. The long-lived Johnnie Lee Wills Tulsa Stampede rodeo died with him.

A second reunion show was held the next year in the same venue, with Billy Parker emceeing, and then, in 1986, Bob Wills' Original Texas Playboys dissolved. The old-timers had made a pact that when one of them died, the group was over, and they were as good as their word, disbanding after the death of pianist "Brother" Al Stricklin. It wasn't until 1988—the year, incidentally, McAuliffe passed away—that another major Wills event was staged in Tulsa, and this time, it was back at the ballroom where it all started.

In a story by John Wooley done for the October 20, 1988, issue of the *Tulsa World*, longtime KVOO engineer Jack Moore described the show and dance, which was a benefit for the Tulsa Press Club, as "a recreation of the old western-swing styled broadcasts that used to be done from the Cain's." Set for October 29, it featured the young western-swing band Stonehorse, with guest appearances by Parker and nationally known fiddler Jana Jae. The first hour was broadcast over KVOO. Moore had also engineered the airing of the Haggard show four years earlier, which he called "phenomenal."

"I couldn't believe I was sitting there listening to what I was listening to," he added. "Merle Haggard didn't even want his name mentioned in the broadcast."

Moore, Cain's, and KVOO were at it again the next year, airing the first hour of a show and dance by the Texas-based Alvin Crow and the Pleasant Valley Boys, one of the successful young acts—along with the likes of Asleep at the Wheel and Commander Cody and His Lost Planet Airmen—that had helped fuel a western-swing revival in the mid-'70s. The free event was held March 11, 1989, foreshadowing the annual Cain's shows that would later be staged around the day of Bob Wills' birth. (Crow's show had been scheduled for March 4, but a major snowstorm pushed it forward a week.) Then, in September of the same year, an 11-piece group and two vocalists—all alumni of Johnnie Lee Wills bands—played a tribute concert at the Cain's before a standing-room-only crowd.

Meanwhile, several former Bob and Johnnie Lee sidemen, along with other players in the Wills style, were getting together in loose-knit groups and staging shows around the Southwest. The very early '90s found some of them doing annual engagements in the Oklahoma towns of Pawhuska and Eufaula. One of those aggregations was fronted by vocalist Truitt Cunningham, who'd been with Bob Wills for several months in the mid-'50s, during the latter's time on the West Coast; Cunningham and his band played, among other dates, a successful engagement at Eufaula's Belle Starr Theatre in September 1992. It's probably that show that brought him to the attention of Larry Shaeffer, although Cunningham may have actually contacted Shaeffer first. "It could be that he called me and inspired me to do it, or vice versa," Shaeffer told Wooley. "I don't remember. All I knew was that Truitt had some experience with Wills, but the main thing he had was the ability to reunite certain ones [from the Wills bands]."

For the first official Bob Wills Birthday Party at the Cain's, held on March 6, 1993—the 88th anniversary of Wills' birth—the lineup was heavy on men who'd racked up more of their bandstand time with Johnnie Lee than Bob, including pianist Clarence Cagle, fiddler Curly Lewis, and saxophonist Glenn "Blub" Rhees. Roy Ferguson, who had led Johnnie Lee's *de facto* group after Wills had let his own band go, and who had helped reorganize that group in the early '90s, was on hand as well.

The Saturday night event went over well enough for Shaeffer to expand it to a two-day celebration the next year, which also reinstated the free KVOO noon broadcast For this one, Luke Wills, the only of the four musical Wills brothers left alive (the youngest, Billy Jack, had died in 1991), traveled to the Cain's from his home in Las Vegas. Steel guitarist Bobby Koefer also came in to join the band, as did such ex-Wills luminaries as Lewis, Rhees, Cagle, Eldon Shamblin, and drummer Casey Dickens. Jody Nix, son of Bob Wills contemporary Hoyle Nix, brought his band in from Texas as well.

In an interview with John Wooley for the March 6, 1994 edition of the *Tulsa World*, Cunningham acknowledged that the joy of the occasion was tempered by the knowledge that it couldn't go on forever. "The Playboys are getting fewer and fewer," he said. "Since I started coming back 10 years ago, it's been two or three of them going every year. I'm 63, and so are Casey and Bobby, and we're the youngest. Luke's 73. Eldon's 78."

Yet, remarkably, it *did* continue. At this writing, a quarter of a century after that interview, the only ex-Playboy of that group left standing is Koefer, the celebrated steel-guitarist, who lives in the Pacific Northwest and doesn't tour much. However, Bob Wills' Texas Playboys have persevered. That's the name of the official band, sanctioned by the Wills family. For decades, some time after the dissolution of the first, Leon McAuliffe-led group, it was fronted by longtime Wills vocalist Leon Rausch—who joined the Cain's event in 1995—and guitarist-producer-songwriter Tommy Allsup, whose affiliation with both Bob and Johnnie Lee Wills stretched back to the early 1950s. They continued squarely in the Wills style, delighting old fans and making new ones, until 2018, following the death of Allsup and the retirement of nonagenarian Rausch.

The current Texas Playboys aggregation is led by two-time Grammy winner Jason Roberts, hand-picked by both the Wills estate and Rausch, whose nearly two decades in the famed western-swing band Asleep at the Wheel includes an eight-year stint actually playing Bob Wills in the Wheel's nationally touring musical-theatre production, *A Ride with Bob*. (And in the interest of full disclosure, we note that this book's co-author, Brett Bingham, manages the band.) That group, which includes several former members of the Allsup and Rausch-led band, continues to play a full slate of concerts and dances—including the annual celebration of Bob Wills's birth at the Cain's—the House That Bob Built.

Davit Souders, who began working closely with Shaeffer and the ballroom in the '90s, coined that phrase, inspired by Yankee Stadium's longstanding nickname, The House That Ruth Built.

And while Souders would become known primarily for bringing younger, alternative rock acts to the Cain's, he said that "one of my favorite experiences, period, as far as good vibes and stuff, was working with the Texas Playboys.

Bob Wills' Texas Playboys led by Jason Roberts - March 2, 2019

"There's that feeling of true, real history that you can feel and see," he explained in an interview for this book. "To see the Playboys up there—it was like traveling back in time. It's as real and tangible history as you can get, and that's an important thing. It was a super highlight for me."

"The first time we did it," Shaeffer said, "I was seeing people who had traveled from a lot of different states, and that kind of made it a big deal. In the days I had it, it never failed—but it never made money. I didn't want to *lose* money on it, but with my ticket prices probably ten or 15 bucks back then, I just had enough to pay the [advertising] media and pay the guys. It was worth it just to get them all into the same room and listen to the stories being told.

"I can tell you it was never done to make money because it never did," he added. "But that was one of the first times in my life that I realized everything isn't about money."

FRIDAY NOVEMBER 5, 1982

LITTLE WING PRESENTS *Epic* RECORDING STAR

GEORGE JONES

CAIN'S BALLROOM

ONE NIGHT ONLY

Tulsa's Timeless Honky-Tonk

ANCE TIX $ 15.00 NOW ON SALE AT BOSTON AVENUE STREET SKATES   ODYSSEY SMOKESHOP   OZ   AND PEACHES

NORTH MAIN   918 584.2306   PRODUCED BY LARRY SHAEFFER 1982   PHOTO BY ANTHONY DARIUS   ADART BY BRIAN TH

CHAPTER 16

The Cain's Ballroom, Tulsa's famed honky tonk, is about to become the home of big name New Wave Music.

Cain's owner Larry Shaeffer said Tuesday he has decided to revamp his established New Wave schedule to offer the biggest, hottest bands in the country.

The lineup for May includes INXS, Bowwowwow, The Ramones and the Blasters—all major forces in the New Wave movement.

— FROM AN UNBYLINED ARTICLE IN THE APRIL 28, 1983 *TULSA WORLD*

I feel like maybe I could say one of my contributions to Cain's was Larry allowing me to reintroduce the Cain's ballroom to a whole other generation.

— DAVIT SOUDERS, IN AN AUGUST 17, 2010 INTERVIEW WITH BRETT BINGHAM AND JOHN WOOLEY

As Larry Shaeffer said about the ill-fated Pig Time Racing event, "We were pretty much throwing things up against the wall to see if they'd stick." Indeed, throughout the 1980s, there seemed to be little that the Cain's owner *wouldn't* try. A roster of the events from 1982, for instance, compiled by Russ Florence and Steve Higgins, lists around a hundred acts—including the ubiquitous lady mud wrestlers —featured on 46 nights, most of them Fridays and Saturdays. (A Summer Closing Party marked the end of the first half of the season on June 5, with the aforementioned Johnnie Lee Wills show opening the ballroom back up on September 2.) Although the lineup was heavy on rock and blues-rock (big names included Head East, Ozark Mountain Daredevils, Huey Lewis & the News, Rare Earth, Johnny Winter, and hometown heroes Leon Russell and Elvin Bishop) and cosmic cowboys (Michael Murphey, Jerry Jeff Walker, David Allan Coe, Asleep at the Wheel, and Alvin Crow & the Pleasant Valley Boys), there were also veteran rock 'n' rollers (the Ventures, Mitch Ryder), country music both classic (George Jones) and contemporary (Juice Newton), soul (Peaches & Herb) and lots of local performers from all sorts of different genres. Nineteen-eighty-two was also the year that Shaeffer began working with Hank Williams, Jr. across the country, which further stretched his time and energies. However, that job was—as Shaeffer noted in an earlier chapter—more suited to how he'd envisioned his career.

"When the opportunity with Junior came up for me, I was going to keep Cain's, because I wanted to office there, but it was not a priority," he said. "I was stepping up to what I wanted to step up to, and the money [with Williams] became so big."

Shaeffer's earnings as one of Williams' promoters far eclipsed what he was making at the Cain's. As he remembered it, "I went from having the electric turned off to making 90 grand on three dates with Hank Jr. And while I was doing that with him, I was powdering a few shows into Cain's, primarily the ones the agents needed me to showcase. So I was kind of where I wanted to be."

With the ballroom playing second fiddle in Shaeffer's plans, he thought it fair to give Scott Munz the opportunity to seek other employment. For a while, Munz had been pursued by the colorful ex-wrestler and promoter Cowboy Bill Watts, whose Mid-South Wrestling had made stars out of such characters as Steve "Dr. Death" Williams and Sylvester "Junkyard Dog" Ritter.

"Bill Watts loved Scott and had already asked him if he'd leave me," recalled Shaeffer. "I went to Munz and said, 'Scott, we're not making money here, and if Bill Watts wants to hire you, now would be the time to jump ship, because I don't know which way this place is going.'"

So, with Shaeffer's blessing, Munz went to work for Watts in 1985.

It was only a few years after that, however, that Shaeffer began to have second thoughts about the ballroom and where to put his energies. He'd gotten married in the late '80s, and he'd begun to feel that he needed to spend more time around Tulsa instead of on the road with Hank Williams, Jr. and others.

"Jake, my first son, was born in '89, and by 1990, I'd decided to draw back in and try to make my living at Cain's," he told Brett Bingham. "I thought I was going to settle down. So at that point I started taking it real seriously and began doing anything I could to rent the building or do a show." (By "rent the building," he was referring to the practice of letting outside promoters bring their own shows into the Cain's for a set fee.)

"I had enough money then, and I didn't feel like I had to make that much more. I just needed to make some at local shows at Cain's, maybe 10 or 15 grand a month," he added. "Why I quit Hank Jr. I don't know, because I was still making a lot of money. But I quit and came back with the necessity of making Cain's a little more scientific and proactive, to make it work."

As the new decade wore on, however, Shaeffer found that generating the cash flow he needed was becoming increasingly problematic. "In the mid-'90s, for me to count on making money, I had to bring in the young modern rock acts," he explained, "which I just didn't have much interest in."

Davit Souders, however, did. And the young promoter and rock singer would become one of Shaeffer's most trusted allies during the Cain's modern-rock period, which lasted through most of the 1990s.

Souders had first encountered the Cain's at the beginning of the previous decade. In 1981, he was the lead vocalist in a Tulsa band called Lynx, which had earned a substantial local following. The group, all either high schoolers or college freshmen, had been booked to open in November of that year for another Tulsa outfit, the David Dover Band, at a benefit show at the Cain's that raised money for multiple-sclerosis research and treatment.

At the time, Souders wasn't at all sure about the booking, or about the venue itself. "The whole wrong-side-of-the-tracks thing was going on, and it just seemed like this scary place to be," he recalled. "We didn't know if our crowd would go there. It was just this *place*, you know. We had no idea of its significance; we were just excited to play a show."

He got even more excited after a late sound check, finished not long before the doors opened for the actual show. "My

father and I went back through the office door, and when we walked out, there was a huge line. I was just blown away that our crowd had actually made the journey to the wrong side of the tracks."

Souders had known about Larry Shaeffer for some time; he even remembered, as an eighth grader, listening to his mother on the phone with Shaeffer, "asking him if he couldn't do something about all the smoke at his concerts." But he didn't actually become acquainted with the Cain's owner until 1986, after Souders had graduated from Oklahoma State and promoted himself into a job at a Tulsa club called SRO, taking tickets and learning about the band-booking business.

He was a quick study. Working his way up to manager, Souders began doing "small shows" at SRO, which led to his forming

Diabolical Productions—named after an adjective that caught his attention when it was uttered by the announcer for the *Batman* TV series—in anticipation of promoting his first concert at the Cain's. That was in January 1990, and it came about because Souders found an opportunity to book the industrial-rock band Ministry in Tulsa— and couldn't get SRO or Shaeffer interested in coming aboard.

"I happened to be a big fan of the band, but the veteran guys were saying, 'I'm not touching this,'" Souders recalled. "They didn't want anything to do with that band on a Monday night. But I was familiar with the band, and they were not. So it came to myself and my partner, Mark Matthews, and we said, '*We'll* do the show.'

"Then," he added, "we got this contract that looked like an encyclopedia. I had been dealing with [contract] riders and stuff like that [at SRO], but this was for a full 30-man crew, and you've got to feed them breakfast, lunch, and dinner. It was just over-whelming. We were like, 'What do we do?'"

What they did was contact Shaeffer. Although his official involvement didn't extend beyond renting the Cain's to the nascent Diabolical Productions for that Monday night, Shaeffer ended up giving the tyro promoters a crash course on how to deal with rider-laden contracts. (Riders deal with the things an act asks for above and beyond the basic contract, and the requests can go well beyond reasonable. Perhaps the most infamous example was the rider entry in Van Halen's 1980s contracts that called for M&Ms candy backstage—with all the brown pieces removed. Failure to adhere to this rider stipulation reportedly caused the band members to trash their dressing rooms at a big venue in New Mexico.)

"Mark and I met Larry at one of the auto shops in town—he was getting work done on one of his cars—and we sat there on car hoods," remembered Souders. "Larry looked at the contract and started marking through stuff—'not this, not this, we're not gonna do *this*, this is okay'—just like nobody's business. It was my first working situation with Larry."

Shaeffer, Souders added, assisted the fledgling producers in other ways as well, especially on the night of the show, when they came up against a legendary tour manager named Jolly Roger.

He was a big tall guy—6'7", 6'8". He'd worked with KISS and lots of other bands, and he was very, very hard on us two little fresh-faced promoters. Food ran out at one of the meals, and the show got delayed because the band wanted a non-alcoholic beer—I believe it was O'Doul's—and we didn't get it. So he's giving us this lecture, and we're on the phone in Larry's office, calling everybody we could think of. Somebody finally brought it to us, but they were literally holding the show up for this one item.

Almost as soon as he gets the O'Doul's, they go onstage—and then they throw it out to the audience!

After the show, we were really getting the business from Jolly Roger again, and Larry took him into a side room. Clearly, he said something like, 'Work with these guys; I'm here to mama-bird 'em,' because the level went down considerably after that.

But I learned a lot from Jolly Roger, and we became really close friends. Years later, if I did a show and Jolly Roger was happy, then I knew I was really good at what I was doing.

The concert, with another industrial act, KFMDM, opening for Ministry, sold out the Cain's, an experience Souders likened to "having your first record go gold or platinum." His first swing at promoting a major concert had yielded a home run, and he was now officially in the business—with considerable thanks to Shaeffer.

"Larry was looking out for me from day one," Souders said. "When I started working with agents and they'd ask Larry, 'What's with this kid Dave Souders?' he would apparently speak very highly of me, which got them to give me attention. I think Larry's nature is to nurture anyone who wants to do something. That was the key."

At the time of the Ministry show, Souders was in his late twenties; Shaeffer was 15 years his senior. They weren't quite a generation apart, but Souders was attuned to the younger rock bands and the emerging musical styles like the industrial genre of Ministry and KFMDM, which combined hard rock and electronic sounds with tough, often aggressive, lyrics.

Souders also had a familiarity with and affinity for the dance culture, which was a major part of the SRO milieu. However, his attempts to transplant DJ nights to the Cain's—a place that was, after all, named after a dance figure, albeit of a far different era— didn't take.

"[Promoter and former SRO head] Tim Barraza wanted to put on a couple of dance events at the Cain's, and he had myself and Zach Matthews, Mark Matthews' brother, put them together," recalled Souders. "I don't remember if it was going to be a series, but we did one night and decorated the Cain's, trying to make it 'clubby' and 'hipsterish,' and it didn't do well. We just didn't have the turnout.

"Zach and I were left alone to kind of wonder what we were doing with all these big, bad, seemingly Harley-riding guys—and I'm talking about the staff," he added with a laugh.

By the end of that year, Souders would start Ikon, a well-remembered Tulsa club that featured both modern rock acts and DJ-driven dance music. Ikon would move downtown in 1994, to a location just over a mile southeast of the legendary ballroom. But, as the decade wore on, the connection between the two venues would become even closer than that.

* * * *

Although Souders and Shaeffer remained friends, there were no more Diabolical Productions events at the Cain's during 1990. Souders kept busy doing smaller shows in other Tulsa halls, but, he said, "I was always looking toward doing more at Cain's."

"Then," he added, "in December of '90, I officially opened Ikon. So I had my own place to go and do the kind of stuff I wanted to do."

I ended up doing shows by myself—I didn't have a partner anymore—and I was just learning the ropes, so to speak. But [Ikon] took off really, really well.

I wanted to do a club that was to Tulsa in the '90s what SRO was in the '80s. The original goal was to be a bigger SRO, and be careful what you ask for, because that's what I got—times 10. It just kind of filled a niche, and I learned a lot of skills at Ikon on how to run a venue the correct way.

Immersing himself in the day-to-day operations of his own club, and still figuring out how to run the business end of things with maximum efficiency, Souders had little time in the first couple of years to try and promote acts anywhere else in town. Then, in 1993, Barraza, his former boss at SRO, and Shaeffer asked

Souders to come in on the latest version of the event that had initially kicked off the rock era at the Cain's back in 1974—the Freakers' Ball.

Larry Shaeffer had kept the Halloween event going after taking over the Cain's, usually pairing a national headliner with a local or regional opening act for the night's entertainment. The year before Souders came aboard, for instance, it was the Kentucky HeadHunters, with the Otis Watkins Band opening. In '91, it had been the Fabulous Thunderbirds with the Steve Pryor Band. Superficially, then, the talent lineup for the Freakers' Ball looked pretty much like what you might find on many other weekend nights at the ballroom.

But the entertainment value of the Freakers' Ball had long since transcended the acts that appeared on its stage. As Thomas Conner succinctly wrote in an October 27, 1995 *Tulsa World* piece, "the real show probably will be standing next to you." Throughout the '80s, the costumes had gotten more and more inventive and/or outrageous, perhaps helped along by significant cash prizes given for the best attire. As a result, Shaeffer told Conner for the *World* article, "It becomes more of a costume party than a music show."

Armed with this realization, Shaeffer and his co-promoter Barraza saw that, for this particular event, area bands might be just as good as big names—and using local bands would help keep their overhead down.

They knew, however, they needed the *right* groups, or at least the right genres, and that was Souders' area of expertise. "They brought me in because I had been working with local bands," explained Souders, who immediately expanded the number of acts on the bill. "For many years, it was generally a band or two. I was the guy who said, 'I'm gonna do a bunch of bands.'"

Souders' first few years with the Freakers' Ball relied heavily on area alternative and modern-rock acts. In 1994—celebrated as the 20th anniversary of the event—there was still a national headliner, the British power-pop band Fretblanket, but 13 local and regional bands also appeared on three stages in and around the Cain's. The next year, the Freakers' Ball talent roster featured Pit Bulls on Crack, Jawbreaker, Shannon's Tub, Superfuzz, Good, Cabbage, Dead Orchestra, and Jify Trip—all hailing from the area. And, as the number of acts grew, and the other stages opened up, Souders began casting further afield for talent—not geographically, but generically.

"I decided that this was going to be a showcase for Tulsa bands, Oklahoma bands," he said, "and after many different configurations, I figured out that it should be a variety. You want to come see mariachi music? Celtic? Rock and blues? This is your night to experience it all."

The Freakers' Ball continued well past the end of the 20th century, as did Souders' involvement in the event. But back in '93, it turned out to be the vehicle that got him back into the Cain's Ballroom, this time for a nice long run.

****

Just as Shaeffer had promoted virtually all his shows, to good effect, on Tulsa's rock-radio powerhouse KMOD, Souders found that the acts he brought in to Ikon could best benefit from spots on local outlet KMYZ (104.5 FM). After starting life in the mid-'80s as a hard-rock challenger to KMOD, the station had undergone a transformation in the early '90s, changing its name to Z-104.5—the Edge—and switching to an alternative-rock format. In addition to advertising on the Edge, Souders became a deejay there as well, helming "Homegroan," a weekly show featuring area bands. As he recalled:

> Around '93, '94, Z-104 went to the Edge format, and modern rock became this thing that just blew up. I started doing the radio show, and I was kind of the guy for Larry to go to, because I knew that music. We started doing shows together [at the Cain's], and everything was selling out: Offspring, Rancid, all these bands.
>
> So we just eased into this natural thing. Larry realized that this music they were calling modern rock was just alternative music stepping up; it was the same music, but now it had become the mainstream. With the Edge just going crazy, we were able to go after these bands and get them and supply them with an instant venue. And we started doing tons of shows.

They also began appearing together weekly in the morning-drive slot on Z-104.5, talking about their upcoming concerts—not just at the Cain's, but also at Ikon, which was still percolating along nicely. It was during these early- to mid-'90s years that the relationship between the two nightspots took on a symbiotic quality. Although Souders was pretty much solely responsible for the acts on Ikon's stage, Shaeffer occasionally lent a hand.

"He always said, 'That's your thing, you do it,'" recalled Souders. "But sometimes there would be a band that came across his plate, and he'd want a small showcase for it. That's where Ikon would come in. Or there would be a show booked at Ikon, and then they'd come back around and we'd move them to Cain's. It was such a good coupling, and it worked really, really well."

As for the Cain's bookings, he added, "I never minded playing Robin to Larry's Batman, and I always looked at Ikon as maybe Cain's younger hip brother. Cain's was the US and Ikon was England. We each had our worlds."

* * * *

Souders' Ministry show foreshadowed the alt-rock and modern-rock concerts that would become an important part of the Cain's entertainment throughout the '90s. But the few months around the Ministry date, from winter of 1989 through spring of 1990, were important in the ballroom's history for at least two other big reasons—one harrowing, the other heartwarming.

Just after midnight on the Sunday morning of May 6, 1990, Steve Munson was returning from the Cain's after helping with the sound for a show by actor Dennis Quaid—who had recently portrayed rocker Jerry Lee Lewis in the biopic *Great Balls of Fire*—and Quaid's band, the Mystics. In addition to being a ticket-office manager, sound technician, and production manager for Shaeffer, Munson was also a well-known bassist. In fact, at the time he was playing in the Mike Bruce Band, which had been scheduled to open for Quaid.

The actor, however, citing time constraints, had asked Bruce and his group not to perform. The members had agreed, but Munson had remained at the Cain's. "We were having some problems with the PA," Shaeffer told John Wooley for a May 11, 1990 *Tulsa World* story, "and he stayed and tried to keep the sound going for Dennis Quaid's set. For no charge, he was helping us get the show done. That's what he was all about.

"He left at 12 midnight," Shaeffer added. "By 12:09 he was dead."

A stolen van, driven by thirteen-year-old Jermell Jordan and filled with his friends, had slammed into Munson's Ford Escort station wagon as the juveniles attempted to elude police pursuit. The youths scattered, leaving behind two dead and one dying in the car they'd hit. Munson's longtime girlfriend, Annette Trigalet, was one of the casualties, along with her sister Constance Trigalet, who passed away at a Tulsa hospital within the hour. All had just left the ballroom.

The deaths prompted local outrage regarding juvenile justice in Tulsa, especially after it was learned that Jordan had been arrested 14 times in the previous two years. Some of the most furious voices belonged to members and former members of the Tulsa music community, where the likable Munson had many, many friends. That group included singer-songwriter Rance Wasson, who told Wooley, "Everybody loved him, and everybody's going to miss him, but everybody's so angry that it's hard to talk about it."

Wasson, a former Tulsan then living and working in L.A., was one of dozens of performers who banded together at the Cain's on Sunday, May 13—a week after the crash—to give a benefit performance for the Trigalet sisters' four children. According to a next-day *Tulsa World* story by Barbara Hoberock, the show was sold out, with a line waiting to get in throughout the night, and the musicians not only played for free, but also paid the $5 admission fee. Rock station KMOD suspended its regular programming to broadcast the entire event live, with volunteers manning phone lines for people who wanted to donate to the cause.

The Cain's concert, which ended up raising $20,000, was the first and biggest of several benefit shows held around town, including one with former Tulsan J.J. Cale at another Tulsa club, the Sunset Grill. When all the money was counted, nearly $30,000 had been raised for a newly formed trust fund in the children's names.

Almost a year later, in an April 29, 1991 *Tulsa Tribune* article headlined "Furor goes on" (referring to the juvenile-justice situation in Tulsa spotlighted by the Munson-Trigalet deaths), Brad Sultan wrote:

> *Larry Shaeffer, Munson's boss for more than 10 years at Little Wing Productions, said Munson was a "miracle worker" who took care of most of the technical work at Cain's and the Brady [Theatre, another Tulsa venue]. Munson was the only person who knew how to fix the old, temperamental sound system at Cain's, Shaeffer said.*
>
> *"You might think it's silly, but I still keep Steve's card in my Rolodex,' he said. "I have to stop myself and realize he is not going to walk around the corner."*

Less than three months before Munson's death, Shaeffer had begun a Christmas Eve toy giveaway at the Cain's, with the idea of gifting kids from low-income families. In a recent interview for this book, Shaeffer explained why he began the event. "My motivation was that I had gotten into a lifestyle where Christmas had turned into a 20,000-or 25,000-dollar shopping spree," he said. "It had become a miserable time of the year for me, just because of the overindulgence. The toy giveaway was my reaction to that."

Partnering with Mother Tucker Ministries, which served the underprivileged, and the Tulsa Angel Society, a provider of gifts for needy children, Shaeffer opened the doors of the ballroom for the debut of the Christmas at Cain's Toy Giveaway on December 24, 1989. Aimed at children 12 and under, the event from the beginning welcomed anyone who wanted to drop by— not only for toys, but food and drinks as well. Shaeffer explained the ground rules—or lack thereof—to Thomas Conner in a December 20, 1998 *Tulsa World* piece:

People are always calling us and asking, "Well, what do we have to do to be able to come down there?" I tell 'em, "Just smile, and please bring your kids." It's open to anyone. I don't care if you walk down here in stocking feet or you drive up in a Mercedes. It's not about showing us your DHS card. It's not about writing it off—which I don't do. It's not about deciding who's qualified to receive a toy. It's about giving toys to kids. Period.

Several hundred youngsters showed up on that first Christmas Eve at the ballroom, and by 1992, there were more than 4,000 passing through the doors, with volunteers giving out toys until 7 p.m. That year, the line had begun forming outside at 8 a.m. for a noon opening. *Tulsa World* reporter Kelly Kurt's December 26 story told of "mounds of free toys...[and] crates of baked goods and hot dogs to be handed out to the crowds...[and] Subway donated sandwiches." However, she added, "it was the toys that drew the most interest." Her opening paragraphs summed up the wonder of the event for its young beneficiaries:

> *Five-year-old Ruben Coffee's eyes widened at the sight of a huge pile of toys on the Cain's Ballroom stage.*
> *"What would you like?" a volunteer asked.*
> *Ruben pointed to a simple plastic truck, immediately tore it from its package and settled on the ballroom's old wooden floor to play.*

On the same date next year, Kurt returned to paint another vivid word-picture of the event, writing, "A little girl in a pink-hooded jacket stretched on her tiptoes to peek onto the stage of the Cain's Ballroom. Her eyes grew wide when she saw the pile of toys on top. Dolls in bright evening gowns, books and puzzles and games, teddy bears and squirt guns and heaps of candy canes and suckers."

Later in the story, a nameless unemployed mother, after selecting a few toys for her three children to complement the one gift each she and her husband had been able to buy for them, told

Kurt that the event was "showing the kids that there are people out there who care for children. It shows them there is hope in the world."

The toy giveaway continued for 15 years, going on even after Shaeffer had left the Cain's. Although the money for the giveaway had mostly come out of his pocket, at least in the first several years, Shaeffer was always quick to credit others who'd stepped up to help, from the volunteers who gave out the toys and kept the lines flowing smoothly, to the local businesses and radio stations that had pitched in, to the owners and managers of the stores where he shopped, who not only always seemed to give far more than the dollar amount warranted, but also often donated toys, food, and drink free of charge.

Gary Thomas worked security at the Cain's during those years, starting his own GT Security company in 1997. Showing up to help with the giveaway, he told Brett Bingham in a March 2011 interview, "made you feel great."

The doors didn't open until noon, and some people would show up at 6:30 or 7:00 in the morning—and on many of those Christmas Eves, it was nasty weather. These people are standing out there with blankets, coats, little kids... sad, but still good that everybody got a lot of stuff. And Larry made it possible. He opened the room up and got all the funding for free food, pizza and popcorn, candy and chips. He just did everything he could. Truckload after truckload—semi-trucks—of toys. Just unbelievable amounts of toys.

I know there were a lot of kids who came in there that had nothing, and passing all that stuff out to those kids made you feel good. It did me.

In 1998, when Shaeffer talked to Conner for the *World* story, he estimated that the Cain's had accumulated some 20,000 toys for the upcoming Christmas Eve's giveaway.

The event came, however, at the end of a challenging year for Shaeffer. Legal troubles had begun a couple of months before the holidays, and they'd end up becoming such a drain on his finances, and on his psyche, that he would find himself not only unable to fund the toy giveaway, as he had once done, but also yearning to finally and forever get out from under the Cain's itself.

Over the next few years, others stepped up to help the holiday event continue—sometimes at the eleventh hour. And even after Shaeffer *did* leave the ballroom for good, not long after the last toy giveaway of the century, the event kept on going, moving a few blocks away to the Brady Theatre and then back to the Cain's for a final couple of years.

"I had a lot of selfish reasons to keep doing it, because I felt so good doing it, but it was much bigger than me or Cain's Ballroom," Shaefer reflected. "I think it meant something to people whose names I never got to know—and they didn't know mine, and they didn't need to. They depended on it. It was a blessed event if there ever was one."

CHAPTER
17

There were times when the bands would come in and just be in awe of Cain's. You'd kind of get used to that—how in awe of this historic place they were.

—DAVIT SOUDERS, IN AN AUGUST 17, 2010 INTERVIEW
WITH BRETT BINGHAM AND JOHN WOOLEY

Everything centered around Cain's. That's where it happened.

— LUKE WILLS, QUOTED IN A STORY BY TERRELL LESTER
IN THE MAY 15, 1992 *TULSA WORLD*

Cain's...has the vibe of America.

— WARNER BROS. RECORDS REPRESENTATIVE LINNEA NAN, QUOTED IN A
STORY BY JEFF KAUFFMAN IN THE FEB 18, 1992 *TULSA TRIBUNE*

As noted earlier in this book, from the earliest days of the Shaeffer era, the Cain's had been casting its net exceedingly wide, pulling in acts from just about every genre imaginable. Never would this be better illustrated—at first glance, anyway—than by two things that happened between its walls in early 1992.

Through most of January, February, and March, the members of a hard-rock group called Life, Sex & Death had been ensconced in the ballroom, along with a couple of producers known for their work with heavy-metal bands and a million-dollar mobile recording studio. After looking all around the country, the musicians and representatives of their label, Warner Bros./Reprise, had chosen Cain's as the place to cut the group's first disc.

According to the *Tulsa Tribune*'s Jeff Kauffman, Linnea Nan, production coordinator for the record, had joined with the band's members in conducting "an extensive search of night clubs, hotels and even a mental hospital to find the right atmosphere for a live recording. 'Cain's had it all,' she said."

The group, originally from Chicago, had been playing on the West Coast for the past couple of years, garnering raves in the press. The stories often mentioned the group's lead singer Stanley, whom *Billboard* magazine called "a grimy, twitching, reputedly homeless apparition," and while he certainly smelled and looked like an unstable street-dweller, it's possible he also could've been a gimmick.

"I always thought it was just his schtick, that he probably had a Mercedes Benz back home," Shaeffer said. "But it could have been real."

As evidence of the latter, Shaeffer cited the relationship that Stanley had with the Cain's Ballroom's highly eccentric clean-up man, a janitor named Jack. "Stanley was always dirty, he smelled, and he talked in riddles. You didn't know what he was talking about. But somehow Jack and Stanley formed a friendship. Jack would start talking about some crazy interplanetary shit, and Stanley would understand him. Then Stanley would talk, and Jack could understand *him*. You wouldn't believe some of the conversations they would have. They were on the same wavelength."

The other three members of the band, Shaeffer added, "were easy to get along with. They loved Cain's. They'd borrow my Marshall amps, and I'd loan them guitars."

Life, Sex & Death made the Cain's their home for several weeks, and not all that long after they left, several other notables moved in—if only for a couple of hours. These musicians had also inhabited the ballroom, albeit in another era, and they'd come back to help honor the man for whom most of them had played: Bob Wills. Included in the group were fiddler Curly Lewis, pianist Clarence Cagle, saxophonist Glenn "Blub" Rhees, bassist Ted Adams, guitarist-vocalist Jimmy Widener, steel-guitarist Speedy West, and drummer Paul McGhee, along with former Cain's owner O.W. Mayo, who was then 91 and wheelchair-bound. He got a standing ovation from the crowd, which included Oklahoma Speaker of the House Glen Johnson, State Representative Betty Boyd, Tulsa mayor Rodger Randle, and many other friends and dignitaries, not the least of which was Bob Wills' longtime attorney David Milsten.

The reason for the gathering was the May 16 dedication ceremony for Bob Wills Main Street, a newly renamed portion of Main that ran from First Street to Easton Street, right in front of the ballroom. Wills fan and friend Bud Stefanoff, owner of Tulsa's Bounty Lounge, had gotten the ball rolling, with the *Tulsa World*'s

Terrell Lester helping attract the attention and participation of Randle, Boyd, and Johnson via his column.

"I'm not an official spokesman for the Wills family, or for any of the Texas Playboys," Mayo told the crowd. "But I don't know if any of us ever expected something like this to happen at Cain's Ballroom."

Of course, if he'd been around a couple of months earlier, he probably could have said the same thing about the recording of Life, Sex & Death's disc, which included several songs whose titles couldn't have been printed in the family newspaper that covered the dedication. But perhaps the chasm between the O.W. Mayo era and the hard-rock recording artists wasn't as vast as it appeared.

"After being in this environment for a while, I've noted my guitar licks changing," commented Life, Sex & Death's Alex Kayne with a smile, speaking to John Wooley for a February 28, 1992 *Tulsa World* story. "It's like the ghosts in this place are saying, 'Play more like the Bob Wills band, and less like Eddie Van Halen.'"

(Life, Sex & Death's debut disc, *The Silent Majority*, came out from Reprise in 1992. Although the group garnered something of a cult following, no other albums were forthcoming, and the band has long since split up.)

****

You could draw another line from the era of O.W. Mayo, Bob, and Johnnie Lee Wills to the '90s. In 1937, after leasing the Cain's from Madison Cain, O.W. Mayo and Bob Wills had put in a ceiling, vents, and an evaporative water-cooler. (Mayo called it "washed air" in his 1986 interview with Wooley.) Although it was

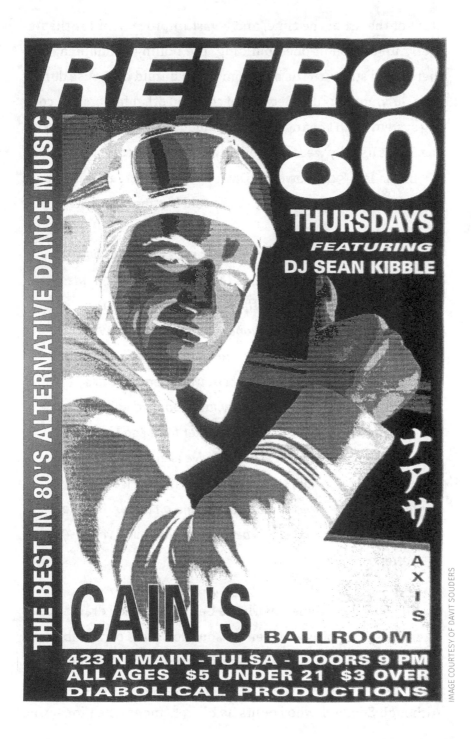

RETRO 80

THURSDAYS

FEATURING
DJ SEAN KIBBLE

THE BEST IN 80'S ALTERNATIVE DANCE MUSIC

ナアサ

AXIS

CAIN'S BALLROOM

423 N MAIN - TULSA - DOORS 9 PM
ALL AGES $5 UNDER 21 $3 OVER
DIABOLICAL PRODUCTIONS

state-of-the-art at the time, and a vast improvement for the formerly un-air-conditioned building, the boiling Oklahoma summers could still turn the ballroom into a humid hothouse during June, July, and August. Because of cost and other factors, the cooling system hadn't changed all that much through the decades, so the Cain's usually went dark during the summer months.

In the late '90s, however, Davit Souders' increased influence in the Cain's changed all that. As he told Bingham and Wooley:

> When I first started working with Larry, Cain's shut down every summer. It had to. I was the guy with the bright idea: "Hey, we can increase the revenue of the ballroom for an extra two or three months out of the year." We'd have to do the right kinds of shows, and I felt like the only crowd that would endure the heat was the alternative modern-rock crowd. So that's what happened.
>
> I remember Dave Grohl, the singer from Foo Fighters, saying "that's the hottest place we've ever played." It probably still is. The Cain's would have like its own weather system in there. It was hard on people and on bands, but the good thing was that Cain's became a year-round venue—for better or worse.

Souders' involvement with the Cain's increased dramatically after the spring of 1997, when he shut down his own club, Ikon, following what he termed dissatisfaction with his landlords. (The venue would rise again in 2004, but only for a few months.) Although Souders, who counts as his role model the pioneering rock 'n' roll disc jockey Alan Freed, has long affirmed his affinity for all kinds of music—"I love Ministry, but I also love Elvis Aaron Presley," he said—the closing of Ikon and Souders' subsequent emergence as the Cain's production manager and second talent buyer heralded an intense time for modern rock at the venue. Souders explained how it all started:

> *Because I was already doing stuff at Cain's [as Shaeffer's partner], I thought I'd move Ikon to its big brother's place. So I just kind of transferred all of that. I instantly started doing '80s Retro Nights there, introducing the dance aspect of the ballroom to another generation. They'd been a big success at Ikon, but when we moved it to Cain's, it quadrupled in size. We were doing 700-900 people every Thursday night for two, almost three years.*

So the concept of the dance night, which had flopped at the Cain's in the early '90s, took off a few years later in its second incarnation. And since the Retro Nights drew a lot of the same crowd as the modern-rock acts, Souders and Shaeffer found they could keep the dance events going during the summer months as well. "It just got bigger and bigger and bigger," noted Souders. "It was so hot in there, but the kids just came out in droves. I couldn't believe that first summer. They didn't have Ikon, and a lot of them were calling it ICain's."

When he and his father had first walked through the Cain's office space some 16 years earlier, happily surprised to see a line of patrons outside, Souders had probably never dreamed he'd one day have his own desk in that same area. But now he was officially working for the ballroom, a part of the mystery and the magic of it, with rows and rows of famous and not-so-famous black-and-white faces—faces that had all gazed out from the stage of the Cain's at one time or another—looking down at him daily from their places on the office walls. And often he was joined in the space not only by Shaeffer—who, Souders said, had given him "another awesome moment of acceptance" by hiring him as production manager—but also by the acts themselves.

"They'd usually relax there, because it was behind the scenes," Souders explained. "To sit there with folks like David Byrne and show him his photo on the wall from [his former band] Talking Heads, or Henry Rollins, these folks who were in awe—I never got tired of that. And there were crew guys, guys selling t-shirts, who would say that their whole reason for being on that tour was having that one night at Cain's Ballroom."

"I had Beck, an extremely talented rock act, on an outdoor show, and I brought him to Cain's Ballroom [in 1996]," Shaeffer added. "At load-in, he came in and he stayed all day. He sat in front of each portrait—in some cases, for a long time. When I went out to visit with him—and he was already selling huge amounts of tickets at the time—he said, 'I don't want to play anywhere else in my life but here.'"

****

By the late '90s, many acts had a history with the Cain's, and with Shaeffer himself, who had been the owner, operator, promoter, and talent booker for the ballroom for more than two decades. (Only O.W. Mayo had owned it longer—from 1944 through 1972—but he had begun leasing it out to other operators, including Bob Wills himself, from 1958 on.) One of those performers was the archetypal rock 'n' roll wild man, Jerry Lee Lewis, who had staged a memorable show there back in 1976, many years after playing his first Cain's show. More than three decades later, in his interview with Bingham, Shaeffer remained impressed not only with the show, but also with Lewis's legendary appetites:

> *I forget what I paid him—10 or 20 grand, and something like $3,000 extra for a Learjet and his pilot. So they fly in from Memphis and show up at Cain's at about 11:00 in the morning. Load-in was at four, so it was like, "Okay, what do we do now?" Jerry Lee asked if I had any whiskey. I went and got him a fifth of Jack Daniels, and he sat and visited. Never smiled, but he was very talkative, and he drank that whole bottle of Jack Daniels.*
>
> *Part of my deal was to get him a hotel suite, and I had him at the Ramada or somewhere. He said, "No, I want to stay where Elvis did."*
>
> *I swear, Jerry Lee had Elvis on his mind every hour of the day. To him, Elvis was the guy who bumped him out of the way.*
>
> *Anyway, that was the Mayo, so I called and got a suite. Who knew if it was Elvis's? But he was all happy about it. We took them to check in, and he wasn't staggering, he wasn't slurring a word, after drinking a whole fifth.*

After I'd gotten back to the Cain's, Jerry Lee called and said, "Hey, back in '56 I was here in this same hotel, and right around the corner there was a coney place. Is that still there?" I said, "Yes, sir." So he went down there, and the guy at the Coney Island said he sat down and ate 12 hot dogs.

Shaeffer had Emmylou Harris performing in a sold-out show a few blocks away at the Tulsa Performing Arts Center, so he left the Cain's to check on her show that night. Lewis was already performing when Shaeffer returned to the ballroom.

When I come back, Cain's is packed, with 1,000 people outside trying to get in, and he's up there playing my old Vose piano with bogus Steinway stickers on it. The wood's chipped on it, it's got old strings mixed with new strings, and he's literally burning down the house. He's playing like he did in 1956. He's slinging his greasy hair around, he's playing with the heel of his shoe, his knuckles, his elbows. It literally was one of the most electric live shows I've seen— one of the top three shows I've ever seen.

Given the vibe from that historic performance, it was only natural that Shaeffer would want to have the same vintage instrument on stage for Lewis 20 years later, when the then-sexagenarian rock 'n' roller was rebooked into the ballroom. "I pulled out that old Vose piano, knocked the dust off of it, had some strings replaced on it, and I had it waxed," he said. "I knew Jerry Lee loved it. I knew he was ready to pound it."

As it turned out, Shaeffer's optimistic predictions weren't quite on the money—a situation that wasn't entirely his fault.

"Jerry Lee had been fighting with his wife or girlfriend all through the day," Shaeffer remembered, "and when he got up there, he was cursing me on the microphone between every song because I'd stuck him with that piano."

"Larry tried to take the old piano that was there at the ballroom and put some new strings on it just for Jerry Lee," added Steve Turner, who'd just become the Cain's sound man at the time, in an interview for this book. "I tried to discourage him. I told him we just needed to get a Yamaha CP80 and have a decent piano for Jerry Lee to play. But Larry wanted him to play that old piano, with the history and everything."

Turner, who was on duty that night, recorded the whole show, including Lewis's uncensored commentary, off the sound board. In the subsequent years, a few CDs of that recording —which Turner titled "Jerry Lee Bitches about the Piano"— have made their way into the hands of rock 'n' roll and Cain's Ballroom aficionados.

"It's something to charge you folks to get in to a club to hear an artist sing and play a piano, and it's another thing having a piano to play," Lewis mutters after his first couple of songs, the drummer firing off rim shots as though his boss is doing a comedy routine. "And this is one big pile of crap. This thing should have been hauled off 75 years ago, when they opened up."

And, later: "I can't believe I got this much out of that piano. This must be one of the first pianos brought over on the Mayflower— by the pilgrims."

After telling the crowd that he'd demand his money back if he'd paid to "hear an artist play a piano like this," Lewis launched into his two signature tunes "Whole Lotta Shakin' Goin' On" and "Great Balls of Fire" and then left the stage. Since he'd been on for less than an hour, the crowd expected him to return for at least a long encore. Instead, said Shaeffer, Lewis left the building, found the limo, and headed for the airport, leaving his band—which included former Elvis guitarist and rock 'n' roll heavyweight James Burton—playing on stage.

"He did a horrible show—only played 48 minutes," Shaeffer remembered. "The crowd's packed, waiting for the next hour [of music]. James Burton just keeps cooking, all the band members are looking over their shoulders, and finally it's, 'Okay, good night, folks, I guess this is it. Thank you for coming.'"

By the time Burton made it to the Cain's office, Shaeffer had received a telephone call from Lewis. "I said, 'James, I don't know how to tell you this, but Jerry Lee just called and said if your ass isn't at the airport about 15 minutes ago, you're fired and you're walking back to Memphis.'

"Burton just started chuckling. 'Oh yeah,' he said, 'he fires us every night.'"

****

The cowboy singer and yodeler Don Walser didn't have a long relationship with the Cain's—at least, not a physical one. But, like so many other Southwesterners, he had grown up listening to the Wills broadcasts, creating in his mind an image of the way this epicenter of western-swing music must look.

Walser finally got his chance to play the ballroom on November 16, 1996, as the opening act for Asleep at the Wheel, which had been playing the Cain's regularly since the '70s. Earlier, Walser had talked to Davit Souders on the phone, sharing his excitement and joy about the booking.

Souders recalled what happened the day of the show:

Asleep at the Wheel was done with the sound check, and there was about an hour and a half of quiet time. Tables were in the ballroom, it was quiet, we had the fans going—
it was the calm before the storm. I decided I was going to sit in the ballroom and watch Don Walser come in.

So the door opens, and it's him and his wife, and it was just awesome. He's looking at the pictures [on the wall], and when I went up and introduced myself, he was already crying.

He said, "I know these people."

I took him on a tour, and I got him some copies of the reproduction posters of Hank Williams and Bob Wills shows, and you'd have thought I'd handed him a million dollars. He said, "My two dreams in the whole world, my whole career, have been to play the Cain's Ballroom and the Grand Ole Opry. I'm here tonight, and I'm playing the Grand Ole Opry next week."

For me, the modern-rock alternative guy, to watch him in the ballroom—it was so awesome.

But Shaeffer had brought Souders in to be that modern-rock alternative guy, and that's how he spent most of his time as the ballroom's other in-house booking agent for the Cain's. "Larry said it best: 'You've got to hit those things when they're hot,' and modern rock was so hot that it was a pretty sure bet for a period of time," explained Souders. Luckily for the ballroom, Shaeffer had found a partner who was not only competent and experienced, but knew his way around the new rock bands. Shaeffer didn't—and, while he told Bingham that "some of them were great," he also admitted that a few that took the Cain's stage mortified him.

"I'd look up and see Bob's face on his portrait [beside the stage], and I'd say, 'Damn. I'm embarrassed. I ought to be shot,'" he recalled. "That's the real reason I wanted out of Cain's; I almost felt like if this is what I've got to do to make cash flow, I don't want it. So, by '95, I wanted out of Cain's."

Shaeffer had made noises about selling the place before, of course. But this time, he was serious. It was more than just the constant drain on his time and energy and resources, and it was more than the passing of a musical generation.

A few years later, as intimated in the last chapter, those and other forces conspired to drive him away for good.

****

In addition to dealing with the everyday running and booking of the Cain's, Shaeffer found himself in legal trouble in the late '90s. A teenaged girl who'd been selling t-shirts in the ballroom came forward to claim that Shaeffer had raped her in his office. The accusations were sensational, as were the whispers that the Cain's owner had been set up by someone very close to the operation. On October 23, 1998, a Tulsa jury—after five hours of deliberation—cleared him of all charges.

By that time, Shaeffer's wife of seven years had divorced him—over the alleged incident, according to his testimony in the courtroom. She had even been a witness for the prosecution. Later, he faced other charges, including possession of a controlled dangerous substance, which was dismissed, and public intoxication, for which he received a fine.

And while Shaeffer had a number of loyal and supportive employees, certain elements in the day-to-day operations of the Cain's weren't positive, as Souders saw when he moved in. "I was surprised at the element of negative staffing," he said. "It was obvious that things weren't running as smoothly as they should. Larry was kind of knocked off course [by his legal issues] and couldn't see it. But I did. I was doing my best to make him aware of some of those elements, but then when he got knocked more off course, it became a struggle. I think there were advantages being taken because Larry's attention was diverted."

Sound man Steve Turner, who came in around the same time as Souders, had a more succinct description of the scene at Cain's in the late '90s. "I describe it to people as a body with its head cut off," he told Bingham, "just bleeding all over itself."

By late 1999, virtually all of Shaeffer's legal troubles were behind him. He'd been acquitted of the rape counts, and the drug charge had been dismissed earlier in the year. He had survived it all, and even though his finances were in bad shape, he resolved to, this time, *really* get away from the ownership and day-to-day operation of the ballroom.

****

At this time, a young man named Danny Finnerty was working as a staffer for Tulsa-based U.S. Senator James Inhofe. And, in addition to his political savvy, Finnerty also had more than a nodding acquaintance with the entertainment business. His father, Hugh, had been deeply involved in minor-league baseball and auto-racing and had also been a creator of the Indoor Fun Fairs (later called Indoor Super Fairs), mini-carnivals successfully staged all across the country.

Danny spent significant time working in his dad's businesses as well as on his political job. Then, in 1995, following his father's passing, Danny began running the Indoor Super Fairs with his brother Mark. That led, according to a 2011 interview Danny gave Brett Bingham, to his first-hand acquaintance with the Cain's Ballroom:

> *We decided to add some talent to the shows. So I went over to Cain's and talked with Shaeffer, rented a [portable] stage, and borrowed Rick Smith, who at the time was his stage manager, and [staging boss and longtime Shaeffer associate] Jerry Bockman. We had a couple of small but national acts—I think it was Ricochet and Diamond Rio— playing at the fair, so I started spending a little bit of time at the Cain's just getting that deal structured—the timing and the dollars and the setup and tear-down, that kind of stuff. Larry was in a situation where he was interested in selling, so we got to talking about it.*

308   TWENTIETH-CENTURY HONKY-TONK

At this point in Shaeffer's life, Finnerty may have looked like the answer to a prayer. Shaeffer was serious about not wanting to be the man in charge of the Cain's Ballroom any more. On the other hand, he didn't want to see it go under, either.

"I chose Finnerty to come in because he showed interest," Shaeffer said in a separate interview. "He'd been a distant friend of mine, I thought he had some talent, and he showed extreme support and enthusiasm. Remember, I'd been up for trial. I'd just been through all that. It was over, and once it was, I decided that I wanted away from Cain's."

According to Finnerty, as Shaeffer began showing him the intricacies of booking acts into the ballroom, the conversations between the two about the Cain's changing hands "got more serious, and I got more interested."

I started spending more time at Cain's on show days, load-ins, and working with Larry on some of the offers, bouncing ideas back and forth—would this work, would that work? I learned a lot from Larry. At the time I didn't know very much about making offers and how much to estimate for stagehands and security and all those things that went into the elements of making a reasonably good offer [for an act].

Then, before long—I had nothing to do with Cain's, wasn't getting paid, hadn't bought it—I found myself doing shows and offer sheets and settling shows. So I thought, "Well, if I'm going to do this, I may as well see if I can make a dollar out of it instead of doing it for fun." So Larry and

I started talking seriously, and it just happened. I got the money together, and we closed, and I bought it from Larry.

The agreement, Shaeffer said, was that Finnerty would be a 50-50 partner. That arrangement happened near the very end of the century, around the time Shaeffer staged another of his Christmas toy giveaways. Over the succeeding few months, Shaeffer functioned primarily as a consultant and talent buyer for the ballroom, and Finnerty began hiring some new people as staff members. As Finnerty and his own people began taking a bigger and bigger part in the proceedings, Souders decided to leave—feeling, he said, that Finnerty "was not going to want to do all the shows" that Souders and Shaeffer had been doing. "We'd kept things so busy, and I just thought this would be a good time [to leave]," said Souders. "Danny called me about two weeks after I left and offered me my job back. I told him I just needed to take some time off, but the reality of it was that I knew what was going to happen, or not happen, at Cain's. I just knew, and that's why I left."

As is usual in these sorts of situations, disagreements arose between new management and former management re: how things should be done, and while Shaeffer hung on for several months, it ultimately proved to be an untenable situation for him.

"It was just time to separate," Finnerty said. "No hard feelings at all. It was just time to move on. I think it was one of those things where he'd owned it for so long, and if I had been in his position, I don't know if I'd have wanted to hang around either."

"The day that Larry finally said [he was leaving] to Danny was long overdue," observed Souders. "When Larry finally got himself enough together to do it—that was a great thing."

"Danny never said to me, 'Hey, you're out of here,'" Shaeffer stressed. "When I left, Danny met with me at a cafeteria down on Boulder and 15th and tried to keep me in it. I said, 'No, you keep the Cain's. I'm done. It's yours.'

"I was at a vulnerable place," he added. "I was worn out on it. Cain's represented my failure and my impropriety. I was drinking myself to death. I'd lost my wife. I was losing my house. I was broke. I saw the writing on the wall, and I'd just made up my mind one day that this was it. So I walked away from Cain's and threw my keys into Main Street—and I was okay with it."

EPILOGUE

I lived half my life in that building. It was more home than any house I ever owned. In fact, I didn't own the Cain's. It owned me.

– LARRY SHAEFFER, IN AN INTERVIEW WITH JOHN WOOLEY
FOR A JANUARY 21, 2001 *TULSA WORLD* STORY

At the time he turned Cain's over to Danny Finnerty and his new management team, Larry Shaeffer had owned the ballroom for some 23 years—close to one-third of the combined lifetime of the Cain's and the Louvre. (O.W. Mayo—along with Bob Wills—had taken over Madison Cain's lease in 1937, giving Mayo about 35 years as owner or co-owner. Neither of the other two owners from the 1900s—Marie Myers and Cain—had it for more than a few years, while the man who built it, Tate Brady, held on to it only for the final several months of his life. He passed away on August 28, 1925.)

After exiting the Cain's, Shaeffer continued to produce, promote, and book shows, setting up an office down the street in the Brady

Theater for a time before moving his operation to the Tulsa suburb of Sand Springs, where he and his Little Wing Productions continued working with a number of acts in venues all across the country.

"Here's what I learned that was so fulfilling," he recounted. "I could sit there in Tulsa and wait 10 years to get a Willie Nelson date—or I could pick 10 cities and call his agent, and he'd tell me, 'Route 'em.' Willie would usually get one or two big dates on a weekend, and I had the rest of 'em. I was the handy man."

And then, because of his success with the Nelson dates, others began calling.

"Gordon Lightfoot's agent started chasing me because everywhere he'd go, it seemed like I was coming in [with Nelson]," said Shaeffer. "So he called me and said, 'Would you please book Gordon Lightfoot?'

"I said, 'I'm not into it.'

"He said, 'Well, you should be.'

"So I said, 'Here's what I'll do. I'll give you no guarantees. We'll take the expenses off the top. Lightfoot takes 80 percent and I take 20.' And all of a sudden, I'm doing 40 dates a year with Lightfoot."

The great thing about it all, he added, "the redemption," was that he had finally become a bona fide national promoter. And that's what he remains to this day. Although his place in American music history has long been assured by what he did during his time at the Cain's, Larry Shaeffer seems happy that his time with the venerable hall is now simply a memory.

"The best thing that ever happened to me," he said, as this book was being completed, "was to get out of Cain's and do what I'm doing now."

Nineteen-ninety-nine may not have foreshadowed the Y2K computer malfunctioning that many predicted would happen when the century turned over, but, as far as the Cain's Ballroom was concerned, the penultimate year of the 20th century was nonetheless an important one. It not only marked the final months of Larry Shaeffer's ownership, it was also the diamond anniversary of the building, which Tate Brady had constructed back in 1924.

Following Shaeffer's departure, Danny Finnerty continued to run things until 2003, when the Cain's was bought by the Rodgers family of Tulsa. Since then, with Chad and Hunter Rodgers doing the booking, the Cain's has continued to enhance its reputation with fans and performers alike as one of the best small venues in the world. The trade publication *Pollstar* regularly rates it as one of the nation's top-grossing club venues ("club" designating halls with a capacity of 3,000 or fewer). And while Shaeffer, Munz, Souders, and several other staffers from the last century haven't been a part of the ballroom's management for many years, others have weathered the decades as they continue to help build the Cain's legacy.

There is, for instance, Gary Thomas. In 1985, well before he was the head of GT Security, Thomas was a welder, still in his teens, working occasionally at the ballroom as a security guard. In his interview with Brett Bingham, Thomas recalled his nearly three decades of being in the building on a regular basis. And even though he came there to work most of the time, his words reflect the experiences of many, many more people—patrons and employees alike—for whom the Cain's Ballroom will always be a cherished and important part of their lives.

Said Thomas:

One thing I have definitely enjoyed about doing this is how it's broadened my appreciation for different types of music. I remember the first time we did Blues Traveler at the Cain's. I'd never heard of Blues Traveler, but I show up and there's a huge line of people; their video had just come out on MTV and they'd just really hit.

That's an example of the many who've come through and I had no clue who they were, and then I got to see them and became a huge fan.

I've also known several people who've gotten married at the Cain's. And a lot of the guys who've worked for me over the years have come up to me and said, "Well, I'm still married."

I'll be like, "okay," and they'll say, "Don't you remember? The night I was working for you at the Cain's, I met my wife."

So that's kind of neat—seeing people involved with the ballroom who've met wives or husbands or whatever there, who've gotten married because of the Cain's, who've had kids, who've gotten divorced, who've gone through all that kind of stuff.

You know. Life.

JOHN WOOLEY

JOHN WOOLEY has written, co-written, or edited more than 40 books, including *Shot in Oklahoma*, named Outstanding Book on Oklahoma History for 2011 by the Oklahoma Historical Society. A three-time finalist for the Oklahoma Book Award, he was the first writer to be inducted into the Oklahoma Music Hall of Fame. His other books include the critically acclaimed biographies *Wes Craven: A Man and His Nightmares* and *Right Down the Middle: The Ralph Terry Story*, along with the current horror novels *Seventh Sense*, *Satan's Swine*, and *Sinister Serpent* (all written with Robert A. Brown) and the classic *Old Fears* (written with Ron Wolfe), currently under option to Sony Pictures Television.

BRETT BINGHAM

Legend has it that when BRETT BINGHAM was born, he could see the Cain's Ballroom out of his hospital window. And it's a fact that he came into the world while Johnnie Lee Wills and His Boys were playing an engagement at the Cain's; his father made it to the ballroom that same night to sing a couple of numbers with the band. Before he was even in high school, Brett was running the national fan club for Bob Wills' Original Texas Playboys; as an adult, he's worked with dozens of musical acts, doing both management and booking and specializing in western swing. Currently, he's the business manager for Bob Wills' Texas Playboys, under the direction of Jason Roberts.

INDEX

CPSIA information can be obtained
at www.ICGtesting.com
Printed in the USA
LVHW081229040421
683394LV00009BA/1300